Up North Michigan Wines by the Bay

Leelanau and Old Mission peninsulas explored

William Allin Storrer

with Patricia A Storrer

Foreword by Sommelier Michael Richmond
of the Boathouse Restaurant, Traverse City

WINEWRIGHT MEDIA — TRAVERSE CITY, MICHIGAN

William Allin Storrer lives in Frankfort and Traverse City, Michigan with his wife Patricia.

Cover photo by Tom Petzold.
Photography and cartography by William Allin Storrer

ISBN: 978-1491267295

Library of Congress Cataloging-in-Publicantion Data
Storrer, William Allin
    Up North Michigan; Wines by the Bay
     Leelanau and Old Mission peninsulas explored
            p. cm.
     Includes Bibliographical references
     ISBN- 9 781491 072479 (paper)
1. Wineries—Michigan 2. Wine and wine making—Michigan 3. Patricia A. Storrer

 663.2—dc22

Printed in the United States of America

Although the authors and publisher have made every effort to provide accurate, up-to-date information, they accept no responsibility for loss, injury, or inconvenience sustained by any person using this book.

CONTENTS

For updated information on the wine scene in the two Up North Michigan AVA's, Leelanau Peninsula AVA and Old Mission Peninsula AVA, the subject of this book, go to www.winewright.net on your computer, tablet, iPhone, whatever . . . !

Enjoy the wine that gave us such pleasure in doing this book for you.

Bill and Pat Storrer

FOREWORD BY MICHAEL RICHMOND, SOMMELIER

AND GENERAL MANAGER AT THE BOATHOUSE RESTAURANT ON PENINSULA DRIVE JUST SOUTH OF BOWERS HARBOR ROAD, OLD MISSION PENINSULA

One of my favorite places in the world is up north Michigan wine country. To be more exact, this gorgeous region, the greater Grand Traverse area, is home to two of the finest American viticulture areas (AVA): the Leelanau Peninsula and Old Mission Peninsula. An AVA is described as a "designated wine/grape-growing regions in the United States distinguishable by geographic features with boundaries defined by the Alcohol and Tobacco Tax and Trade Bureau of the United States Department of Treasury."

So what makes northern Michigan wine country so special? It's the area I call home, where I work at The Boathouse Restaurant, where I play, and where world-class wineries make some of my favorite varietal wines.

The wines of these two AVA's share some similarities due to the glacial-tilled, sandy loam soil, the lake-dominated cold climate, and the northern latitude which it has in common with other great wine-producing areas. Northern Michigan wineries are predominantly family-owned and operated, each offering their own unique wine and winery experience.

The Leelanau Peninsula Vintners' Association (LPVA) and the Wineries of Old Mission Peninsula (WOMP) are the two organizations that are designed to promote their wine and the wineries which are clustered along the trails of these AVA's. The LPVA is Michigan's oldest and largest wine trail dedicated to producing world-class wines and wine touring. As they describe themselves, the LPVA's 20 wineries and 100 miles of Lake Michigan shore, its unique villages and shops, the Leelanau Peninsula is wine country. The WOMP is much smaller in size and number of wineries, only representing seven distinctive wineries and is a beautiful peninsula situated between two bays.

One of the varietals most predominantly represented is Riesling, one of the world's most famous white wine grapes. Most northern Michigan wineries produce an excellent dry Riesling, as well as the better-known late harvest sweeter style. As a restaurateur and sommelier, I am pleased to recommend Riesling, as its characteristics are great paired with many styles of cuisine. These two AVA's also produce many other varietals, including Chardonnay, Pinot Gris/Grigio, Gewürztraminer, and, yes, even some red varietals such as Pinot Noir, Merlot, and, in my opinion, a promising Cabernet Franc.

The wine tours and tasting rooms are as different and unique as each wine. The winemakers' personalities are evident not only in the wine but in the wineries, the vineyards, and the tasting rooms, thus offering the traveler a one of a kind experience. Come discover the UP North Michigan wine area and create your own wine trail, wine story, wine experience.

An ancient European wine press

Hello!

I'm Bill Storrer, author of this book (with lots of editing and research by wife Pat). Why would we create a book on the wines and producers of the wines of Up North Michigan's two parallel peninsulas, Old Mission and Leelanau? There is no other region anywhere on our planet like these two pieces of land nearly surrounded by and infiltrated with water. That alone would justify a book, but another reason is that here in these two peninsulas of Up North Michigan (peace be unto Uppers of even further north Michigan, who also think they are "Up North") are grown some of the world's finest white wines and some very worthy reds.

I can't help but notice that Michigan wines receive virtually no attention in international wine books and magazines while the Missouri wine scene does manage to garner space – this in spite of Missouri ranking less than Michigan in terms of acreage, number of wineries and gallons of wine produced. I could say that Michigan wines are better than those of Missouri, but that must be left up to those of you who, after reading this book, really want to drive across the Mississippi on a taste-touring expedition.

Let me tell you what this book is and is not.

It is not a wine-tasting tasting book - you must do the tasting. Nor is it about food-pairing per se. Locally, individual wineries host multi-course "wine dinners" for which the winemakers, sommeliers and chefs combine their expertise to create ideal food and wine pairings. Additionally, many tasting rooms participate in a variety of promotional food-and-wine "small taste" events. We have included food-and-wine-pairing menus for some of these in the tasting room listings. We have also included a section that includes recipes from those who make the wines.

Importantly, this book does not presume to rate wines. That is best done by Masters of Wine and Sommeliers who have specific training and credentials. Lacking such expertise, these authors feel unqualified to judge wines – no matter how many hundreds of wines have been tasted at tasting rooms or enjoyed at dinners and wine-pairing occasions. There are many excellent and reliable wine-specific publications available. We do not, however, point you to "wine critics," such as the famous Robert Parker Jr, 'The Nose." We find any wine system that rates wines by points to miss the point about wines; each person's taste is a wonderful personal palate, and no other person has the same palate, so no one can tell you what you will like.

A sommelier, however, knows the characteristics of each wine in the restaurant wine cellar and can, with some information from you, the wine drinker, help you choose a wine that is suitable to your palate and price range.

Here, I should add, an experience I had in this respect. At Annecy, in France between Lake Annecy and the Swiss Alps at l'Auberge du Pere Bise, I ordered a wine for my wife and myself at dinner. L'Auberge du Pere Bise is one of the destinations of the haute couture of Europe, south of Geneva. The sommelier offered that the wine I had chosen could be served, but he thought I would prefer another, which he named. The price was THE SAME as what I had ordered, so he was not trying to price-gouge me, but offer me a better taste selection. We ordered his choice, and were delighted with the result.

A good sommelier will provide you the best taste treat possible in your price range. Elsewhere, trust your own taste buds, but listen to the person serving you at the tasting room for useful hints.

While history is not the book's primary focus, much personal history is woven into the individual stories. With our survey occupying a whole year and then some, our book snapshots the single year, 2012, with all the known vineyards and every tasting room and its offerings. Some of the vintages are as recent as 2012 and others date back several years for wines that have taken several years to mature before being bottled and released.

What this book does do is to celebrate the vines, vineyards, wines, wine producers of our two Up North Michigan parallel peninsulas, the Leelanau Peninsula and Old Mission Peninsula – the vision, the hard work and the skill of the people who make it all possible. In America it had always been French wines, or maybe German, until, back in the 1970s, California wines first commanded worldwide attention. Since then, Argentina, Chile, New Zealand, Australia. Now Michigan! I want to give you, the reader, an appreciation of the vision and sheer hard work that go into the wines that you taste and buy, the production processes, the unique local risks, and the gift of our *terroir* and climate conditions. I hope to convey the wine producers' enthusiasm for their product and to foster an understanding of the value of our local wines.

Wine is a growing business in two meanings of that word. It is farming, and that means hard work. The "romance of the grape" may be on your mind, but the wine from that grape comes from hard work day after day starting before the sun is up. And, here in Up North Michigan, the business keeps growing. Several new labels have appeared during the year, as well as new vineyards that, in three years, will yield their first harvest.

This is a "go-to" book about our wonderful wines and their producers, and the tasting rooms where you can find out for yourself just how good these wines are. While there are many excellent, detailed books for the dedicated oenophile, this is for you who are already in, or planning to enter, a tasting room.

The "biographies" of the wine businesses presented in this book come from personal conversations augmented with information provided on each winery's website. *There is no set format for the articles as each reflects the owner's or winemaker's personality and approach to the business of making wine. This involved "off the cuff" meetings with the personalities of Up North Michigan wine production.*

Thank you!

I feel so very privileged to have been welcomed by hundreds – yes hundreds –of vineyard and winery owners, winemakers, tasting room staff and others who are involved in the business of bringing to you, the reader, the grape in its finest expression, wine. I have heard the stories of triumph, defeat, rapture and disappointment that come with living with and pampering a vine that has been with us for millennia, but only for a couple or so decades in Up North Michigan. So many individuals have shared their time, their stories, insights, photographs, enthusiasm, and encouragement for this project, so now I must finish putting what I have learned on to paper and into print.

Tasting rooms and wineries are usually not hard to find. Vineyards, on the other hand, can be a challenge. They hide behind houses and hedgerows or are sheltered behind forests or orchards, or maybe simply over the next hill. I have driven every road that is a road on the two peninsulas, and some "roads" that are but two tracks in the sand. I cannot count the number of times, seeking this or that vineyard that I already knew about, a friendly farmer would say something like "that's just up the road behind the yellow house on the left. Oh, by the way, did you know about such-and-such?" And off I would go, finding yet another vineyard. I may now not remember your names, but when you see this book, you'll know who you are and when I met you. To you, also, I owe a big "thank you".

To all of you, I am truly grateful for your constant encouragement in what has turned out to be a challenging, rewarding and enjoyable project. I can only echo Louis Pasteur's "a bottle of wine contains more philosophy than all the books in the world".

How Wine came to Up North Michigan

Anyone in Up North Michigan who knows anything about wine knows that Bernie Rink – Boskydel - started it all. He threw 35 hybrids, 10 vines each, into the ground and watched to see what would grow. That was back in 1965. While this story has achieved the status of legend, it is only part of the real story.

Why hybrids? Because MSU (Michigan State University, for out-of-staters) Extension services said *vitis vinifera* vines (the ones you know from Europe, Pinot Noir, Cabernet Sauvignon, Chardonnay, Sauvignon Blanc and so on) would not grow in the northwest Michigan climate. How wrong they were.

Ed O'Keefe – Chateau Grand Traverse on Old Mission Peninsula– noticed, in Germany, that the cold climate of Riesling-growing areas was no impediment to producing wonderful wine. So he brought Riesling (a *vitis vinifera* variety) to his farm..

Then Bruce Simpson – Good Harbor – decided to bring *vitis vinifera* vines to Leelanau Peninsula and tried Chardonnay. This produced great wine! (This is as the tale is told by Dan Matthies – Chateau Fontaine).

The early Leelanau winemakers – Bernie Rink, Bruce Simpson, Larry Mawby, Dan Matthies and others – would gather often in Traverse City for a couple of hours, "talk shop", taste wine and develop their palates.

Listed in no particular order from an early photograph (of which I've not been able to obtain a copy), the original twelve Leelanau Peninsula winemakers were: Charles E. Edson of Bel Lago Vineyard and Winery, Bernie Rink of Boskydel Vineyard, Joanne M. Smart of Chateau de Leelanau Vineyards and

Shawn Walters — Warren Raftshol — Bryan Ulbrich — Bernd Croissant — John Crampton — Bruce Simpson — Mark Johnson — Lee Lutes — Adam Satchwell — Dr. Charles Edson — Dan Matthies

Spencer Stegenga — Larry Mawby — Bernie Rink — Silvio "Tony" Ciccone — Roberta Kurtz

2

Winery, Silvio "Tony" Ciccone of Ciccone Vineyard & Winery, Dan Matthies of Chateau Fontaine, Bruce Simpson of Good Harbor Vineyards, Larry Mawby of L. Mawby Vineyards, Adam Satchwell of Shady Lane Vineyards, John Crampton of Willow Vineyard, and Lee Lutes, Winery at Black Star Farms.

A similar photo, made in 2004 by Jo Crampton, shows the winemakers of both peninsulas. To the list above, add: Warren Raftshol of Raftshol Vineyards and Shawn Walters of One World Consulting on Leelanau Peninsula; and, from Old Mission Peninsula, winemakers Bernd Croissant of Chateau Grand Traverse, Mark Johnson of Chateau Chantal, Spencer Stegenga of Bowers Harbor and Bryan Ulbrich of Left Foot Charley. The only one in the photo not still making wine is Roberta Kurtz, who sold her winemaking facilities and property to Chateau de Leelanau.

The *terroirs* of these two peninsulas allow winegrowers to select grape varieties that will grow not only well, but also spectacularly, where they are planted. Microclimates abound. Bryan Ulbrich of Left Foot Charley, recognized as a master winemaker, suggests that Leelanau Peninsula is so large, though always within a few miles of open water, that it can be defined best by microclimates rather than general *terroirs*. The narrow old Mission Peninsula has three general *terroirs* based on soil and climate.

Each of these microclimates constitutes a local *terroir*.

So what is a *terroir*? Climate, soil type and topography are its chief defining components, though other plants growing in and around the vines might be considered. This is important, as Northwest Lower Michigan is also a center of cherry growing, as well as of apples, pears and peaches.

The local climate is, to winegrowers, cool. This means that the wines of Burgundy (Chardonnay, Pinot Noir), Mosel (Riesling) and Alsace (Gewürztraminer) can grow as well here as in their European *terroirs*.

With the locations of Bordeaux, France, and of northern Italy – both historical settings for quality wine production – on the 45th parallel, much is made of our location on that same parallel. What makes our location different is the proximity to water, with no vineyard more than a few miles from water. This aspect is crucial to Northwest Lower Michigan, somewhat relevant to Bordeaux, and largely unimportant to northern Italy. Northwest Lower Michigan has a continental climate moderated by Lake Michigan, Lake Leelanau, Grand Traverse Bay (West Arm and East Arm, usually called just West Bay and East Bay), and even Elk and Torch Lakes further east. Even the most isolated of vineyards in the north part of the Leelanau Peninsula is hardly three miles from a large lake.

Our sandy soil, sometimes rich loam, sometimes clay, but created by the Laurentide Glacier, plays an important part. Working with these conditions, the layout of each vineyard must be designed to meet the cultural needs of each selected grape variety and clone for the best wine to emerge from the grapes grown thereon.

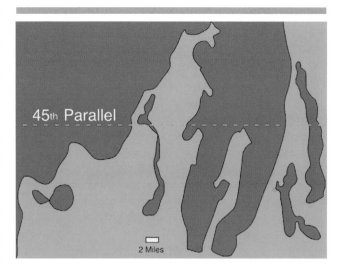

Wine Grape Statistics for the Two Peninsula AVA's

Wine grape growing Up North Michigan began at Bernie Rink's Boskydel Vineyards, and so the first Up North Michigan AVA (and second in Michigan) came to the Leelanau Peninsula. But first, a word about the AVA.

An AVA is a unique area in terms of its viticulture. The Leelanau Peninsula AVA was established on March 30, 1982. It came about by petition of Bernie Rink of Boskydel Vineyard, Lake Leelanau, Larry Mawby of L. Mawby Vineyards, Suttons Bay, and Bruce Simpson of Good Harbor Vineyards, Leland. Rink and Mawby were co-writers and submitters of the petition. The need for AVA designation came from the requirement that, to call a winery an "estate winery," it had to be part of an AVA. The Leelanau Peninsula AVA excludes the offshore islands of Leelanau County.

The Old Mission Peninsula AVA came about in 1987 by petition of Ed O'Keefe of Chateau Grand Traverse, the only winery on the peninsula at that time.

The number of *Identified* Grape Varieties, including those grown in both AVA's is 53. This represents wine grapes grown in vineyards devoted to commercial production. Statistics are derived from the vineyard maps contained in this book. Both AVAs are included in this presentation.

In terms of the acreage planted in Wine Grapes, the 2011 Michigan Fruit Survey reports state-wide numbers: 1,765 acres planted in *vinifera* varieties with 675 acres in hybrids. The same survey reports 680 acres in Leelanau County and 700 acres in Grand Traverse County; this number is marginally high because it includes Juice and Table Grapes even though almost none are grown. Northwest Michigan acreages for the main Wine Grape varieties, with only 70 acres outside the two counties, are: Riesling 485 acres; Pinot Noir 196 acres; Chardonnay 165; Pinot Gris/Grigio 155; Cab Franc 92; Merlot 62.

On Old Mission Peninsula (OMP), the *number* of vineyards planted in Riesling (57) was twice that of the next three: Pinot Gris/Grigio (28), Pinot Noir (28) and Chardonnay (26). Gewürztraminer (18) outpaced Cabernet Franc (17) and Merlot (17). Note, this is number of vineyards, not acreage. It represents popularity among wine grape vineyard owners.

Over on Leelanau Peninsula (LP), a similar pattern adheres with a clear exception. Old Mission Peninsula's number one (Riesing) is Leelanau's number four. OMP's "next three," are all grown in more LP vineyards than Riesling (34)! Pinot Gris/Grigio (37), Pinot Noir (36) and Chardonnay (34). Here Gewürztraminer (15) falls well below Cabernet Franc (25) and Merlot (22). Leelanau vineyards tend to be much larger than those of Old Mission, so these figures are again popularity among wine grape vineyard owners.

Wine Grapes of the Two Up North Michigan AVAs

This list is a compilation of the grapes identified on this book's Vineyard maps. It does not include such classification groupings as Experimental, Test, Red, White, Red-Skinned, etc. It also does not include the vines grown for test purposes at the MSU Horticultural Station.

Let's start with the grapevine "hierarchy" Within the flowering plants family *vitaceae*, *vitis* is a genus, subdivided into approximately 60 species, such as *vitis vinifera* (also known as Common Grape Vine and European Grape Vine), *vitis riparia* (an eastern North American species, also known as Riverbank Grape), and *vitis labrusca*. Most wine grapes, except hybrids, are cultivars of *vitis vinifera*. *Vitis riparia* can withstand very cold temperatures. *Vitis rupestris*, native to the southern U.S., is used for breeding phylloxera-resistant rootstock. Hybridizers look to a variety of different *vitis* species to produce new hybrids incorporating the best features of each.

A hybrid grapevine variety is created by a crossing between one *vitis* species (e.g., *v.vinifera*) and another *vitis* species (such as *v.riparia*), or between a species (such as *v.vinifera*) and another hybrid.

A cross is created by a crossing between two other vine varieties within the same species.

A cloned grapevine is produced by taking one or more cutting(s) from a single mother vine.

Information for this section has come from the encyclopedic *Wine Grapes, A Complete Guide to 1,335 Vine Varieties, Including Their Origins and Flavours*, by Jancis Robinson, Julia Harding and José Vouillamoz (New York: Harper Collins Publishers, 2012.) Also, from the Professional Friends of Wine website.

A grape grown only on Leelanau peninsula is shown in red,
A grape grown on both Old Mission and Leelanau peninsulas is shown in green.
A grape grown only on Old Mission peninsula is shown in blue.

Vitis Vinifera Red Wine Grape Varieties:

1. Blaufränkisch, also known as Lemberger: Austro-Hungarian variety, the "fränkisch" coming from "Franconia" in what is now modern Germany (the Duchy of Franconia being established in the early 10th century). *(Grown by 3 Leelanau Peninsula (LP) growers and 6 Old Mission Peninsula (OMP) growers, as identified in this book's vineyard maps.)*
2. Cabernet Franc: one of the most important and ancient of Bordeaux varieties. Parent of Cabernet Sauvignon, the other being Sauvignon Blanc. . *(LP = 25; OMP = 17) Cabernet Franc*
3. Cabernet Sauvignon: quoted by *Wine Grapes* as "the world's best-travelled red wine variety". *(LP = 3; OMP = 1)*
4. Dolcetto: from Piedmont region of Italy. "Dolcetto" means "little sweet". *(LP = 1)*
5. Dornfelder: *Wine Grapes* says "the most successful of modern German crosses". *(LP = 3; OMP = 2)*
6. Gamay Noir: an ancient variety from Burgundy, first quoted by name "Gaamez" in 1395. *(OMP = 6)*
7. Lemberger: see Blaufränkisch above.
8. Malbec, also known as Cot: The Cot variety is a native of southwestern France, where it is not much now grown, but is successful in Argentina. *(LP = 1)*
9. Merlot: first mentioned 1780s in Libourne (Gironde, southwestern France), as "Merlau". According to the *Wine Grapes* and translated from French, the "the name Merlot was given to this variety because the blackbird likes this

grape very much. Indeed, the blackbird was called *merlau* in Occitan". (the Langue d'oc, an old language still spoken in southern France.) *(LP = 22; OMP = 17)*
10. Nebbiolo: This ancient variety from Piedmont region of Italy was recorded in the 13th and 14th centuries. According to *Wine Grapes*, the best etymological explanation is that "nebbia" (Italian, fog) is "probably referring to the thick natural bloom covering the ripe berries, as if they were covered in a layer of fog". *(LP = 1)*
11. Pinot family: Pinot comes from French word for pine. Certainly, the clusters are pine-cone shaped. Though Pinot has been around for a couple of millennia, giving it plenty of time to evolve and mutate, its origin(s) remain a puzzle to ampelographers. Ampelography is a field of botany devoted to identifying and classifying grapevines, most often *vitis vinifera*.
12. Pinot Meunier: this French variety is named for the flour-like hairs under the vine-leaf's underside, "meunier" being French for "miller". *(LP = 1; OMP = 4)*
13. Pinot Noir: French Burgundian variety. "Noir", French for black. *Wine Grapes* mentions the name as identified "in 1394, a letter of dismissal issued by Charles VI reported that a fifteen-year old boy, who had been hired for the harvest in Saint-Bris-le-Vineux and who had disobeyed the order given to the harvesters to set aside the Pinot Noir grapes to prevent them from being mixed with other kinds of grapes, was hit by the owner so brutally that he died". *(LP = 36; OMP = 28)*
14. Schönburger: German cross between Pinot Noir and another *vitis vinifera* cross. *(LP = 1)*
15. Teroldego: variety from Trentino region of northeastern Italy, first mentioned in a 15th century sales contract. *(LP = 1)*
16. Zweigelt: an Austrian *vitis vinifera* cross. . *(OMP = 1)*

Hybrid Red Wine Grape Varieties:

1. Baco Noir: French hybrid. *(LP = 1, OMP = 3)*
2. Chancellor: French-American hybrid, obtained from crossing two Siebel hybrids in Eastern France. It was named "Chancellor" by New York State. *(OMP = 1)*
3. Corot Noir: American hybrid, from the Cornell University's Geneva research station. *(LP = 1*
4. De Chaunac: French hybrid. .*(LP = 1)*
5. Foch, also known as Marechal Foch: French hybrid, developed in Colmar, Alsace, France. Named for General Foch, a WWI general who was named Marechal de France in 1918. The same crossing that produced this hybrid also produced the hybrid Leon Millot. *(LP = 5; OMP = 5)*
6. Frontenac: American hybrid, from the University of Minnesota. *(LP = 2}*
7. Geneva Red, synonym "GR 7", American hybrid, from Cornell University, New York State. *(LP = 1)*
8. Leon Millot: French hybrid. *(LP = 3; OMP = 1)*
9. Marechal Foch, also known as Foch. See above.
10. Marquette: American hybrid, from University of Minnesota's Horticultural Research Center. *(LP = 4; OMP = 3)*
11. Noiret: American hybrid from Cornell University, New York State. *(LP = 2; OMP = 1)*
12. Regent: German hybrid. *(LP = 5; OMP = 1)*

Vitis Vinifera White Wine Grape Varieties:

1. Auxerrois: name probably from "Auxois", an early name for Alsace, France. Not from "Auxerre", a town in France's Yonne River valley. *(LP = 5; OMP = 2)*
2. Chardonnay: supposedly first mentioned in late 16th century, spelled as "Chardonnet", its name deriving from the village of Chardonnay in southern Burgundy. Late in 17th century, described as making the best wine. *(LP = 34; OMP = 26)*
3. Gewürztraminer: first mentioned in 1827, likely a natural mutation. *Wine Grapes* says "Thought to be an aromatic mutation of Savagnin Rose, observed in the German Rheingau region." *(LP = 15; OMP = 18)*
4. Grüner Veltliner: Austrian variety. *(LP = 6; OMP = 3)*
5. Kerner: German cross between Riesling and another *vitis vinifera* variety (Trollinger, also known as Schiava Grossa), from Baden-Württemberg, southern Germany. *Wine Grapes* says the new variety was "named after nineteenth-century Württemburg medical doctor and writer of drinking songs Justinius Kerner who used to recommend that his parents drink a glass of wine as the best natural medicine". *(LP = 1)*
6. Muscat: not a single variety, but about 200 distinct and often unrelated *v.vinifera* varieties. *(LP = 4; OMP = 1)*
7. Muscat Ottonel: French variety, developed from *vitis vinifera* varieties in mid-19th century by a breeder who omitted to record the names of its parents. *(LP = 4)*
8. Pinot Blanc: a color mutation of Pinot Gris, "blanc" being French for "white". *(LP = 9; OMP = 15*
9. Pinot Gris/Pinot Grigio: a color mutation of Pinot Noir. "Gris" and "Grigio" are, respectively, French and Italian for "grey". Each of these is the same grape variety, the difference between the two being that that their varietal wines are vinted in the French style or in the Italian style. *(LP = 37; OMP = 28)*
10. Prosecco: north-east Italian variety, probably from the Istrian peninsula. Renamed "Glera" in 2009, to prevent sparkling wines of other origins being named as "Prosecco" by using the grape variety's name. *(LP = 1)*
11. Riesling: one of the oldest German varieties, probably from the Rheingau region. One of many 14th century references is to the inventory of Count John IV of Katzenelnbogen (close to today's Rheingau) with "22 shillings for Riesling vine cuttings for the vineyard". *(LP = 34; OMP = 57)*
12. Sauvignon Blanc: the *Wine Grapes* authors believe, and DNA evidence appears to support, that the variety originated in France's Loire Valley. Parent of Cabernet Sauvignon. Name probably from French "sauvage", wild. *(LP = 4; OMP = 2)*
13. Siegerrebe: German cross. *(LP = 1)*
14. Viognier: from northern Rhone region of France. *(LP = 2)*

Hybrid White Wine Grape Varieties:

1. Bianca: Hungarian hybrid. *(LP = 3)*
2. Cayuga: Full name Cayuga White. American hybrid developed from crosses of Schuyler and Seyval Blanc hybrids, from Cornell University's New York State Agricultural Experimental Station in Geneva, New York (Cayuga being the lake in the New York State's Finger Lakes region that is overlooked by the Cornell University campus). *(LP = 3; OMP = 5)*
3. Chardonel: American hybrid, from the Geneva research station (full name, under Cayuga), cross of Seyval Blanc hybrid with Chardonnay. *(LP = 1)*
4. Frontenac Gris: a color mutation of Frontenac. *(LP = 5)*
5. La Crosse: American hybrid, obtained by Wisconsin breeder, presumably named for La Crosse, Wisconsin. A sibling of St. Pepin. *(LP = 1)*
6. Seyval Blanc, also known as Seyval: French hybrid. *(LP = 3, listed as Seyval, plus 2 listed as Seyval Blanc)*
7. Seibel 10868: hybrid from Ardeche area of south-central France. *Wine Grapes* says "Ardeche hybrid found only (rarely) in Michigan today"; also that Boskydel has a few hundred vines left that are used for Soleil Blanc blends. *(LP = 1)*
8. St. Pepin: American hybrid from Osceola, Wisconsin. *(LP = 1)*
9. Traminette: American hybrid from University of Illinois, Urbana-Champaign. *(LP = 3; OMP = 3)*
10. Vidal Blanc, also known as Vidal: French hybrid. *(LP = 1; OMP = 1)*
11. Vignoles: French hybrid. *(LP = 12)*

Grape Varieties Not Classified:

1. Crimson Cabernet: not referenced in *Wine Grapes*. Grown by Boskydel. *(LP = 1)*
2. Le Crescent: not referenced in *Wine Grapes*, though the name is licensed by the TTB. Grown by Boskydel. *(LP = 1)*
3. NY 76 White: a New York hybrid, not referenced in *Wine Grapes*. Grown at Norvick for Motovino. *(LP = 1)*

What's on a label, and why you should read it!

Here is a label. What does it tell you?

Who? The brand name – "Herding Cats"

What? Chenin Blanc/Chardonnay, specifying the wine's grapes

Where? South Africa, Western Cape

When? 2011

Here is another, "Lady in Red".

Who? Brand name – "Kestrel Lady in Red"

What? "Red Wine"

Where? Washington State, Columbia Valley

When? Not listed on front label.

Michigan, with the whole United States, has specific requirements for its wine labels. The rules for labeling are designed to help you know exactly what you are getting. The label is worth reading.

When you visit a tasting room on Leelanau or Old Mission peninsulas, you probably want to know whether the wine that you taste was made from grapes from either of those peninsulas. A Michigan wine label will tell you that. It will also tell you specifically, whether or not it is made of 85% grapes of that peninsula but only if it has the peninsula identified. If a winery's label names a year and it is a Leelanau or Old Mission winery, 95% of the grapes must be from that winery's vineyards. Those are the general rules that are followed on both our peninsulas.

There is a lot more to be learned from a label, so here follows a detailed explanation for the connoisseur or techie. Note, what is good for the U.S. is not quite the same as for Michigan or specifically the two AVAs of Up North Michigan – the point being that a Michigan "appellation" is more restrictive than the U.S. as a whole, and our two Up North Michigan AVAs are more restrictive than "Michigan".

An American wine label, for foreign and U.S. wines, contains information controlled by the U.S. Department of the Treasury's Alcohol and Tobacco Tax and Trade Bureau (TTB); the intent being to advise buyers what's in a bottle of wine. The label may also carry information that the winery tells of itself and its product – such as winery story; vineyard location and *terroir*; grower identification; blend components; suggested food pairings; wine sweetness

who

what

when

where

(or otherwise). With this book addressing only the Up North Michigan Leelanau and Old Mission Peninsula AVAs, this article addresses only domestic U.S. wine labeling.

With its combination of mandatory and optional information – all of it TTB-approved - the label identifies the wine's <u>who, what, where, when.</u> In 2012, the TTB approved over 300,000 labels.

Who? The TTB requires brand or brand name identification, which must not mislead in terms of the wine's age, character, identity or origin and may not duplicate any foreign wine's brand or trade name. The TTB also requires, as a minimum, "Bottled By", with bottler's name/trade name and address.

- If the bottler made at least 75% of the wine, "Produced and Bottled By" may be stated, which says that the winery must have crushed the grapes, fermented the juice and bottled the wine.
- Phrases like "Vinted By and Bottled By" and "Cellared and Bottled By" can mean the winery bought the wine from another winery or vintner and may then have blended it and/or aged it before bottling.
- An "Estate Bottled" wine label must list an AVA. The winery must be in that AVA, the winery must have grown 100% of the grapes on land owned or controlled by the winery (i.e., long-term lease) within the same AVA, and the winery must have crushed the grapes, fermented the resulting must, aged, finished, and bottled the wine in a continuous process.
- "Grown, Produced and Bottled By" may be used by a winery meeting all the "Estate Bottled" requirements but is not located within an AVA.

What? The TTB requires definition of Class, the most common being Table Wine – which is defined as not less than 7% and not more than 14% alcohol content by volume. Labels can alternatively specify a "semi-generic" name, such as "light wine" "red table wine" "light white wine" "sweet table wine" etc., which are Table Wine subsets. Generic names (such as Bordeaux, Burgundy, which represent a wine style in their home country) are rarely used in the U.S. Another alternative for the Table Wine class is for labels to carry a "varietal" identification of the wine's dominant grape, such as Chardonnay and Riesling varietal wines from Chardonnay and Riesling grape varieties. If a varietal is named, then appellation listing is also required (in Up North Michigan, the Leelanau Peninsula or Old Mission Peninsula): this says that at least 75% of the wine's grapes are of that variety and grown in the named appellation (51% for *vitis labrusca* grapes, such as Concord).

Where? "Appellation of Origin" says where the grapes were grown. An "appellation of origin" for an American wine can be the entire U.S., or a single State or two or not more than three contiguous States, or a single county or two or not more than three counties within the same State, or an American Viticultural Area (AVA). Each AVA is geographically distinct and possesses distinct growing conditions - such as climate, elevation and soil. With AVA as the smallest and most strictly defined appellation, the most stringent appellation regulations apply at AVA level.

"Leelanau Peninsula" and "Old Mission Peninsula" are each an AVA: naming of one of these on the label says that at least 85% of the wine's grapes were grown in that AVA. Vineyard identification, also optional, says at least 95% of the grapes come from that vineyard. "Michigan" says at least 75% of the grapes are Michigan-grown.

When? If listed, year says when the grapes were harvested (picked) and crushed. For grapes harvested late one year and vinted early the next, year means vinting year. A wine's year is also known as its "vintage". If year is shown, an appellation is also required. If the listed appellation is an AVA, 95% of the grapes must be from that year – 85% if the appellation is a U.S. State or County.

Also mandated by the TTB are:
- Alcohol content in percent by volume. For table wines, with their defined not less than 7% and not more than 14% alcohol content, many bottlers instead label their wines as "Table Wine", "Light Wine", "Red Table Wine", etc. Alcohol content is required for other classes of wine.
- Net volume of contents, almost always 750 ml (25.4 fl.oz.).
- "Contains Sulfites", required for any wine with 10 or more parts per million for wines intended for interstate commerce but not required for wines for intrastate commerce. With sulfur occurring naturally in grapes and with yeast fermentation producing a 15-20 ppm sulfur level even before adding further sulfur, there is no sulfur-free wine.
- The fixed "Government Warning" wording, required on all alcoholic beverages.

The label tells what a bottle of wine contains but not what the wine tastes like. This is where thoughtful tasting, talking with tasting room staff, reading the whole label come in. Some labels give tasting notes, sweetness/dryness indicators and other helpful information. The label might also include words that imply a certain quality but have no defined legal meaning. All label information is not created equal!

The TTB's www.ttb.gov site has a useful introduction: search for "Wine Grape Label". The Professional Friends of Wine website www.winepros.org has a comprehensive treatment of labeling and associated terminology.

Taste-Touring

But Why Taste?
There are books and videos on "how to taste."
But, why do you taste?
Ask yourself, "When do I drink wine?" Most often, the answer is, "at mealtime." Lunch, dinner. Yet at a tasting room, you taste wine after wine, judging each wine against other wines.
Well, if you only drink wine sitting on the deck of your summer cottage, or in front of the fire on a cold winter's day, that's fine! But if, more often than not, it is with a meal, you should ask yourself, as you sip, "with what would I serve this?" That is the "why?"

But what do I taste in a wine?
"Barrel aging, hang time, and blends" is all you need to know to train your palate to wine.
70% of red wines are blends, 30% varietals. If you are into blends, learn your winery. If you are into varietals, learn the grape. ("Varietal" refers to wine made from a variety of grape – mostly, though not always from a single grape variety. "Chardonnay", for example, on a label refers to wine produced from the Chardonnay grape variety.)

Here is how Don Coe of Black Star Farms explains wine tasting.

Barrel aging. At a tasting room, try an unwooded Chardonnay (the French call this Chablis, but American Chablis is not the same), then a barrel aged Chardonnay. Ask the tasting room server to serve you the same vintage and same vineyard if possible. This will clearly show you what barrel aging does to a wine. Note: reds are almost always barrel aged.

For hang time, taste a dry Riesling, then a late harvest Riesling. The dry will have been picked early and have little sugar. The late harvest Riesling will have hung on the vine longer so will have more sugar.

For blends, try a white or red blend. Check the label to see which wine varietal predominates, and then try that varietal by itself to compare with the blend.

Given that there are more wines that are blends than varietals, a blend might be your choice. Bordeaux is all about blends, but Burgundy is Chardonnay, Chablis and Pinot Noir . . . which are varietals. So, if you are interested in varietals, learn the grape by tasting that grape at every tasting room, and take notes on what you taste: barrel or not (if a red, how much tannin . . .), dry or sweet or in-between, and don't forget aroma.

Now to the where of tasting

Tasting wines comes in at least two situations that concern us; at home and in the tasting room. In the former, you control the pouring and tasting, in the latter it is the rules set by the tasting room manager. Since you are touring tasting rooms, we will consider that first.

How should I get to the tasting rooms?

Sounds simple - you will just drive to each. Might be okay if you have a refrigerator in your car to keep any wine you purchase cold until you get home or back to your motel. Otherwise, consider renting a tour. There are several tour organizations, some run by wine producers. Use the Yellow Pages or go online. You might want to check websites of the wineries you plan to visit before arriving on the doorstep. If you are a large group, say, over six, you might want to call ahead. Indeed, the tasting room might request this.

Touring Tasting Rooms

So the great day (weekend) has come. You are going out on a tasting tour of Up North Michigan wines.

So, where do you start, Leelanau or Old Mission, at the bottom of the peninsula or the top? There are 29 tasting rooms on Leelanau, 9 on Old Mission, and 3 in Traverse City.

It would be pushing it to do ten a day. So you probably have to make choices. Look at the wine offerings listed in this book for each tasting room. What wines do you really want to taste and which tasting rooms offer them? If you want to taste Riesling, Chardonnay, Pinot Gris/Grigio and Cabernet Franc, you have a problem, as most winemakers do these four, so there are too many for you to get to all. (Yes, there is a tasting room where Riesling is not served and one that does not offer Chardonnay.)

Now, if you really want to taste Baco Noir, you will find only Leelanau Cellars offers it.

If you want to taste a dozen wines, you will find there are a few tasting rooms that can meet your desire, but they may limit you to five tastes, so check ahead.

One of the marketing organizations, Leelanau Peninsula Vintners Association suggests that visiting eight tasting rooms is about the best one can, or should, do in a day. So think about five days of touring if you want to visit every one on both peninsulas.

But then . . .

So you have decided your starting point and the seven others you will go to today. At the first you fall in love with a particular wine. Should you buy a case?

How many bottles of wine are you planning on buying today, or on all the days you tour? This is a quandary that few can answer. That wine you have chosen may be a great wine and you will love it back home, but will you find another that is even greater? Maybe you won't, and then you'll be disappointed you didn't buy more of the one you now have with you.

So this is one quandary out of which this author cannot help you.

In a tasting room, how should I taste?

First, smile at the person who is serving you. You are there to learn, to taste, and your server wants to help you. Listen. Treat your tasting room server with respect. He, or she, wants to help you find the kind of wine you want. Seek advice, don't give it! You are there to taste, not to get drunk.

There are many ways to taste wine, but most sommeliers and masters of wine with whom I am familiar have somewhat consistent standards. The first taste of any wine will shock the mouth, so it is the next taste that you should trust. Take enough into your mouth so that it touches the front and back of the tongue, and the sides of the mouth, to get all the flavors the wine might offer.

Since you don't control how much wine will be poured into the (usually) small tasting glass, your best bet might be to decide on tasting, at most, four wines at each stop. Taste the same wine varietal or blend at each tasting room. Take notes on what you taste and with what you might serve the wine. The amount that is poured in tasting rooms is usually not enough to allow you a first taste to get the "mouth shock" that a first taste imparts and then a second taste to really understand the wine, so try by taking a small sip first. The reason for the small pour, by the way, is to ensure that you taste but not get drunk after a few tasting rooms. If you don't rent-a-tour, have a designated driver.

This author's own personal suggestion is that, before you taste a wine, create an image in your mind's eye of what you will serve it with (or not, if it is for Summer sipping or to be taken by the fire in Winter). If you do this, while in a tasting room, you are less likely to arrive home with a case of wine that won't fit in with your dinner.

Before you taste, smell. Then smell again. Test the aroma. Hold the glass at your waist. Can you smell it? Then move it to your chin. Again, can you smell it? Finally, put your nose into the bowl of the glass. (Might look funny, but it works!) The aroma should give you a hint of what with you might serve the wine. If you cannot think of anything, and can't imagine this wine as a sipping wine for the back deck or for in front of the winter fireplace, then, today at least, this is not the wine for you.

Tasting notes: Barrel aging, hang time, blend. Remember these three.

Do not be too charmed by "the romance of the wine." Wine grapes involve farming and risk. Whatever you eat or drink, in most instances it has been farmed. Honor the farmer by cherishing what s/he offers you.

Getting your wine home

Don't put that case (or bottle) in your car on a hot summer's day and leave it there while you are in the next tasting room and expect the wine to be good when you get it home!

HEAT is the worst enemy of wine. If you are serious about your wine (or even if you are not, but don't want your wine ruined), purchase a portable refrigerator that will work off your car cigarette lighter (make certain that you have one; some recent automobiles do not!). It should be big enough to hold twelve bottles stacked out of their case. A store that sells camping goods is most likely to meet your needs.

If you have filled the fridge and still have more tasting rooms on your list, drive back to your motel (or Up North Michigan cottage/home) and leave your purchase there before continuing your tour.

Then, over the next months, enjoy.

At home with your wine

Should wine be refrigerated?

Yes, if you intend to buy lots of wine and keep some for drinking in years or decades ahead, a wine cooler is suggested. Most often basements are cool enough, even for long-term storage. Measure the temperature in mid- to late-Summer. If it is 58° or cooler, your basement is suitable for storage. (I have found this solution to be acceptable in Up North Michigan with our lower temperatures, though professionals generally do not recommend it.) A wine cooler is certainly the best solution.

Should the wine be decanted?

The better the wine and the older it is, the greater the importance of decanting. Some suggest this is less important for white wines than red. Decanting exposes the greatest possible wine surface to the air. Why is this important? Air releases a wine's complexity (the character of a quality wine as it "matures") and its aromatics (what the nose senses of the wine) and softens the wine's tannins. Any red wine will "soften" if aired in a decanter or in wine glasses. An hour before drinking is enough to soften the wine and release the flavors, particularly a red, often beyond your wildest expectations. Any sediment (not a bad thing, but not good drinking) should be allowed to settle in the bottom of the decanter – or the glass, if it got that far. If you don't have a decanter, you should open the bottle at least an hour before serving and pour the wine into glasses.

How much should one pour?

Various suggestions can be made from filling the glass to ⅓ or ½ of its capacity. Though the shape of the glass makes it difficult to determine the exact third or half point, such a suggestion misses the point. The simplest pour is to fill the glass to the point where the glass is widest, namely, the point where the curve turns inward. Why? This provides the greatest surface for airing the wine.

Serving Your Wine: Temperature and Airing

Temperature and air: they both affect how your senses perceive a wine's flavors and aromas.

To keep things simple, the traditional rule has been to serve wine at room temperature. Many of our wine appreciation books come from Europe so they say that, too. But that is based on the temperatures maintained in European homes, traditionally lower than in our American homes. Europeans put on a sweater if it feels cold!

While some authorities on wine service quote very specific temperatures for different wine types, I have chosen instead to quote a range of temperatures that work for the various wine types.

White wines deserve chilling to the mid- to upper-40°s Fahrenheit. Sparkling wines deserve 39°F to 52°F, with the sweetest ones getting the coldest chill.

The general rule for red wine is to serve between 50°F and 65°F. Also, any red wine needs airing – decanting, as mentioned– and that alone will raise its

temperature as it airs for about an hour. Room temperature in American homes tends to run between 68° and 77°F, so one hour is plenty. If you don't have a decanter, still open your wine an hour before drinking and pour it into glasses, up to the level of the widest air surface in the glass. Simply opening your bottle and leaving the wine in the bottle until drinking time does not provide sufficient airing.

In general, for reds, the greater the wine's complexity, the warmer you serve it. But – and this is a big "but" – if the wine (red or white) gets too warm, its alcohol evaporates which in turn destroys the balance that the winemaker worked so hard to achieve.

Please resist the temptation to put a wine in the freezer for quick cooling. Don't even think about it! Your wine will get too cold. You don't ever want a wine to get colder than the normal 38°F refrigerator temperature. If you need to cool your wine in a hurry, there are "jackets" available (that you can store in your refrigerator) that will wrap around your bottle and cool it rather quickly. Never put ice cubes in your wine!

Do not ever, please, lose sight of the artistry, knowledge and care that went into your bottle of wine – from the siting and planting of the vineyard, to the growing and the harvesting of the fruit, and finally to the complex process of making your wine. As a reflection of its life story, your wine should be treated, enjoyed, shared, as the work of art that it is.

Stemware

So you don't drink that much wine but, once a year while in Traverse City, you tour the tasting rooms and buy a few bottles. So why worry about the glass you will use to drink your wine; just put it your everyday water glass.

Well, not exactly! It won't taste as good as if you drink it from a well-designed stemmed wine glass.

You don't believe me! Well, the Austrian company Riedel tested all manner of shapes with all the standard wines, and then some, and found that the shape of the glass changed the flavor of the wine. And when Robert Parker, "the Nose" as many call him because he can differentiate just about any wine from any other just by its aroma, tried Riedel wine glasses, he agreed; "The effect of these glasses on fine wine is profound. I cannot emphasize enough what a difference they make," said Robert M Parker, Jr., in *The Wine Advocate* magazine.

Let us first touch on the stem. If you hold the bowl of the glass, you will warm the wine (and correct temperature is one aspect of good wine serving and tasting). You will have seen people who manage not to hold the stem at all, holding the base of the stem instead. Unless you are practiced at this, especially if you have a big "bowl" full of Cabernet Sauvignon, you would do better to choose a glass with a stem long enough that you do not warm the wine in the bowl as you hold the stem.

If you an occasional drinker, a single "big red" glass, the large and somewhat tulip-shaped Bordeaux, could serve as your all-purpose glass. This same single all-purpose glass is used by no less an authority than Master of Wine Jennifer Simonetti-Bryan in her video exploration of wines, *The Everyday Guide to Wine*.

Another option for the occasional drinker is to choose one general-purpose glass for red and another for white. Riedel (full name, Riedel The Wine Glass Company) introduced an inexpensive line of machine-made wine glasses including a generic Red wine and a generic White wine glass in 1990. (I do not mean to "advertise" Riedel, but they were the pioneers. Other glassmakers have since followed suit.)

If you drink more white than red, you might go for a Chardonnay glass – or a Riesling glass, if that's your primary white wine.

Expanding from there, and depending on your wine-drinking style, you may go for any or all of those illustrated. The question is: how much wine do you drink, and which type of wine. Not just "red or white?" but which red(s) and which white(s). So, for your reds, you might choose, the Bordeaux and/or the Burgundy glasses; and, for whites: the Chardonnay and/or the Riesling glasses.

Let's look now at four basic wine glass shapes.

Left to right:

Riesling/Sauvignon
Bordeaux/Cabernet Sauvignon/Merlot

Burgundy/Pinot Noir

Chardonnay/Chablis
(Unwooded Chardonnay)/
Viognier

Riesling/Sauvignon
Blanc/Zinfandel/Chianti

Why are there different glass shapes for red and white wines? It all goes back to what Professor Claus J. Riedel discovered in the 1950s; that "the bouquet, taste, balance and finish of wines are affected by the shape of the glass from which they are drunk". Red wines – especially if properly aired - tend to be more aromatic than whites, so a large rounded glass will help capture the aromas and direct them to your nose. The whites are less aromatic, so a smaller straighter-sided glass works best for them.

The Riedel Company has made a science of this. Their initial exploration of wine glass shapes dates from 1961 with a catalog of wine glasses of different shapes and sizes for different wines. In 1973, they introduced their Sommeliers lead crystal, mouth-blown, hand-made glasses. In its extensive 50-page 50th anniversary catalog, Riedel offers multiple lines of stemware, such as their Vinum, Tyrol and Sommeliers lines – the last named, with 38 stemmed glasses and four stem-less black tasting glasses! One of the glasses is for single malt whiskey (Scotch).

A wine drinker who wants the "right" glass doesn't have to buy everything. The more wine you drink, and the more different types of wine you drink, the more different glasses you might WANT to have. At least, don't waste an expensive fine wine on the wrong glass. Essentially it is all a question of the shape of the bowl that determines how the wine flows into your mouth.

A true wine glass has no rolled rim. The rolled rim of inexpensive wine glasses strengthens the glass so it can go in the dishwasher. Without that rim, the maker will probably say, "hand-wash." So why do you want a rim as thin as the walls of the glass? Because that allows the wine to flow freely into your mouth. The rolled rim causes turbulence at the wrong moment before tasting. Or so say the experts.

There is also the champagne flute (not pictured). Whatever glass you use for sparkling wine, it must be narrow and tall, or the bubbles will quickly dissipate.

Please don't agonize over stemware. Above all, wine is to be enjoyed and, to paraphrase Leelanau Wine Cellars' "If they want MerloTT, we'll serve them MerloTT," then try, "if you want your wine in a water GLASS, serve your wine in a water GLASS" and enjoy it

Leelanau Peninsula

Because it all started at Bernie Rink's Boskydel Vineyards, and because it was the first Up North Michigan AVA (and second in Michigan) our survey starts on the Leelanau Peninsula. But first, a word about the AVA.

Leelanau Peninsula American Viticultural Area

An AVA is a unique area in terms of its viticulture. The Leelanau Peninsula AVA was established on March 30, 1982. It came about by petition of Bernie Rink of Boskydel Vineyard, Lake Leelanau, Larry Mawby of L. Mawby Vineyards, Suttons Bay, and Bruce Simpson of Good Harbor Vineyards, Leland. Rink and Mawby were co-writers and submitters of the petition. The need for AVA designation came from the requirement that, to call a winery an "estate winery," it had to be part of an AVA. The Leelanau Peninsula AVA excludes the offshore islands of Leelanau County.

The Tasting Rooms of Leelanau Peninsula

The list below identifies each Leelanau Peninsula tasting room, with the number that is assigned to each cross-referencing to its location on the peninsula map. Tasting room numbering commences with those open at the beginning of 2012, assuming a starting point in the southeast of Leelanau County and driving north on M-22, and then south down the west side of Lake Leelanau. Tasting rooms offering primarily fruit wines or cider come next in the numerical order, followed by tasting rooms that opened during 2012, then by a vineyard planted in 2012, and finally by the MSU Horticultural Research Station (which does not sell its products). Research for this book was completed in 2012. The order of listing implies no special designation or ranking:

On the individual vineyard maps, the direction of the vine rows is shown. There is no indication of the number of rows. North is always at the top of each map. The vineyard maps shown here represent the prime vineyards of each Michigan State registered winery. Additional maps of vineyards that provide grapes to each of these are in a separate vineyard section.

A Note about tasting room listings and Wine offerings

The headers in the following pages give the name and address, phone number and website information of the named business. Vintages for wines are not provided because often there are two or more vintages of a wine being offered at the same time. Some wines in the listings may be sold out. The listings are designed to show what, in any given year, you might find at each tasting room. The listing of wines offered in each tasting room follows these groupings:

1. Ice wines
2. Sparkling wines
3. White wines, including desert wines
4. Rosé wines
5. Red wines
6. Special blends and unique offerings
7. Fruit wines including cider

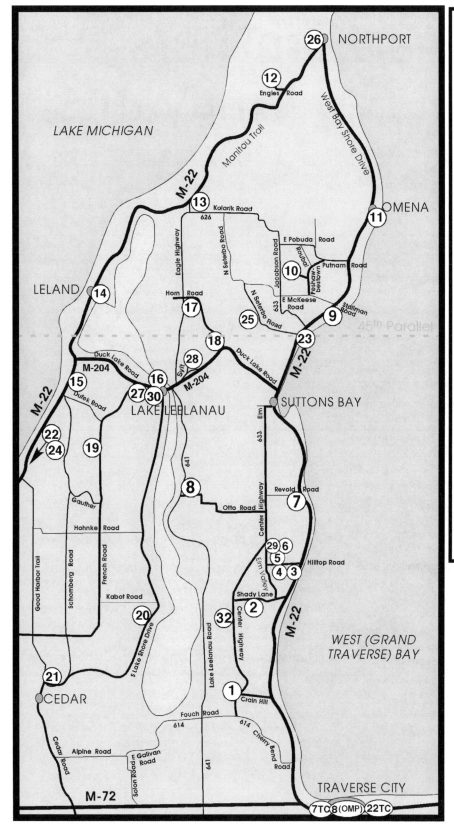

Leelanau Peninsula Tasting Rooms

A Western tour:
24 M22
22 Cherry Republic
21 Longview
20 Bel Lago Slope & Overlook
19 Chateau Fontaine
18 Forty-Five North
17 Circa Estate (closed)
28 Blustone
16 Boathouse
30 Bella Fortuna North Restaurant
27 Laurentide
15 Good Harbor
14 Verterra
13 Gill's Pier
12 Good Neighbor Organic

An Eastern tour:
26 Motovino Cellars
11 Leelanau Cellars
10 Silver Leaf
9 Raftshol
25 Tandem Ciders
23 French Valley (Corky's Bistro)
7 Black Star Farms
8 Boskydel
6 L Mawby +
29 Big Little
5 Ciccone
4 Willow
3 Chateau de Leelanau
2 Shady Lane Cellars
1 Brengman Brothers
7TC TASTES of Black Star Farms
22TC Cherry Republic Traverse City

Northern Wine Loop tour:
The "Loop" features tasting rooms on or north of Route 204.
32 is the NW MI Horticultural Station, MSU extension. There is no tasting room.

There are many ways to wine-tour Leelanau Peninsula. One may start a wine-tasting tour at any tasting room. Head to the top of the peninsula and work your way back. Or do the north half one day, the southern section the next. Given the number of tasting rooms, one might be advised to allot three days to visit all 31 tasting rooms.

Not all roads on the Leelanau peninsula are shown, only those necessary to reach the tasting rooms with the least time in travel.

Tasting rooms in Traverse City:
7TC TASTES of Black Star Farms, their Tasting Room in The Village on the Commons in Traverse City's west side.
8(OMP) Left Foot Charley, also in The Commons
22TC Cherry Republic on Front Street

13

1. Brengman Brothers at Crain Hill Vineyards

231-946-2764
9720 S Center Highway
Traverse City, MI 49684
www .brengmanbrothers.com

Owners: Robert and Ed Brengman, with brother Gerald handling the heavy equipment. Wines are made both at the winery and by Bryan Ulbrich at Left Foot Charley in Traverse City.

Tengo famiglia. Loosely, it is Italian for "I support a family," but more than that, it is about being a man, providing for the wife and children, and thus a good reason for being alive. It applies equally to the Brengman family who were farmers from Belgium who came first to Detroit, then Up North Michigan. In Detroit, they entered the entertainment industry. Pleasing people was a passion they've now brought to Up North Michigan.

The 45-acre vineyard property was bought in 2004 by the Leelanau Land Conservancy and passed to the Brengmans with a proviso allowing a tasting room to be sited on the Crain Hill property. Two parcels, yet unplanted, on the peninsula have been added – Cedar Lake Vineyards and Timberlee Vineyards. Brengman labels will continue to name vineyard and block number, such as Crain Hill Block 65, Cedar Lake Vineyards, Timberlee Vineyards; the Brengmans believe *terroir* is important to each wine's character and want the buyer to be able to identify his or her favorites year after year.

Learning from family in Ontario and uncle/aunt Tom and Linda Scheuerman (See Old Mission Peninsula 8b), the brothers practice what is called "viticulture raisonée," a compromise between conventional and alternative agriculture such as organic or biodynamic approaches. This involves minimal use of fungicides, herbicides and insecticides and prefers composting to chemical fertilizing. Guinea hen and baby doll sheep, for instance, help keep out pests.

According to the Brengman Brothers' published statement, this involves:
1. Preservation or restoration of the physiological balance of the vine by traditional means such as pruning, nutrition, composting, and exposure of the grape clusters to ventilation through canopy management.
2. Estimation, throughout the countryside, of the risk level of a specific viticultural threat and adaptation of interventions according to the necessary risk level.
3. Choosing a product that respects the environment when synthetic treatment does become necessary.
4. Minimization of environmental impact through application of a treatment with respect to the code of good practices while scrupulously managing the effluents and losses.

On a September 16 visit, Robert Brengman informed me that Chardonnay had just been picked and crushed and was now in The Egg (see photo, opposite), the one-and-only-concrete-east-of-the-Mississippi fermentation tank.

For Sip & Savor, a.k.a. "Sip o' de Mayo," the annual Spring May 5 celebration by members of the Leelanau Peninsula Vintners Association, Brengman Brothers served their Runaway Hen Late Harvest Riesling with French Puff Pastry.

For the Harvest Stompede event, the Brengmans offered a variety of cheeses paired with any of their Brengman Brothers wines.

For Toast the Season, the Brengman Brothers paired their Riesling Med-Dry with a Vanilla Cream Puff with Caramel and their Runaway Hen Syrah with Spicy Chili. Officially, however, Brengman Brothers were scheduled to serve Cheese Carmandy Raclette and Moody Blue Cheese with Runaway Hen White Late Harvest, and Rosso Red Blend. It is always good to check with the chef!

For Taste the Passion, a chocolate truffle made with their Valpanessa Refrosco from their italian sister winery.

Tastings are offered in rimless glasses chosen to enhance the varietal character of each wine.

Brengman Brothers label:
Riesling Dry Reserve
Riesling Med-Dry Reserve
Riesling Med-Sweet Reserve
Block 65 Blend*
Gewürztraminer Gary's Reserve

Pinot Noir Rose

Cherry Wine
Egghead Mead

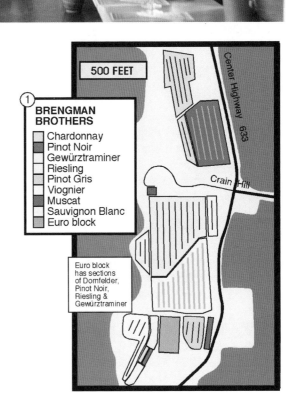

* 65% Chardonnay, 20% Viognier, 15% Sauvignon Blanc

Runaway Hen label:
White
Late Harvest Riesling

Syrah Red
Rosso Red

The lead to this article is cribbed by the author from the play, "Over the River and Through the Woods," by Joe DiPietro, which he (the author, not the playwright) directed for Old Town Playhouse January 2013.

In 2013-2014, Brengman Brothers will be planting their two new Leelanau Peninsula vineyards: Cedar Lake in 2013, Timberlee in 2014.

500 FEET

① BRENGMAN BROTHERS
- Chardonnay
- Pinot Noir
- Gewürztraminer
- Riesling
- Pinot Gris
- Viognier
- Muscat
- Sauvignon Blanc
- Euro block

Center Highway 633

Crain Hill

Euro block has sections of Dornfelder, Pinot Noir, Riesling & Gewürztraminer

2. Shady Lane Cellars

231-947-8865
9580 Shady Lane
Suttons Bay, MI 49682
www.shadylanecellars.com

Dr. Joe O'Donnell is the owner of Shady Lane Cellars. He came north from Grand Rapids with buddy Bill Stouten to fish on the Manistee River. The idea of growing wine grapes followed and a hundred-year-old fruit farm was purchased in 1987 and peach trees were removed to plant 11 acres of vines. Since 2001, the total acreage has grown to 150; the vine plantings grew to 41 acres and now stand at 52 acres. The first sales, in 1992, of methode champenoise wine, helped along with advice on production of "bubbly" from Larry Mawby, took place in a renovated hundred-year-old chicken coop. The farm is an environmentally certified farmstead system.

Ohio-an by birth, Michigander by choice, Adam Satchwell is a longtime winemaker (in France he would be called a wine grower) and is certified as Sommelier by the London, England, Court of Master Sommeliers. Fresh out of high school, and taking an interest in wine, Adam enrolled in the Viticulture/Vineyard Management program at Santa Rosa Junior College, California. At Edmeades Vineyards in the Anderson Valley of Mendocino, he worked with his uncle, Jed Steele. Adam continued his studies at the University of California, Davis. Seven years in Washington, D.C. found Adam managing a specialty wine store. He then went to work for several years as the winemaker at Benmarl Vineyards in Marlboro, New York, which dates back to 1788, and is the oldest continually operating winery in the United States. Adam's next stop was Dearborn, Michigan, where he managed a specialty wine and food store. In 2000, he became winemaker and vineyard manager at Shady Lane Cellars.

"The one thing I have to do is produce wines that are different enough that people will turn left on their way up M-22 at Shady Lane Road," was how Adam explained how he shapes his wines.

"I sometimes use two yeasts," he continued, "but one always dominates. One might begin fermenting quickly while the other has a slower response that will dominate. Hybrid yeasts are available to shape what you want from the grapes."

One tends to think that "blending" means mixing two or more varietals, such as they do in Bordeaux, France, each providing the product with some desired characteristic. But Adam goes further; "I will often put Riesling in up to different seven tanks each with a different yeast. Then I blend the seven different Rieslings to get what I think is commercially worth producing."

Further, "the Riesling from one clone is different from another clone. The Riesling from one side of the vineyard is different from that from the other side of the yard." So each gets its own fermentation.

For the long term, Adam asserts that, although they currently produce 5.000 or so cases each year, "We have the equipment to produce over 8.000 cases. We want to expand, but one does that first by increasing sales." He'll also tell you that his "Pinot Noir is like no other; it is the best!"

Most winemakers on the two Up North peninsulas talk of their local *terroir* and how great it is. Adam doesn't deny that, but says also "I'd love to make wine from grapes grown outside the region. Why not? I'm a winemaker and I like to experiment. I'd love to make wine from German Riesling! But we grow everything in our vineyards to make our wines." Yes, everything is done on the Shady Lane property, from vine to wine.

For the most recent Harvest Stompede, Shady Lane Cellars paired their 2010 Franc'n Franc with Sacchettini Carbonara, made by Chef David Slater of Bluebird Restaurant. These "Little Purses" consist of pasta topped with Sauce Carbonara: bacon, cream, celery, carrots, white pepper and spices.

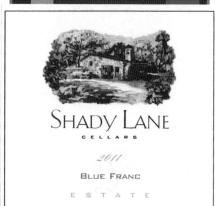

For Sip & Savor, a.k.a. "Sip o' de Mayo," Shady Lane Cellars served Pulled Pork with Pico de Gaio and their Semi-dry Riesling.

Brut (58% Pinot Noir, 42% Chardonnay)

Chardonnay   Semi-Dry Riesling   Coop de Blanc *

Cabernet Franc/Merlot Rosé
Franc 'n' Franc **   Blue Franc ***   Cabernet Franc
Pinot Noir   Coop de Rouge

* 60% Vignoles, 40% Riesling
** 65% Lemberger = Blue Franc, 29% Cabernet Franc, 6% Merlot
*** Blue Franc is trademarked in California.
    Adam Satchwell is the only vintner outside California who can use the name. "Blue Frank" refers to Blau Frankish, which is also known as Lemberger. It has lower alcohol than Pinot Noir.

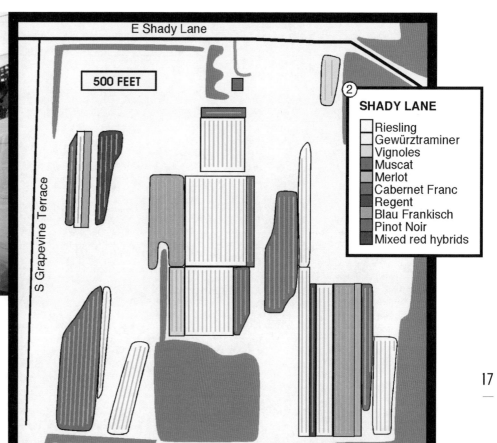

E Shady Lane

500 FEET

S Grapevine Terrace

② SHADY LANE

- Riesling
- Gewürztraminer
- Vignoles
- Muscat
- Merlot
- Cabernet Franc
- Regent
- Blau Frankisch
- Pinot Noir
- Mixed red hybrids

17

3. Chateau de Leelanau Winery & Vineyard

231-271-8888
5048 S W Bayshore Drive
Suttons Bay, MI 49682
www.chateaudeleelanau.com

It would be hard to miss the Chateau de Leelanau tasting room. It is the first one you meet on M-22, ten miles from where US 31 makes a right turn at West Bay. But you might need a genealogist to understand its history!

First, Chateau de Leelanau is part of Cherry Bay Orchards, which has been around since 1968. The whole Gregory family tends the winery, located at the entry to the vineyards. Matt manages the day-to-day operations of the wine business.

Don Gregory and Matt's father Bob Gregory purchased the winery properties from Roberta Kurtz in 2009. Joanne Smart and Roberta had purchased land in 1987 and, in 1989, began pulling out fruit trees and replanting with grapevines. They became the first all-woman owned winery in the region. At the time of the Gregory family purchase, the winery's juice was being processed at a custom wine processing facility. It was not a wine with a popular name, so they labeled it Hawkins Red, after the property on which is located the Chateau de Leelanau tasting room.

So began the tradition of labeling some of the wines based on long-time Leelanau Peninsula farms. As to "Solem", both Farm White and Farm Red, that is Dan Gregory's original connection to cherries; Solem Road is west of Peshawbestown and north of Suttons Bay and just south of the Cherry Bay Orchards fruit processing facilities.

But that brings us back to Matt Gregory, the general manager. You will find him at the tasting room for every special event and on many other days too. But come hunting season, he just might leave the room to his assistant, Makena. Then there is Roger Veliquette, the prime overseer of winemaking, Mark Miezeo, Don's son-in-law, and Andrew, Matt's brother. All are partners in Cherry

Bay Orchards. They see the winery as a boutique operation, making a limited bottling of high quality wines.

Chateau De Leelanau introduced Bianca, a Hungarian white wine, to Michigan. Note that only 44 cases were made.

For Sip & Savor, a.k.a. "Sip o' de Mayo," the annual Spring May 5 celebration by members of the Leelanau Peninsula Vintners Association, Chateau de Leelanau served Pulled Pork Tacos paired with their Solem Farm Red.

For the LPVA Harvest Stompede, Chateau de Leelanau presented a Smoked Bacon-wrapped, Apple-stuffed Pork Tenderloin with Riesli Chimichurri Sauce featuring apples from the Gregory farm and paired with their 2011 Pinot Gris.

For Taste the Passion, Chateau de Leelanau unveiled their new release 2011 Select Harvest Riesling, paired with a Savory Chocolate Mystery.

Peach Fizz

Pinot Gris
Schaub Farm White (house blend)
Pinot Grigio
Chardonnay Sur Lie
Bianca (their prime wine)
Riesling Harvest Select

Pinot Noir
Cabernet Franc
Hawkins Red

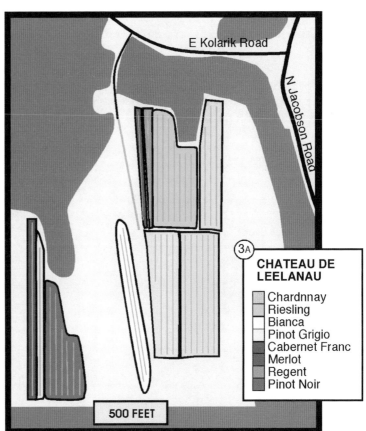

4. Willow Vineyard & Winery

231-271-4810
10702 East Hilltop Road
Suttons Bay, MI 49682
www.willowvineyardwine.com

One doesn't exactly "drive up" to Willow's tasting room. The gravel drive goes downhill before it turns right, and one can look uphill to the tasting room. Once in the tasting room, however, it will be tempting to forego tasting and just purchase a glass of wine and go out to the patio and sit in the sun, admiring the view over the vineyards to West Bay.

Though John and Jo Crampton's Willow Vineyard was established in 1992, it wasn't until 1995 that the tasting room was being built – by John, a landscaper from Holly, Michigan (near Detroit) - into a hillside overlooking the vineyards and West Bay. Owners John and wife Jo, from Union Lake, Michigan, began their operation by first planting vines, then by having the grapes vinted by Larry Mawby back when Mawby was still doing some table wines. John learned from Mawby for two years. To create their own winery to make their wines, the Cramptons cut into the hillside and placed the winery under their house.

The winery operation opened in 1998, becoming the fifth winery on Leelanau Peninsula with Chris Guest (of Seven Lakes Vineyard in the Holly-Fenton region) as early winemaker. Now, he and John make the wine.

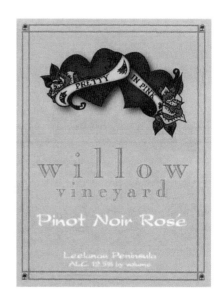

John recalls that, in the early days when his planting of new vines was just starting, he took five boxes of rootstock to be stored in Dave Hansen's Suttons Bay cold room. The problem was that the grafted varieties had to be ordered a year in advance and either immediately planted or protected from dying. In March 2003, with Lake Michigan and West Bay frozen over, the temperature plunged to about 25 degrees below zero for thirty hours, killing much of Willow's vineyard and the vines of almost every other vineyard in the two-peninsula region, requiring much replanting.

While growing only three *vinifera* varieties, Willow thrives as a small producer (they think they may be the smallest in Michigan) with just five offerings. In the heart of the Great Recession, Willow bottled half bottles so prices could be made reasonable. Despite the winery's small size, Willow's patio is likely to be well populated on warm summer days. Weddings have been celebrated on and around the rocks that form part of a wall.

Though dogs seem ubiquitous at wineries, Willow has the wisdom of a cat in their patio. Frankie seems quite content in her private bed!

20

For Sip & Savor, a.k.a. "Sip o' de Mayo," Willow served Mexican Strawberry Crunch with Strawberry Fondue, paired with their Baci Rosé.

For Toast the Season, Willow served French Vanilla Pumpkin Squares with a Butterscotch Fondue, paired with their 2011 Pinot Gris. For all such events, Willow produces the food they serve in their own kitchen.

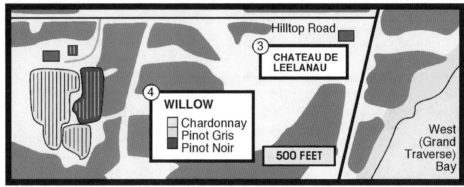

Willow's wine list is not long, but the wine all comes from their own vines on the hillside next and below their house, winery and tasting room.

Pinot Gris   Reserve Pinot Gris   Chardonnay

Baci Rosé   Sweet Rain   Pinot Noir Rosé

Pinot Noir

5. Ciccone Vineyard and Winery

231-271-5553
18343 E Hilltop Road
Suttons Bay, MI 49682
www.cicconevinewayrd.com

Ciccone Vineyard has the only Up North Michigan planting of Dolcetto. Why is that important? Because it is the perfect wine for a simple cheese pizza! Dolcetto is slow to ripen, but produces huge clusters of grapes. One knows the berries are ripe when they start to fall off the cluster on their own: that is when to pick, and that is when pure Dolcetto is made and bottled at the Ciccone Winery.

Ciccone Winery is a true Mom & Pop organization: no outside investors. Silvio "Tony" and Joan Clare Ciccone, do everything by hand! They even bottle by hand (no machine). They hand cork. They put the cap over the top and seal by hand. They put front and back labels on in the barn. Only in the spring does Craig Cunningham help prepare the vines.

Tony is originally from Pittsburgh, then moved to Rochester, Michigan, where a half-acre plot in his back yard was his first vineyard.

When Tony and Joan Clare came Up North, where they and their eight children had vacationed, they looked for a place to start a winery. They found Old Mission Peninsula was too expensive - $10,000 per acre was the asking price but, as soon as Tony offered it, someone overbid him. So, he was shown a site on the Leelanau Peninsula, an old fruit farm with 40 to 50 year old trees, many of them dead. He did a soil test, found it to be mostly clay with some pockets of sand. He bought 40 acres, of which 14 are now in vines, with expansion planned. On the Leelanau Peninsula, Tony's $10,000-per-acre outlay included the land – and the costs of planting the vines, putting in the posts and wires to hold them – in other words, an acre of producing vines. The property came with a house that was nearly new, having been lived in for just one year.

6,000 vines were purchased from Warner in the Finger Lakes of New York and planted in the spring of 1996. Tony went through three augers, digging every one of the 6,000 holes, with Joan, on her knees, and two others doing the planting. Ciccone Vineyard grows Cabernet Franc, Pinot Noir, Chardonnay, Pinot Grigio, Gewurztraminer, Dolcetto, Pinot Blanc, Riesling, Merlot, Cabernet Sauvignon, Muscat, Malbec, Marechal Foch and De Chaunac. The vines are rooted in soil characteristic of the region: clay and sandy loam. Most of the vineyards face west to benefit from the long summer days. The vineyard climate is moderated by Lake Michigan to the west and Grand Traverse Bay to the east. A lake effect natural downdraft delays both blossoming, minimizing blossom damage, and first frost,

Tony grows not what everyone else thinks will sell, so much as "what the soil wants to produce" and which he can make into a wine he'd want to drink. The fruit is picked and sorted by hand. The wines are made using traditional techniques under Tony's direction. He embraces the "European" style of wine, and most of Ciccone Vineyard wines are dry and off-dry. For the customers preferring late harvest Riesling, that is planned for, perhaps, 2013.

Though the term has marketing pizzazz rather than regulatory significance, Ciccone strives to operate entirely as an "estate winery," namely a winery where everything from the vines to the production facilities is on site. Only in bad years when they need product to sell do they import grapes: "Michigan" on the label reveals when this is the case. A normal annual output is 2,500 to 3,000 cases.

Tony takes particular pride in his 3-clone Pinot Noir, which he asserts would go well with lamb or veal.

The Ciccone family hails from Pacentro, Italy; Pacentro is the name of a new Pinot Blanc Moscato blend to be released in 2013.

There is a story told by Traverse City's Tuscan Bistro. Back in the fall of 2011, an opera singer came to Traverse City to sing at the First Annual Traverse City Wine & Opera Festival sponsored by the Ciccone, Tabone (Old Mission Peninsula) and Grossnickle (Forty-Five North) families. After the concert, Tony invited the singer to be the guest celebrity at a late night dinner. Off they went, all forty or so persons, to the Tuscan Bistro at 11 pm. They sang, ate and drank until 4 in the morning. Yes, Tony is a true opera-loving Italian. After all, while America created jazz, Italy created opera. The "second annual" Wine & Opera Festival is scheduled for 2013.

Ciccone's offerings at the Tasters Guild Auction in February at Northwestern Michigan College's Culinary Institute

Ciccone Vineyard & Winery

Reserve
Cabernet Franc
Leelanau Peninsula
Estate Bottled Table Wine
2001

For Sip & Savor, a.k.a. "Sip o' de Mayo," Ciccone Vineyard & Winery served a Taco Salad paired with a Sangria featuring their house Dolcetto.

For Toast the Season, Ciccone served Italian Bruschetta with Ripe Tomatoes, Fresh Garden Basil and Garlic, served on Toasted Italian Baguette. This was paired with their 2011 Pinot Noir.

For Taste the Passion, Ciccone Winery paired Italian meatballs with their 2011 Cabernet Franc. Games include cork fishing and wine bottle ring toss. Prizes awarded.

Chardonnay   Pinot Grigio   Gewürztraminer
Michigan Riesling   Nectar **

Pinot Noir   Cabernet Franc   Due Rossi*
Lee La Tage

Starboard (brandy)

Bella Ciliegia (Balaton cherry wine)

* Marechal Foch & De Chaunac
** 50/50 Chardonnay & Pinot Grigio

Food pairings are suggested for all Ciccone wines.

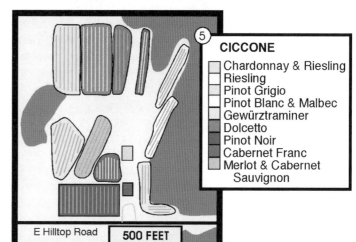

CICCONE
Chardonnay & Riesling
Riesling
Pinot Grigio
Pinot Blanc & Malbec
Gewürztraminer
Dolcetto
Pinot Noir
Cabernet Franc
Merlot & Cabernet Sauvignon

E Hilltop Road   **500 FEET**

23

6. L. Mawby Vineyards

231-271-3522
4519 South Elm Valley Road
Suttons Bay, MI 49682
www.lmawby.com

Larry Mawby is both owner and winemaker of L. Mawby.

Wines are living things, raised with care, giving voice to our joie de vivre. "There are people who use grapevines as landscaping. Some are interested in grapevines as 'an agricultural enterprise,' and hope to make a living. Then there are those like myself who grow grapes to make a living." Thus spoke Larry Mawby.

L. Mawby. A legend. Yet some would ask, Larry Mawby or L. Mawby, which is the legend? Or is it M. Lawrence, and sex? That misses the point. L. Mawby and M. Lawrence labels are sold well beyond Michigan's borders.

There are four common methods of sparkling wine production, but only two are relevant here. There is the *Metodo Charmat* in which the wine undergoes a secondary fermentation in bulk tanks, and is bottled under pressure; it is known as cuve close in America. Then there is the traditional method or *méthode champenoise*, which involves the secondary fermentation in the bottle. L. Mawby uses the *méthode champenoise*, and M. Lawrence the cuve close method. Production of the latter commenced in 2004.

The first vines at L. Mawby were planted in 1973 with about 20 acres planted currently. L. Mawby has produced "estate grown and bottled" Leelanau Peninsula wines since their first crush in the fall of 1978. The L. Mawby line of sparkling wines made by the méthode champenoise arrived in 1984.

So, how do we get Sex? The wine!

Well, it all started with a pink sparkling wine called Dionysus, after the Greek god of wine. Sold maybe 80 cases a year. Larry received a phone call from a California lawyer advising that he owned the name "Dionysus" for his wine, so Larry had to stop using it. The label changed to simple "Rosé." Sold maybe 80 cases a year.

Meanwhile, the tasting room ladies were complaining about long or otherwise unpronounceable wine names like Chardonnay, Riesling, and such. Yeah! So Larry offered to shorten the names on his labels. He asked, "Would you ladies like to sell 'sex' all day long?" Well . . . So the boss submitted the label to the government for approval, as required, expecting it to be rejected so he could go back and say, "I tried." Three weeks later, "Sex" got governmental approval. Sold 1,200 cases the first year! It remains his best-selling wine.

Of course one must understand Mawby-style labeling. "Detroit" is sold around the Leelanau and Grand Traverse county area, but should you look for it in Grand Rapids, you would search in vain. But you would find "GR." Yes, that's it. Kazoo in Kalamazoo, Buckeye in Ohio, Chi in Chicago, and NYC in New York. Same wine. Oh yes, L. Mawby sells overseas; Denmark regularly takes 50 cases.

L. Mawby is proud of improvements made to the facility in 1998, including additional space and the purchase of new equipment to allow specialization in production of methode champenoise sparkling wines. Their handpicked grapes are whole-cluster pressed in a Bucher tank. A computer-controlled gyropalette, made in Champagne, France, does the riddling. Also from France are additional equipment and the bottles. Larry believes L. Mawby may be North American's largest producer of *méthode champenoise* sparkling wines.

24

For Sip & Savor, a.k.a. "Sip o' de Mayo," L. Mawby served local Xylo Bistro's Ceviche in Scoop Corn Chips (there was a non-shellfish alternative available) and paired it with their 'Wet' Sparkling Wine.

For Toast the Season, L. Mawby served local Apple slices and Black Diamond Cheddar with their Blanc de Noir.

For Taste the Passion, L. Mawby paired Jadore with chocolates from Grocer's Daughter Chocolates.

L Mawby:
Cremant Classic (100% Vignoles)
Conservancyl*
Talisman Brut (Vignoles, Pinot Noir, Pinot Gris & Chardonnay)
Jadore Demi Sec (Vignoles, Pinot Noir, Pinot Gris & Chardonnay)
Blanc de Blancs Brut (Chiefly Chardonnay)
Consort Sec (Chiefly Chardonnay)
Blanc de Noirs (Pinot Noir)

M Lawrence:
Wet Pinot Gris & Riesling)
US Brut (Pinot Noir & Chardonnay)
Sex, Brut Rosé (Pinot Noir & Chardonnay)
Fizz Demi Sec (Pinot Noir & Chardonnay)
Sandpiper (Seyval and others)   Detroit (Vidal & Muscat)
Green (Cayuga & Vidal)

*$2 of every bottle sold goes to the Farmland Preservation Fund of the Leelanau Conservancy.

L. Mawby purchases wine grapes from other vineyards on Leelanau Peninsula. See the Leelanau Vineyard Maps Section.

Big Little's Tasting Room is scheduled for opening in Spring 2013. Their vineyard map is with Blustone Winery.

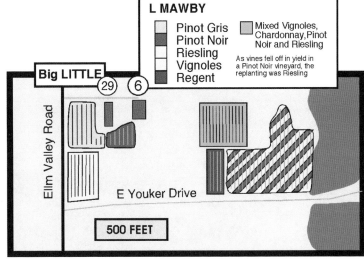

7. Black Star Farms
Leelanau

231-944-1270
10844 East Revold Road
Suttons Bay, MI 49682
www.blackstarfarms.com

There are two other Black Star Farms tasting rooms: on Old Mission Peninsula and TASTES of Black Star Farms located on the Mercato level of The Village at Grand Traverse Commons.

Don Coe and grower Kermit Campbell are the owners, and Lee Lutes the winemaker, of Black Star Farms. The partners purchased Sport Valley Farm, a 120-acre equestrian facility, in 1997. The property included the red estate house, currently the B & B Inn, stables, barns, and paddocks. In March 1998 this became Black Star Farms, named after the stylized star in the marble foyer of the estate house. Lee Lutes, former vintner at Peninsula Cellars on Old Mission Peninsula, was employed as winemaker to process the 1998 vintage in the new winery. Lee is a Michigan native with winemaking experience in Italy.

Lee notes that the first vintage was not from the Revold Road Farm, but from Kermit Campbell's properties, which were planted in 1991 on Old Mission Peninsula. BSF is a cooperative. Each vineyard owner has invested in BSF. Thus, with vested interests and long-term relationships, each cares directly for the quality of the grape crop. One example is the Leorie Vineyard, a former gravel pit and thus with a stable *terroir*, on Old Mission Peninsula, has been with Black Star Farms 15 years. No fertilizer is used. The current manager has been with the property for ten years. With Black Star Farms for 12 years, the Stanton Vineyards grows mostly Chardonnay on beach sand that is rarely irrigated. Their Chardonnay is often offered as "Isidor's Choice."

A 20-25,000 case output is a good year.

"Waterfall," the vines at the entry to Black Star Farms Leelanau when covered with bird netting.

For Sip & Savor, a.k.a. "Sip o' de Mayo," the annual Spring May 5 celebration by members of the Leelanau Peninsula Vintners Association, Black Star Farms offered a Taco bar and with the tacos paired with their Hard Apple Cider or Artisan Red.

For Toast the Season, Black Star Farms-raised Pork and Lamb Cassoulet was paired with their Red House Red. Cassoulet is a hearty, meat-studded dish from south-western France featuring a slow-simmered mix of beans, pork, lamb and pancetta that takes its name from the earthenware casserole in which it was traditionally made.

For Taste the Passion, Black Star Farms served a white chocolate cranberry lollipop with salted pistachio paired with their Sirius Raspberry Dessert wine.

The Black Star Farms website offers suggestions for food pairings.

A Capella Riesling Ice Wine

Sparkling Wine[5]   Be Dazzled[4]
Isidor's Choice Blanc de Noir

Arcturos Pinot Blanc   Arcturos Sur Lie Chardonnay
Arcturos Riesling   Arcturos Barrel-Aged Chardonnay
Arcturos Dry Riesling   Arcturos Late Harvest Riesling
Isidor's Choice Pinot Grigio   Arcturos Pinot Gris
Red House White*

Arcturos Pinot Noir Rosé   Red House Rosé[6]

Arcturos Merlot   Red House Red**
Arcturos Cabernet Franc   Leorie Vineyard Merlot Cabernet Franc
Arcturos Pinot Noir   A Capella Pinot Noir
Isidor's Choice Pinot Noir   Black Star Farms Pinot Noir
Vintners Select***   Artisan Red
Black Star Farms Pinot Noir Chardonnay (70/30)

Sirius Red Desert Wine
Spirits: Spirit of Apple, Cherry, Pear, Apricot, Plum, Vineyard Red Grape Grappa and Vineyard White Grape Grappa

Hard Apple Cider   Hard Apple Cherry
Cider
Cherry Wine   Pear and its Spirit

**Cabernet Franc, Merlot, Pinot Noir and small amounts of Marechal Foch & Regent
***51% Merlot, 39% Cabernet Franc, 5% Syrah & 5% Regent
[4] Pinot Noir, Chardonnay & Pinot Meunier
[5] Chardonnay, Pinot Noir & Pinot Blanc
[6] Cayuga, Marechal Foch, Riesling

Note: the blends shpwn above could be varied in future years.
Black Star Farms manages numerous vineyards on both peninsulas. See the Old Mission Peninsula Maps Section and the Leelanau Peninsula Maps Section for additional vineyards.
Chardonnay, Riesling, Pinot Gris & Pinot Blanc

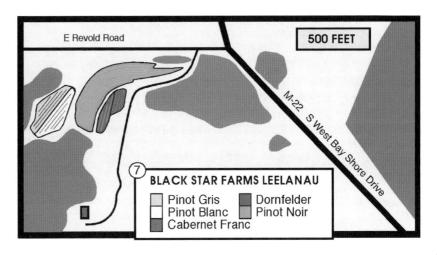

8. Boskydel Vineyard

231-256-7272
7501 E Otto Road
Lake Leelanau, MI 49653
www.boskydel.com

Bernie Rink is the owner. Two of his five sons work the farm. Jim claims to be the wine taster, while Andy, an architect, is the winemaker.

Bernie Rink grew up on a farm and vineyard near Cleveland, Ohio (Avon). Hard work every day. So one day he decided to try something different and moved to Up North Michigan, where he became a library director for 30 years at Northwestern Michigan College

He bought his farmland with no plan to farm it. But, as he says, "Every time I sat on the couch with my wife, we had another son." After four they burned the couch. Still, a fifth son, Andy, arrived.

So, Bernie decided he had to keep them busy so they'd be tired at bedtime. What better way to achieve this than what his boyhood memories conjured up; he created a farm.

The legend goes thus. On his acres, he planted 35 different French hybrids, ten plants each, and those that survived are what he makes his wine from to this day. Why argue with success?

But that is not exactly correct, says Jim. Bernie took vines from wherever he could get them, and this included *vinifera* grapes. But in the winter of 1977 Lake Michigan froze over. It was so cold that the *vinifera* died off while the hybrids survived. Some believe that on a March day, the temperature dropped to 25° below zero. Previous to that, Lake Michigan froze over in 1963, a year before Bernie planted his first vines.

Recently, the farm obtained from Minnesota a cultivar, Marquette, which can survive extreme cold. In 2009, when everything else was hit by frost, this cultivar gave a second bloom that produced a full crop.

If there is an impelling reason for Bernie Rink (his heritage is German and Hungarian) to keep producing wine, it is his belief that wine should be reasonably priced so everyone can drink it! Every summer he looks at what he has lots of, and drops its price to compete with "two buck chuck." In 2012, Aurora Blanc 2008 was offered at $41 (including Michigan tax) a case. That's less than $3.50 a bottle, and it is an easy-to-drink white semi-dry table wine.

All but three of eight Boskydel wines for 2012 are semi dry. Bernie says "Bosky" in some language means "tipsy." "Del" is a shortening and elision from "dell." In another tale, the meanings are reversed and the word Bosky comes from a friend's unpublished manuscript.

Seyval Blanc   De Chaunac Red
Soleil Blanc   Roi des Rouges
Vignoles (dry)
Vin Blanc
Traminette

Rosé du Cru
Rosé de Chaunac

BOSKYDEL

From his original 35 different grape vines, Bernie Rink now has sixteen that he identified for this vineyard map, some recent additions. Nine are unique to his vineyard. The right column is vines identified by their standard color in all these listings. The left & center columns are vines unique to Boskydel..

Corot Noir
Crimson Cabernet
La Crosse   Le Crescent
Chardonel   De Chaunac
Seibel 10868   St. Pepin
                         Geneva Red

Vignoles
Seyval Blanc
Traminette
Noiret
Marquette
Frontenac
Muscat

500 FEET

Lake Leelanau

S Lake Leelanau Drive 641

E Otto Road

8

9. Raftshol Vineyards

231-271-5650
1865 North West Bay Shore Drive
Suttons Bay, MI 49682
www.raftsholvineyards.com

Warren Raftshol is the owner and vintner of Raftshol Vineyards.

A century old farm has been home to three generations of Raftshols. The barn in the photo (below) was built by Anders Raftshol in 1906. The land was first a dairy enterprise, with Anders raising cattle until 1930, and then a cherry orchard. Anders' son Karl and daughter-in-law Jean continued farming, handing over in the course of time to their sons Warren and Curtis (an airline pilot). By 1975, the cherry trees had been pulled out, as unprofitable; now the farm annually produces over 1,000 cases of Bordeaux varietal red wines as well as white wines.

Brothers Warren and Curtis Raftshol began Raftshol Vineyards, the latest incarnation of their family farm, with their 1985 grapevine plantings. They were the first in the area to grow commercial-sized plantings of red *vinifera* grapes, which most local growers believed would fail in our northern climate. The gamble paid off, as the Raftshols are still renowned for Raftshol Red, currently unavailable, one of the first red wines made in Northern Michigan (produced by Peninsula Cellars of Old Mission Peninsula). Other local vineyards have since followed the Raftshols' lead and are now successfully growing red grapes.

A picture of the Raftshols' mother Jean, at age twenty, graces the Vineyards' road sign. It was Jean's foresight in keeping the farm for her children that allowed the Raftshol brothers to continue the long and honorable family tradition of earning a living from the land. The Raftshol Vineyards' wine tasting room is open from noon until 5 p.m., seven days a week, year round.

12 acres produce Cabernet Franc, Cabernet Sauvignon, Merlot and Pinot Noir as well as Chardonnay, Riesling and Gewürztraminer. 2012 offerings:

White

Chardonnay	Dry Riesling
Gewürztraminer	Semi-dry Riesling

Merlot   and Asphalt Red!!!*

Riesling Dessert Wine   Mead
Mama's Boy (port)

*This is a private joke that was shared with this author. At a wine tasting for the North Loop group, Warren was being teased about his grapes ripening early because of the heat generated off the asphalt roadway next his vineyards. But, then, if you look at a Raftshol cork, printed on it you may find "Grapes of Raftshol."

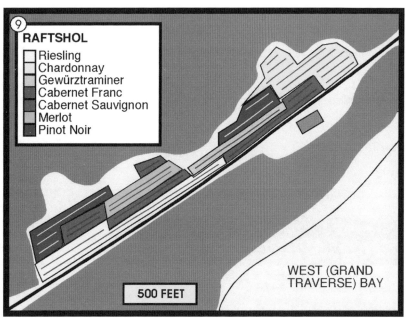

RAFTSHOL
- Riesling
- Chardonnay
- Gewürztraminer
- Cabernet Franc
- Cabernet Sauvignon
- Merlot
- Pinot Noir

500 FEET

WEST (GRAND TRAVERSE) BAY

10. Silver Leaf Vineyard & Winery

231-271-3111
11061 E Silver Leaf Farm Road
Suttons Bay, MI 49682
www.silverleafvineyard.com

Mark & Patti Carlson, owners and winemakers

Chardonnay and Pinot Noir are grown and processed on the site. A neighbor grows the cherries they use.

From an asparagus farm to a horse farm, the Carlsons now make hand-crafted wines, small-batch fermented, hand bottled, hand corked, hand labeled! While growing only Chardonnay and Pinot Noir, traditional Burgundian cold climate *vinifera* wine grapes, the Carlsons currently source additional grapes from carefully chosen Michigan vineyards where a specific *terroir* provides character to the resulting wine. "Great wines begin in the vineyard."

Calling their wines "the next generation of Michigan wines," the Carlsons follow an artisanal approach to winemaking. Not by the book, but by tasting and intuition. Both American and French Oak barrels mature the wines. From vintage to vintage, each wine varietal will change character as it reflects the *terroir* from which the grapes were sourced.

For their wine labels, the Carlsons have asked local artists to provide graphics.

Silver Leaf obtains wine grapes from Harvest Moon vineyard on Leelanau Peninsula. See the Leelanau Peninsula Vineyard Maps Section.

"Fling," by Stefanie Schlatter

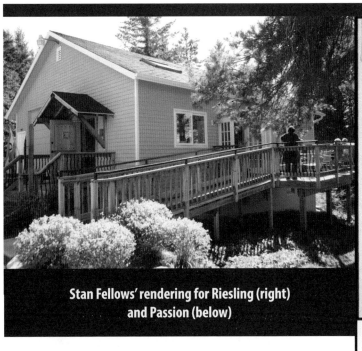

Stan Fellows' rendering for Riesling (right) and Passion (below)

For Sip & Savor, a.k.a. "Sip o' de Mayo", Silver Leaf paired their Purple Passion served as Sangria with a classic Spanish tapas, Patatas Brava, spicy and hot potatoes with a Brava sauce to match, along with another classic, Chorizo Braised in Red Wine.

For Toast the Season, participants enjoyed Silver Leaf's fall specialty of Beer-braised Swedish Meatballs in Hunter Sour Cream Sauce with their Fling Rosé.

For Taste the Passion, Silver Leaf paired their 2011 Pinot Gris with Clam Chowder and welcomed cross-country skiing & snow-shoeing thru their vineyard and on a two-mile trail that crosses Tyler Creek and winds through woods & cherry orchards.

Silver Leaf's website provides suggestions for pairings

Pinot Grigio	Riesling
Chardonnay Sur Lie	Playa Blanca*
Fling	Pinot Noir

*90% Sauvignon Blanc, 10% Pinot Gris

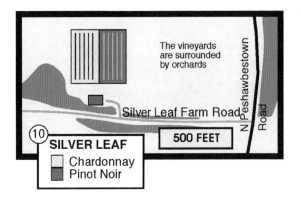

11. Leelanau Wine Cellars

231-386-5201
5019 North West Bay Shore Drive (M-22)
Omena, MI 49674
www.leelanaucellars.com

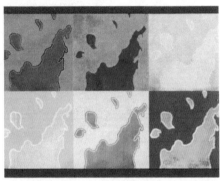

The Leelanau (Wine) Cellars Omena tasting room can be reached not only by car but also by boat, there being a small marina next to the tasting room parking lot.

Mike and Bob Jacobson are the owners of Leelanau Wine Cellars, whose wine label is Leelanau Cellars.

Marcels Lenz is one of the winemakers. Adam Satchwell was winemaker, part-time, until Aug 2012. David Hill moved from Forty-five North to replace him. Winemaking is a year-round process at Leelanau Wine Cellars. Tony Lentych is general manager. Carrie Hanson manages the tasting room

One farm is off M-204, another in Omena, and the original Leelanau Wine Cellars vineyard is southwest of Suttons Bay. These are the basis for all Leelanau Cellars wines.

Leelanau Cellars' wines have evolved over the years from the first release in 1977, but the philosophy has remained constant: to produce both inexpensive wines and affordable quality wines. The philosophy of Leelanau Wine Cellars (the parent company that produces the Leelanau Cellars wines) is to serve all wine lovers, so the cost must be kept down. "If someone comes in and asks to taste MerloTT, the tasting room staff will serve MerloTT."

Accordingly, Leelanau Cellars' labels don't always proclaim "Leelanau Peninsula." Their problem is the popularity of their wines. Tony Lentych explains: "Everything started with local fruit." As the wines became popular and demand exceeded supply, Leelanau Cellars brought in grapes and juice from the West Coast and blended it with their Michigan juice. Nothing is without some Michigan grape juice in the fermented blend. This approach has allowed prices to remain affordable. Over 90 acres of vineyards in Leelanau County support 30 varieties of wines including those that are presented as estate wines.

Leelanau Cellars provides suggested food pairings for their wines, many of which are priced under $10. The varietals command higher prices, yet the highest priced wine in 2012 was the Vignoles, their only wine higher than $14.00, at $18.00. Keeping up with their wine list is always difficult, as new releases are a year-round event. The list below is a combination of the Cellars' online list and their November 2012 tasting room menu, which listed the wines as Table wines, $10 or less, and Premium wines.

For Sip & Savor, a.k.a. "Sip o' de Mayo," Leelanau Cellars featured their Baco Noir Rose with Quesadillas.

For Harvest Stompede, they served a Chocolate Peanut Butter Brownie or an Amaretto Cheesecake with their Great Lakes Red (100% Cayuga).For Toast the Season, **Leelanau Cellars** paired a Sweet Potato Soup with the new release of Late Harvest Riesling.

For Taste the Passion, Leelanau Cellars paired a creamy Brie and Mushroom Risotto with their 2009 Reserve Chardonnay.
How better to celebrate an occasion than at the tasting room counter?

Seasonal Wines:
Autumn Harvest
Spring Splendor   Winter White   Renaissance
Summer Sunset

Fun Wines:
Sweet White   White Sangria
Sweet Red   Great Lakes Red (Concord)
Red Sangria
Witches Brew   Rose Sangria

Vidal Ice Wine   Riesling Ice Wine

Late Harvest Riesling
Semi-Dry Riesling
Dry Riesling Leelanau Chardonnay
Reserve Chardonnay
Late Harvest Vidal

Pinot Grigio   Tall Ship Chardonnay Vignoles
Sleeping Bear White
Tall Ship Select Harvest Riesling

Baco Noir Rosé

Pinot Noir   Meritage*   Baco Noir
Merlot   Sleeping Bear Red** Cabernet Franc
Tall Ship Red

Vintage Port   Strawberry Port   Cherry Port
Raspberry Port

Apple Wine   Blueberry Wine   Cherry Wine
Raspberry Wine   Pomegranate Wine Pear Wine
Strawberry Wine   Cranberry Wine

*Cabernet Sauvignon, Cabernet Franc, Merlot (estate)
**Cabernet Sauvignon, Cabernet Franc, Merlot, Baco Noir & Pinot Noir

Leelanau Wine Cellars owns additional vineyards, and purchases wine grapes from other vineyards, both on Leelanau Peninsula and beyond. See the Leelanau Peninsula Vineyard Maps Section.

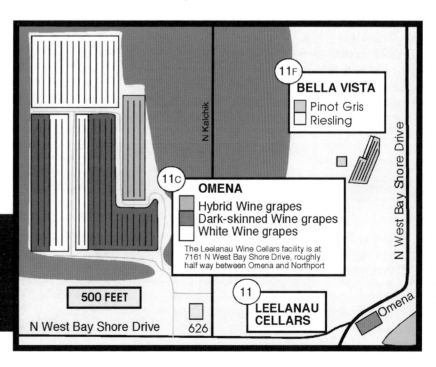

11F
BELLA VISTA
■ Pinot Gris
□ Riesling

N Kalchik

N West Bay Shore Drive

11C
OMENA
■ Hybrid Wine grapes
■ Dark-skinned Wine grapes
□ White Wine grapes

The Leelanau Wine Cellars facility is at 7161 N West Bay Shore Drive, roughly half way between Omena and Northport

500 FEET

N West Bay Shore Drive

626

11
LEELANAU CELLARS

Omena

12. Good Neighbor Organic Vineyard & Winery

231-386-5636
9825 E Engles Road
Northport, MI 49670
www.goodneighbororganic.com

Stan Silverman is both owner and winemaker.

Stan has a Ph.D. Start a conversation by asking him about it! Also, just for fun, ask how many ethnic groups there were on Detroit's east side when he knew the neighborhood.

Good Neighbor Organic Vineyard & Winery is the region's first (and only) totally Certified Organic Vineyard, Orchards & Winery as well as Leelanau's first Micro Brewery. The farm has been selling "certified organic" products since 2001 and produced its first organic wines in 2007!

First and foremost, organic wine is wine made from Certified Organic grapes. The grapes are grown with no synthetic pesticides, herbicides, or fertilizers. By law, the organic wine making process is governed (and certified) by the USDA (through licensed organizations) under the National Organic Program. The NOP includes such aspects as the use of sulfites. Good Neighbor Organic products have NO SULFITES added.

The over-arching goal of organic farming is defined: "The role of organic agriculture, whether in farming, processing, distribution, consumption, is to sustain and enhance the health of the ecosystems and organisms from the smallest in the soil to the human beings" —*International Federation of Organic Agriculture Movement (IFOAM) The Principles of Organic Agriculture Principles of Health*

Stan uses nothing but naturally occurring substances for pest control and soil enrichment. No "poisons" that are not in nature. I asked, "How do you keep the (garter) snakes sober?" Stan just grins.

Organic vines are more widely spaced than in non-organic vineyards, to provide airflow and to assure vines don't cast a shadow on neighboring vines. One cannot manipulate the grape with fertilizers or in other ways.

Organic means no pesticides. This means a lot of insects. Honey bees a-plenty. (This author just had to mention these most beneficial insects.) Lots of frogs around the pond. Birds everywhere. Organic fertilizers are used, as are such things as hay around the roots at ground level to keep away pests.

Google "Organic wine Michigan" and you will get only one: Good Neighbor Organic. Stan's.

Stan notes that, while his costs for wine and cider are similar, his per-bottle profit on cider is approximately half that of wine - $7 versus up to $15.

"Do you guys want clean glasses? I save a lot by re-using them," teases Stan:

For Toast the Season, Good Neighbor served a Spicy Asian Noodle dish paired with their Gewürztraminer,

For Sip & Savor, a.k.a. "Sip o' de Mayo," Good Neighbor paired a cold Spring Chicken & Spinach Pasta Salad with their semi-sweet Peach cider.

For Taste the Passion, Good Neighbor Organic served a culinary rustic slow cooked ham and bean soup with cornbread squares. This dish was paired with the newly released Pinot Noir. For the real taste of passion it is suggested that one try chocolate cherry hard cider- it's like biting into a chocolate covered cherry!

Pinot Gris
Gewürztraminer
Chardonnay
Riesling
Traminette/Vignoles

Cab Franc/Merlot
Noiret

Cheer (cherry wine)

There is also a selection of hard ciders from apples and other fruits.

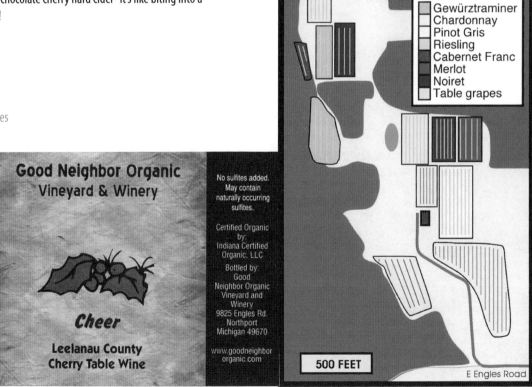

37

13. Gill's Pier Vineyard & Winery

231-256-7003
5620 North Manitou Trail
Northport, MI 49670
www.gillspier.com

Ryan and Kris Sterkenburg own the vineyard, which was founded in 2002. Bryan Ulbrich makes the wine.

Gill's Pier was once a Bohemian settlement. The pier was on the east shore of Lake Michigan. William Gill and his son Wilbur were the owners and operators of a saw and shingle mill. Feeling a connection with the settlers of 100 years ago, Kris and Ryan wanted to honor the name Gill's Pier. Now the Gill's Pier area is known for Gill's Pier Vineyard and Winery, The tasting room is a pole barn, officially opened in May 2004.

It was important to the Sterkenburgs to create an inviting entrance to the tasting room, cutting straight through the middle of the hay fields in which it sits. The potato wagon made in the late 1800s by the Harrison Wagon Company of Grand Rapids, Michigan, sets at the entrance. Two large rocks, original to the property, flank the driveway.

The Sterkenburgs are antique collectors. The story of the mahogany bar (opposite) bears telling. Apparently it came, in three parts (shipped by Kris's uncle), from (Kern) Dail(e)y's Bar and Restaurant in Long Lake, New York, right in the middle of the Adirondacks.

The Gill's Pier Memorial Day Pig Roast (always on a Saturday) provided a thick cut of pork as a sandwich with a choice of wine, coleslaw and cookie, paired with a Merlot 73% Cabernet Franc 27%. Interestingly, author Bill's first great wine love was a Saint Emilion Trottevieille 1959 – a blend, but always with 20% or more Cab Franc. The 2005 vintage retails at $150 per bottle in Michigan; Gill's Pier local version goes for roughly one-fourth that price.

Of course, when a camera appears, the patrons turn to face it! Here is Gill's PierTasting Room on a rare, quiet moment.

2010
Cabernet Franc (27%)
Merlot (73%)

LEELANAU PENINSULA

13% ALC BY VOL

GILL'S PIER

For Toast the Season, Gill's Pier served different pairings each weekend. Weekend I: Sweet & Savory Pumpkin Scones by Bakery Chef/Owner Extraordinaire, Hannah Israel, of Frida's Bakery of Suttons Bay, Michigan. Weekend II: Picadillo de Papa con Chorizo by Costa Rican Chef de Cuisine, Fresia Granados, from Traverse City, Michigan.

For Sip & Savor, a.k.a. "Sip o' de Mayo," Gill's Pier served Gazpacho Shooters paired with their 'Just Unleashed' Red. This red is a blend of three grape varieties: 48% Regent, 38% Dornfelder and 14% Lemberger.

For Taste the Passion, Gill's Pier featured Mexican Hot Chocolate Mini-Pound Cakes paired with their 2011 Riesling. Semi-dry and delicious. Chef Hannah Israel creates a delightful blend of spice and chocolate to pair with this very balanced and very agreeable estate Riesling.

Royce****   Whitewater*   Semi-Dry Riesling

Cabernet Franc Merlot**   Just Unleashed***

Icebox Apple

*100% Vignoles 2011; a blend 2012
**52/48 2011, 27/73 2010
***Regent, Dornfelder & Frontenac Gris
**** Pinot Gris, Seyval Blanc & Sauvignon Blanc
Just Unleashed features always Regent and Dornfelder, then Frontenac Gris or Lemberger, or both, from year to year. Thus the two different listings in the text.

Gill's Pier obtains wine grapes from two other vineyards, which they manage, on Leelanau Peninsula. See the Leelanau Peninsula Vineyard Maps Section.

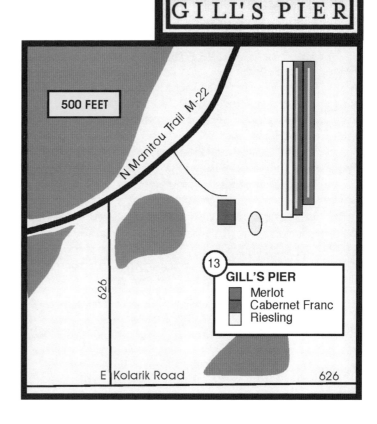

500 FEET

N Manitou Trail M-22

626

13 GILL'S PIER
Merlot
Cabernet Franc
Riesling

E Kolarik Road   626

14. Verterra Winery

231-256-2115
103 E River Street
Leland, MI 49654
www.verterrawinery.com

Verterra Winery may be reached also by boat. From Lake Michigan, dock your boat in Leland Harbor. Head east (up River Street) through Fishtown, cross Main Street (M-22) and find the tasting room on the north side of the road across from the Bluebird restaurant.

If your boat is in Lake Leelanau, head north into the Leland River and dock in either the public spaces by the boat launch or in the slips behind the Bluebird restaurant. Walk across River Street.

Owners of Verterra are the Hamelin family. The wine is produced and bottled by Chaos Vineyards. Paul's son Geoff is the general manager and he has a business degree from Indiana University and an associate's degree from Washington State University in Enology and Viticulture. Shawn Walters is the current vintner. The vineyards are jointly owned by the (related) Hamelin and Telgard families. The vineyard name "Verterra" is a Latin derived word, meaning 'Truth in the Land' signifying the origin of all the grapes from their three vineyards in Leelanau County.

Though his wife comes from a six-generation vegetable farming family down state, Paul Hamelin's career was in pharmaceuticals working for many big companies across the country. But he had been thinking about a vineyard for 30 years. "Are you crazy" was his wife Marty's response as she was thinking about all the physical labor associated with farming, when Paul suggested a winery. In 2005 he and his wife moved to the U.K. and there hatched a business plan. In May 2007, the Hamelins and Telgards, having noticed that the bank had their savings doing nothing much, "plowed" those family savings into the ground as they planted 27,000 plants in 10 days on 18 acres. A former cherry orchard, the Matheson vineyards are three football fields in length and now 65% of Verterra's production. Looking at what they had accomplished by June of 2011, the Hamelin's could count nine different varieties, 28,000 vines in the ground, 27 miles of drip irrigation and 216 miles of wire on this vineyard site. (See also "A Vineyard Tour" article, p. 136.)

Photo looking over the Swede Road vineyard (lower left and center) to Lake Michigan, provided by Verterra.

Vineyards have since been added on Swede Road. From this highest point in the northern part of Leelanau County, there are views west to Lake Michigan and east to East (Grand Traverse) Bay. To be more specific, the views are west to North Manitou, north to the Fox Islands and east to the Northport Bay, Gull Island and even across to the mouth of Little Traverse Bay.

For Sip & Savor, a.k.a. "Sip o' de Mayo," Verterra offered Spicy Pork Enchiladas with red and green sweet bell peppers paired with their Pinot Grigio.

For Toast the Season, Verterra served different specialties for each weekend. November 3 & 4: Local Smoked Whitefish Chowder with New Potatoes paired with the Chaos Red or Unoaked Chardonnay. November 10 & 11: Char-Grilled Individual Pizzetta with Sun-dried Tomato, Fresh Spinach, Garlic, Feta and Mozzarella paired with the option of Chaos Red or Unoaked Chardonnay.

For Taste the Passion, Verterra served Leelanau Apple Tart w/Maple Mousse and Caramel paired with their Chaos White Cuvee.

Verterra's Reserve Chardonnay derives its unique character from its blend of four different clones of the grape, rather than the single or double clone Chardonnay of most wineries. Further, it is aged in oak barrels that are two and half times larger the standard barrel size.

In their tasting room, Verterra uses full-size lead-free wine glasses. The Verterra website provides suggestions for food pairings.

Tundra Ice Wine****

Reserve Chardonnay
Unoaked ChardonnayPinot Blanc
Pinot Gris   Gewürztraminer Medium Sweet
Dry Gewürztraminer
Dry Riesling   Riesling Medium Sweet   Chaos White*

Rosé of Pinot Noir

Reserve Red***   Pinot Noir Chaos Red Cuvee**

* 50% Riesling, 33% Vignoles, 7% Moscato, 7% Cayuga, 3% Seyval
** 44% Cabernet Franc, 26% Merlot, 20% Pinot Noir, 10% Chambourcin
*** Merlot 42%, Cabernet Franc 41% & Syrah 17%
*** 100% Vignoles. Harvested at 48 brix, fermented down to 18 brix

Verterra owns two other vineyards on Leelanau Peninsula.
See the Leelanau Peninsula Vineyard Maps Section.

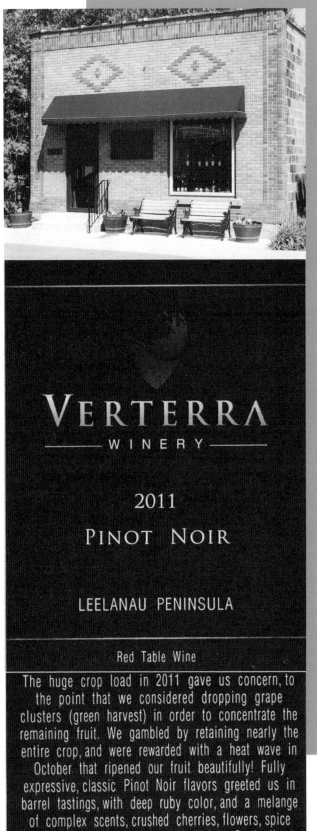

VERTERRA
— WINERY —

2011

PINOT NOIR

LEELANAU PENINSULA

Red Table Wine

The huge crop load in 2011 gave us concern, to the point that we considered dropping grape clusters (green harvest) in order to concentrate the remaining fruit. We gambled by retaining nearly the entire crop, and were rewarded with a heat wave in October that ripened our fruit beautifully! Fully expressive, classic Pinot Noir flavors greeted us in barrel tastings, with deep ruby color, and a melange of complex scents, crushed cherries, flowers, spice and vanilla, with a long, smooth finish. Cool climate Pinot fans will love this wine!

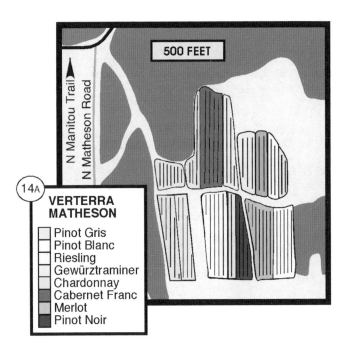

500 FEET

N Manitou Trail
N Matheson Road

14A
VERTERRA
MATHESON
☐ Pinot Gris
☐ Pinot Blanc
☐ Riesling
☐ Gewürztraminer
☐ Chardonnay
☐ Cabernet Franc
☐ Merlot
☐ Pinot Noir

15. Good Harbor Vineyards

231-256-7165
34 South Manitou Trail
Lake Leelanau, MI 49653
www.goodharbor.com

The Simpson family — Debbie and her children Taylor and Sam — own Good Harbor Vineyards. Sam is the winemaker, Taylor the sales and marketing manager.

When you enter the Good Harbor Tasting Room, your first view will be of family, for this is a family operation. Mrs. Simpson, Debbie, is almost certainly at the cash register. Taylor is probably not far away. Oh, you probably won't see Sam. He's down below in the winery part of the building.

Despite working in the winery since 2004, Sam acknowledges a "steep four-year learning curve" since his father, Bruce, passed away in 2009. Sam has reshaped the future of Good Harbor Vineyards, taking it from being winemaker for various other labels to producing entirely for Good Harbor. Sam's winemaking now concentrates on grapes from Good Harbor vineyards and other vineyards for which Good Harbor is a full management service and whose grapes produce the juice that goes into Good Harbor's offerings. The future is growth, expanding markets already established in Ohio, Indiana and Chicago and opening markets in Wisconsin. The Simpson family sees their operation as a mid-Western winery. Every grape that they harvest is from a Michigan vine. You will see "Leelanau Peninsula" on most of their labels.

For three generations, the Simpsons have been on the Leelanau Peninsula, growing cherries on over 300 acres. It was Bruce's father, John Simpson who first had the vision of vineyards and a winery.

Bruce Simpson is known as a founder of Leelanau Peninsula wine production. Graduating from Michigan State University with a degree in agriculture, Bruce went on to study at the University of California, Davis. There he focused on viticulture and enology. Back in the Leelanau Peninsula, Bruce and his wife Debbie in 1980 opened the doors of Good Harbor Vineyard, the fourth winery to be established on the Leelanau Peninsula. 65 acres are currently planted, with one of the largest plantings of Pinot Grigio on the peninsula. The family's goal has always been to produce good unpretentious wines for a reasonable price.

Bruce was instrumental in many aspects of the growth of the wine industry on Leelanau Peninsula. He started the Leland Wine and Food Festival, the oldest running wine festival in Michigan, in 1986. He was an early member of the Michigan Grape and Wine Council, and a founding member of the LPVA.

TRILLIUM

A proprietary blend of white wines
from Michigan's Leelanau Peninsula.
Semi Dry White Table Wine

Produced and Bottled By Good Harbor Vineyards, Lake Leelanau, MI 49653

Many consider the trillium flower, which blankets the forest floor in spring, the emblem of Good Harbor.

For Sip & Savor, a.k.a. "Sip o' de Mayo," the annual Spring May 5 celebration by members of the Leelanau Peninsula Vintners Association, Good Harbor showcased their Trillium wine with a Mexican Corn Chowder.

For Toast the Season, Good Harbor presented a Thai Curry Chicken Soup paired with their 2011 Pinot Grigio.For Taste the Passion, Good Harbor served Chicken Jalapeno soup paired with their Trillium wine.

Moonstruck Blanc de Blanc Brut
Cluster Demi-Sec Rosé

Sleeping Bare Blanc de Blanc
Grüner Veltliner	Tribute	Chardonnay
Pinot Grigio Reserve	Pinot Grigio	Dry Riesling
Fishtown White[6]	Gewürztraminer	Manitou[5]
Trillium[4]	Riesling	

Rosé

Collaboration**   Labernet***
Harbor Red*

*Marechal Foch, Chambourcin, De Chaunac, Pinot Noir and small amounts of other red)
**Cabernet Sauvignon, Merlot, Marechal Foch, Leon Millot, Chambourcin, de Chaunac
***Cabernet Sauvignon, Leon Millot, Pinot Noir, Merlot, de Chaunac, Chancellor   [4]Riesling, Vidal, Vignoles, Seyval ,[5]Chardonnay & Pinot Gris 50:50, [6]Chardonnay, Vidal, Vignoles, Seyval

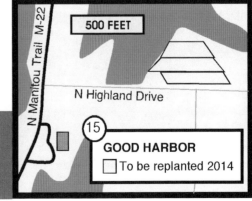

Good Harbor owns additional vineyards and obtains wine grapes from other vineyards on Leelanau Peninsula. See the Leelanau Peninsula Vineyard Maps Section.

16. Boathouse Vineyards

231-256-7115
115 St Mary's Street
Lake Leelanau, MI 49653
www.boathousevineyards.com

The Boathouse tasting room may, of course, be visited by boat. The dock is on the channel between North and South Lake Leelanau.

Jane and David Albert are the owners, with Shawn Walters of One World Winery Consulting as their winemaker. The tasting room opened on April 14, 2012.

The dream of producing northern Michigan wines has been a story of visits and retirement. David and Jane started staying at the Fountain Point Resort in Lake Leelanau late in the 1980s, then came every year until 2002 when they built their Up North Michigan home. Two years later Dave retired and they moved to Leland.

David learned his business acumen as Chief Financial Officer of a small privately-held automotive parts manufacturer in Ionia, Michigan, and retired from there in 2004. "Since we had built our "retirement" home in Leland a few years before, I pursued manufacturing companies in this area but to no avail. At the same time I had an opportunity to work at a winery in Leelanau Peninsula in 2007. I worked in their vineyards, at their Winery and in their Tasting Room for about 6 months. Since Jane and I had always loved tasting the wines up here we decided that growing grapes, producing wine and being able to sell the finished wine with eye-to-eye customer contact would more than offset my desire to go back to manufacturing. Besides, I would love to be a part of producing very good red wines up here.

"So we started from 'scratch'. I asked a winery owner who had grown both cherry orchards and vineyards over the past 40 years: if he were to purchase a piece of land for grapevines, where would it be. He identified three pieces of property for me to check out - none of which were for sale. In early 2008, I was able to purchase one of those properties, land that I believed ideal for growing grapes, and began preparing the land for a vineyard. In December of 2007, we purchased a one-acre plot of land on the Lake Leelanau Narrows in the Village of Lake Leelanau to site our tasting room. We created the "Boathouse Vineyards" company, naming it to reflect the boathouse that was already on the property."

Dave continues: "In 2009 we planted nearly 14 acres of Pinot Gris, Riesling, Auxerrois, Regent, Merlot, Cabernet Franc and Pinot Noir. In 2010 we harvested a small amount of Pinot Noir, Riesling and Pinot Gris. In 2011 we harvested 36 tons of grapes and also planted an additional 2.4 acres of Pinot Gris. In 2012 we harvested over 50 tons of grapes."

"We utilize Shawn Walters, a highly regarded Leelanau Peninsula winemaker, for our winemaking direction. We both knew Shawn's reputation in making excellent white wines. After tasting some of Shawn's Cabernet Franc wines and because of Dave's desire to produce very good red wines from the Leelanau peninsula, we knew Shawn would help us reach our goal."

44

16 acres are planted at Amore Road. Besides the usual northern varieties, the Alberts have chosen the lesser-known vines of Regent and Auxerrois. Dave notes his 16 acres will be able to produce 3,000 cases of wine.

Boathouse Vineyards presents their 2009 Pinot Noir paired with a Mayan spiced brownie covered in single origin Peruvian dark chocolate from "Just Good Chocolate" based in Lake Leelanau.

Pinot Noir	Boathouse Red**	Sunset Table Red***

Sweet Seduction Cherry Dessert Wine

Riesling	Seas the Day" Table White
*Pinot Grigio	Semi-Sweet Riesling
Dry Riesling	

"License to Chill" Pinot Noir Rosé

*35% Riesling, 22% Cayuga, 20% Seyval & 22% Vidal
**50% Cabernet Franc, 35% Merlot, 15% Syrah
***75% Cabernet Franc, 14% Regent, 11% Merlot

Food pairings are suggested for each of these wines.

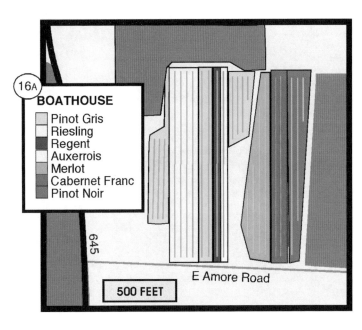

16A

BOATHOUSE
- Pinot Gris
- Riesling
- Regent
- Auxerrois
- Merlot
- Cabernet Franc
- Pinot Noir

645

E Amore Road

500 FEET

45

17. Circa Estate Winery

231-271-1177
7788 East Horn Road
Lake Leelanau, MI 49653
www.circawinery.com

Circa Estate Winery closed at the beginning of 2013. The following describes the winery as we knew it in 2012. David and Margaret Bell are the owners and Margaret the winemaker.

It is but the first of many aesthetic experiences you will meet at Circa Estate Winery's tasting room. Inside you will find art gracing the walls. A piano, too, for Margaret is a professional music teacher and choral director. To her, "winemaking is listening to the song the grape wants to sing. Wine is an aesthetic experience, a work of art in color, taste and smell. Each varietal wine - whether from a unique clone or a blending of multiple clones – and each blend must allow the grape to be what it wants to be, not what some magician with his variety of yeasts chooses." The almost cave-like ambience of the European-style tasting room "cellar" invites a thoughtful sampling of the wines. The wines are served in glasses chosen to release the complex array of flavors of each.

Circa, Latin for "about," a timeless experience, and a name that can go anywhere. Timeless, as winemaking dates back to about Biblical times, perhaps earlier. Having rejected various location-based names, such as Pink House (their late 1800s farm house a short way from the vineyards), it was Margaret who woke David up at 3 a.m. with "Circa."

David and Margaret would head into the two AVA's of southwest Michigan while dating, picking grapes and learning about wine. They added wine grapes to their suburban Chicago home's lot. Summer vacations to Up North Michigan, again picking grapes, led to the Bells' purchase of an abandoned 50-acre farm in the town of Lake Leelanau. Planting vines by hand, adding new plantings year after year, they now offer two styles of wines, artisan and family.

To winemaker Margaret Bell, wine is like a song. You can sing it well, or poorly, depending on how you listen to what the song offers in its words, or the grape in its juice. Sing the song as it is meant to be sung and you have wonderful music. Accept what the grape wants to be and you can make great wine.

Circa manages other vineyards on Leelanau Peninsula, including the Telford Vineyard - from which it also obtains grapes. See the Leelanau Peninsula Vineyard Maps Section.

Seduction ice wine

Pinot Grigio
Chardonnay
Improvisation
Mosaic*

Cabernet Franc
Requisite

* Pinot Grigio, Chardonnay and Muscat Ottonel

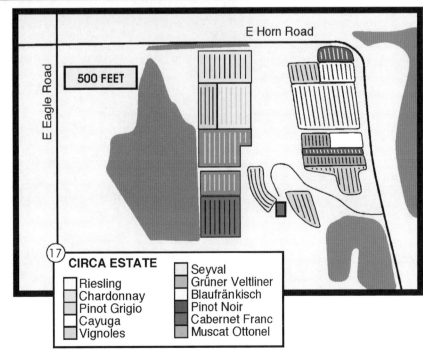

E Horn Road

E Eagle Road

500 FEET

⑰ CIRCA ESTATE

Riesling
Chardonnay
Pinot Grigio
Cayuga
Vignoles

Seyval
Grüner Veltliner
Blaufränkisch
Pinot Noir
Cabernet Franc
Muscat Ottonel

18. Forty-Five North Vineyard & Winery

231-271-1188
8580 East Horn Road
Lake Leelanau, MI 49653
www.fortyfivenorth.com

Since the 1960s, three generations of Grossnickles had been vacationing almost every year Up North Michigan before Steven and Lori with Alanna and Eric decided to plant a vineyard and open a tasting room. Jay Briggs is Cellar Master as of mid-2012. David Hill had served as the winemaker until mid-2012, and continues as consultant. Alanna Grossnickle is the General Manager. She learned about wines in California while Eric was earning his college degree. Channing Sutton, who grew up on the southern end of Lake Leelanau, is the Tasting Room Manager. She learned wine lore from a sommelier in Atlanta, Georgia and achieved sommelier status for herself.

After Steven Grossnickle's leaving the U.S. Navy and establishing an ophthalmology practice in Indiana, the Grossnickles bought a lakefront property on Little Traverse Lake in Leelanau County in 1983. Back then, there were few wineries in the county, but, over time, that changed and the Grossnickles saw the local wine industry growing and flourishing. How could one not be aware of the wine-producing success of the Bordeaux, France, region, 4,500 miles to the east – on that same 45th parallel?

Enter an old high school friend, Maynard Johnson, head of the California State Fair wine judges, who confirmed the quality of Leelanau County wines. What about starting a winery? In 2006, helped by local realtor John Peppler, Steve and Lori bought "a perfect piece of Leelanau", the 100-acre Dean Robb farm on which to found the county's fourteenth winery. The Vineyard is right on the 45th north parallel, hence the Forty-Five North Vineyard & Winery name. 37 acres of grapes and three acres of red raspberries are planted and a production facility with an annual 20,000 case capacity installed.

45 North has a second vineyard on Schomberg Road and obtains wine grapes from Trillium Hill Vineyard on Leelanau Peninsula. See the Leelanau Peninsula Vineyard Maps Section.

Full-sized glasses, with thin rim, are used in the tasting room.

For Sip & Savor, a.k.a. "Sip o' de Mayo," Forty-Five North served Phyllo Bites Topped with Blue Cheese, Dried Cherries and Candied Pecans paired with their Cherry Dessert or Sparkling Hard Chapple.

For Taste the Passion, Forty-Five North presented White Chocolate Brie phyllo shells topped with orange marmalade paired with 45 Gold, an apricot dessert wine aged in Bourbon barrels and fortified with spirits.

Blanc de Pinot Noir

Dry Riesling
Select Harvest Riesling
Riesling
Pinot Gris
Gewürztraminer
Sauvignon Blanc
Chenin Blanc
Semi-dry Riesling
45 White
Unwooded Chardonnay
Reserve Chardonnay

Rose of Cabernet Franc

45 Red
Vintner's Select 45 Red *
Cabernet Franc
Pinot Noir Pinot Noir/Merlot

Cherry Dessert
Sparkling Strawberry
Sparkling Cherry
Peach Cremant
Tart Cherry

Pear Cider Chapple
Hard Cider
45 Gold

* 50% Pinot Noir, 45% Cabernet Sauvignon, 5% Regent

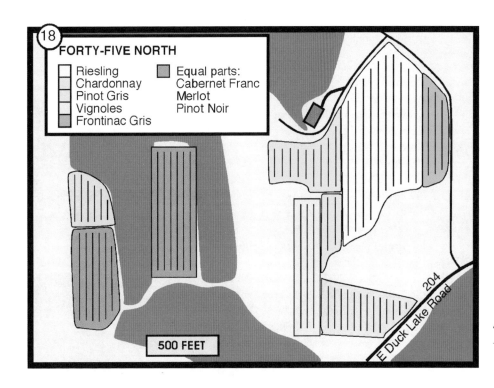

FORTY-FIVE NORTH

Riesling
Chardonnay
Pinot Gris
Vignoles
Frontinac Gris

Equal parts:
Cabernet Franc
Merlot
Pinot Noir

E Duck Lake Road 204

500 FEET

49

19. Chateau Fontaine Vineyards & Winery

231-256-0000
2290 South French Road
Lake Leelanau, MI 49653
www.chateaufontaine.com

"Wine a bit, it makes you feel better" greets the visitor at the entrance to the Chateau Fontaine tasting room.

Getting its French title from proprietor Lucie Matthies' middle name and paying homage to the French immigrants who settled in the area, Chateau Fontaine was a deserted potato farm and cow pasture when Dan Matthies discovered the property in the 1970s with its favorable south-facing slopes for growing grapes. Today, the cow pasture is one of three prime Chateau Fontaine vineyards.

Son Doug Matthies is the vineyard manager, Lucie Fontaine Matthies and Dan Matthies are the owners and Shawn Walters is the winemaker for Chateau Fontaine.

Back in the late 1980s, Michigan State University's agricultural extension programs were looking for south-facing plantable land good for vineyards and checked out the Matthies' properties. They thought it would be good for Cabernet Franc, but it was Bruce Simpson of Good Harbor who made Dan's decision, by offering to buy Chardonnay if Dan would plant it. Well, Lucie did as much of the planting as anyone.

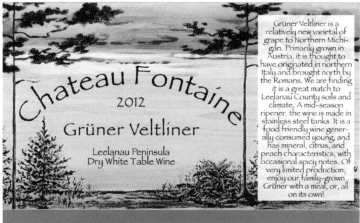

Dan & Lucie poured most all their profits back into the vineyard, planting Pinot Gris next, then . . . their Syrah was the first to be planted in Michigan, his Merlot the first in Leelanau Peninsula. Currently 27 acres are planted in vines.

Then, Dan bought a winemaking kit from Diversions – still on Front Street – and made wine. Some of it was awful, but that taught him how to make better wine.

The cost of equipment to process grapes into wine is very expensive, and only used part of the year. It was the idea of Dan's and Lucie's son Doug to provide, through Big Paw Vineyard Services, a full service program for everything needed from the vineyard pruning to the harvest for those who couldn't do it themselves. Doug learned his trade at Leelanau Wine Cellars, where Shawn Walters was for years the winemaker.

As to Chateau Fontaine's wines, "Mother nature is the wine maker," asserts Dan. He believes one should leave the vines alone, make them strive to grow, so no irrigation. All Chateau Fontaine wines are from family-grown grapes, thus, by definition, estate bottled.

Lucie's sister, artist Sally Biggs, paints the winery labels, and the original was drawn on a cottage wall in the early 1900s. Look closely at its representation in the tasting room; the wood grain is visible behind the paint. The winery's motto is "celebrate the sunset," the theme of the painting. Also on the label, the winery asks buyers to "Please recycle."

Dan Matthies obtained his real estate license while in college. As realtor for Peninsula Properties, Dan specializes in vineyard and winery properties.

The Chateau Fontaine patio, ready for business

For Sip & Savor, a.k.a. "Sip o' de Mayo," Chateau Fontaine paired Chicken Enchiladas with Green Sauce with their 2010 Chardonnay.

For Toast the Season; Chateau Fontaine served Grapevine Grilled Pork Loin on homemade Rosemary Sea Salt Focaccia, topped with Cherry Apple Chutney, and paired with the new release 2011 Pinot Noir.

Dry White Riesling   Chardonnay
Pinot Gris
Gewurztraminer   Semi-Sweet White
Riesling   Woodland White*
Pinot Blanc   Grüner Veltliner

Laughing Waters Dry Rosé

Woodland Red**   Pinot Noir Big Paw
Red***

Cherry Wine

* Auxerrois   **Cabernet Franc, Merlot
& Syrah
*** A blend of three hybrid grapes

Chateau Fontaine/Big Paw Vineyard Services manages several vineyards on Leelanau Peninsula. See the Leelanau Peninsula Vineyard Maps Section.

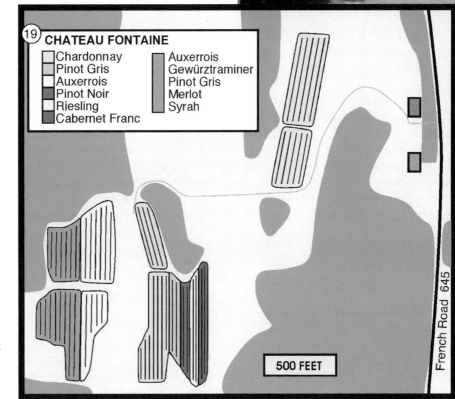

19 **CHATEAU FONTAINE**

Chardonnay	Auxerrois
Pinot Gris	Gewürztraminer
Auxerrois	Pinot Gris
Pinot Noir	Merlot
Riesling	Syrah
Cabernet Franc	

500 FEET

French Road 645

20. Bel Lago Vineyard & Winery

231-228-4800
6530 South Lake Shore Drive
Cedar, MI 49621
www.bellago.com

Original owners; Domenic, Ruth and Amy Iezzoni and Charles Edson. Charles Edson, Cristin Hosmer and Blake Lougheed are the winemakers.

Founded in 1987, Bel Lago – Beautiful Lake in Italian, so named by Domenic Iezzoni (now deceased) – is unique among the wineries of the two parallel peninsulas in that many of their wines are blends of grapes grown only in small quantities and only in their own vineyards. The blends can be of different grape varieties, which can be expected to result in very complex flavors in the style of European wine, or they may feature a mix of clones of a single variety. In each instance, "the wines are made in the vineyard," which suggests that harvesting top quality grapes is paramount – which is not to minimize the equally paramount importance of the wine-maker's expertise.

Charles Edson earned bachelors and master's degrees at MSU before taking the Ph.D. in horticulture. Besides serving as winemaker and manager of the vineyards, he also serves as winemaker for several Leelanau Peninsula vineyards.

At MSU Charles met Dr. G. Stanley Howell, Professor of Viticulture and Enology. Here, then, is the perfect place to introduce Stan. From 1969 to his retirement, Stan brought about MSU's expansion of education in enology and cool climate viticulture, thus helping a seven-fold growth of the industry to 2012. In 2012, Stan was honored with the American Society for Enology and Viticulture – Eastern Section - Lifetime Achievement Award. It was appropriate that the award be presented in Traverse City, since there can hardly be an area winemaker or grower who is not familiar with Stan and some aspect of his work.

Amy Iezzoni also holds a doctorate. She earned a Science Baccalaureate in Horticultural Science from North Carolina State University, then her master's and Ph.D. in Plant Breeding and Genetics at the University of Wisconsin, Madison. While Amy continues as a Professor and is involved at the Northwest Michigan Horticultural Station on Leelanau Peninsula, Charles gives full time to the vineyards and winemaking. Together, Charles, Amy and their vines have achieved the status, within the industry, as their own one-family research station. Consider, for instance, just a few of the uncommon wine grapes grown at the Bel Lago's Farview vineyard: Seyval, Bianca, Regent, Schönburger, Noiret, Dornfelder, Zweigeltrebe/Zweigelt

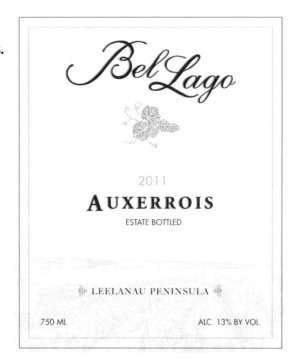

Selecting their varieties to match the climate and soils to produce the finest wines possible, Bel Lago grows over 100 varieties on 33 acres, including such rarely grown varieties as Auxerrois, Siegerrebe and Cayuga White. Also grown are several popular *vinifera* varieties: Pinot Grigio, Chardonnay, Pinot Noir, Cabernet Franc, and Riesling. For one of their varieties, Pinot Noir, Bel Lago grows over 30 clones in their estate vineyards. Several test varieties from the University of Minnesota and Cornell University grape breeding programs round out the mix with tests of eastern European and German grapes.

Balaton and Montmorency cherries for the cherry wine are obtained from Cherry Bay Orchard and are processed in mid-summer, a time when grape wines are not being made.

Work in the vineyards is by hand, not machines. What is known as "Integrated Pest Management", limiting sprays and using netting and electric fencing – "shocker wire" – is employed to control weeds, bugs, birds, raccoons, deer . . . and is minimally invasive to the health of the grapes.

Barrels from France and around the United States are used for red wines and for some whites, to enhance flavors and complexity.

For Sip & Savor, a.k.a. "Sip o' de Mayo," Bel Lago served their 2010 Bel Lago Pinot Grigio with a Spring Minestrone Soup, a hearty chicken stock base with chick peas, orzo and fresh asparagus, spring peas, spinach, kale, new potatoes, diced tomatoes, artichoke hearts and a few ramps finished with pesto and garnished with grated Parmesan.

For Taste the Season, Bel Lago has found a new pairing for 2011 Bel Lago Auxerrois with Light and Lemony Shortbread Cookies. It's not just for dinner anymore!

For Taste the Passion, Bel Lago served Decadent Triple Chocolate Cake drizzled with Chef Hamar's Balaton Cherry Sauce paired with Bouquet, a delightful blend of Pinot Noir and Cherry wines.

From the wide range of grapes and clones are produced the wines of Bel Lago, only some of which may be available at any specific time of year:

Auxerrois
Pinot Grigio   Pinot Grigio Chardonnay
Chardonnay   Semi-Dry Riesling
Leelanau Primavera
Herman Vineyard Pinot Gris, Botrisized Vintner Select

Rosé[5]

Pinot Noir
Bel Lago Red***
Tempesta[6]

Cherry Dessert Wine
Dessert Riesling

Bouquet[4]
Cherry Wine

*Pinot Noir, Auxerrois, Chardonnay & other white varietals
**Cayuga, Vignoles, Seyval & other aromatic and muscat vari

The extremely complex organization of the experimental plantings has required this special map layout.

***Cabernet Franc, Merlot, Regent & up to 15 other select red varietals
[4] Pinot Noir with Balaton and Montmorency cherry wines
[5] 76% Pinot Noir and 24% Auxerrois
[6] Cabernet Franc, Merlot and Regent

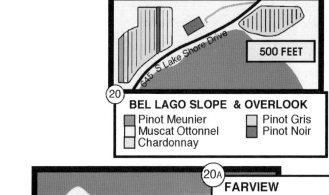

645 S Lake Shore Drive

500 FEET

20

BEL LAGO SLOPE & OVERLOOK

Pinot Meunier
Muscat Ottonnel
Chardonnay

Pinot Gris
Pinot Noir

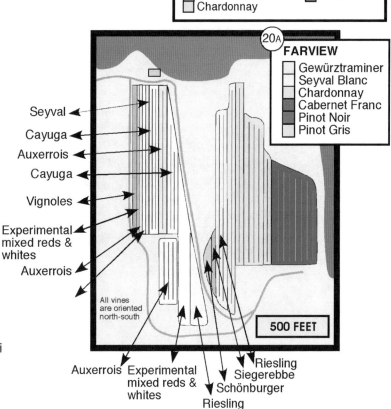

20A

FARVIEW

Gewürztraminer
Seyval Blanc
Chardonnay
Cabernet Franc
Pinot Noir
Pinot Gris

Seyval
Cayuga
Auxerrois
Cayuga
Vignoles
Experimental mixed reds & whites
Auxerrois

All vines are oriented north-south

500 FEET

Auxerrois   Experimental mixed reds & whites   Riesling   Riesling Siegerebbe Schönburger

53

21. Longview Winery

231-228-2880
8697 Good Harbor Trail
Cedar, MI 49621
www.longviewwinery.com

Alan and Linda Eaker are the owners, he the winemaker.

This listing might almost have been relegated to a sidebar! Why? Because Alan Eaker is an important name in the art world, starting with 35 years as an art professor at the University of South Florida, and his wife Linda is an internationally recognized bronze sculptor. Running a winery as a one-man operation is Alan's sideline, but one involving a very large part of his day.

Alan is from San Francisco and has been a Marine and an art specialist. He was living in Florida, Linda in Michigan, when they met at a conference. A long-distance romance ensued.

As Alan told me, he told Linda he loved her so much, he'd do anything for her. Linda said, "Could we buy a farm in the Leelanau Peninsula. "Yes, where's the Leelanau Peninsula?" was Alan's response. They bought the farm in 1998.

The farm is "dry-farmed," namely no irrigation, as the clay soil holds water.

Clockwise from above: Boxing the clusters; stacks of boxes; the Longview facility.

54

Cedar Rustic Inn, the other part of the Longview Tasting Room, serves Longview wines.

For Sip & Savor, a.k.a. "Sippo de Mayo," Longview Winery presented their Pinot Gris with a Roasted Salmon Chowder.

Longview Winery featured a local lake trout pate from Peshawbestown paired beautifully with the premier of their 2011 Semi Dry Riesling for the Harvest Stompede.

Salmon Chowder was served with Pinot Gris for Toast the Season.

For Taste the Passion, Longview served Chef Aaron's Double Chocolate Cherry Brownie made with their Cherry Wine paired with their 2011 Pinot Noir.

Sweet Winter Ice

Dry Riesling   Riesling   Chardonnay
Pinot Gris   Rustic White

Rustic Rosé (Cayuga & Frontenac Gris)

Rustic Red (70% Frontenac Gris, 30% Pinot Noir)
Pinot Noir
Cabernet Franc Barrel Reserve
Cabernet Franc

LONGVIEW
☐ Pinot Blanc
☐ Pinot Gris
☐ Riesling
☐ Chardonnay
☐ Cayuga
☐ Pinot Noir
☐ Cabernet Franc
☐ Frontenac

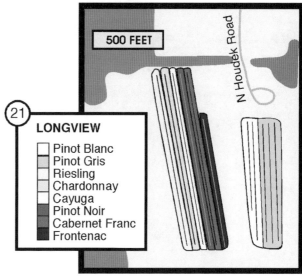

55

Left, Into the de-stemer,
Bottom, the juice

Harvest time at Longview vineyards reveals how much a few people can do to make wine that reflects its terroir. Three work the fields, one the processing!!! This is farming, but when the result reaches the bottle, it is the romance of the grape! But never forget the hard work that brought the elixir to you.

Pumping into the big tanks for fermentation.

22. Cherry Republic

800-206-6949
6026 S Lake Street / 154 E Front Street
Glen Arbor, MI 49636 / Traverse City 49684
www.cherryrepublic.com

Bob Sutherland is the owner of Cherry Republic. Charles Edson produces the wine, and L. Mawby provides the crush and grapes for the sparkler.

Hey, wait a minute, isn't this book about grape-based wines? Cherry Republic makes cherry beverages. But cherry wines? Yes, Cherry Republic produces just about anything you can make from cherries, including six Boom Chuggalugga soda pops. They also make four wines that feature cherry juice in the mix.

Some might suggest these could be very nice introductions to the culture for those who've never tasted wine. Or a nice variant from the sweetness of most fruit wines. Consider that even many grape wines are "flavored" by the wood casks in which they are made, so adding cherry juice is just another flavor. "Easy drinking, fun, easy going" is the idea.

There is a synergy between cherry wine production and grape wine production in that they happen at opposite seasons. During the summer, while the stainless steel tanks are empty at the boutique, then is the time to process the cherries. Bel Lago's Charles Edson is the winemaker for Cherry Republic. The cherries are purchased by Cherry Republic from local growers, and they are non-vintage so that the product style can be maintained year after year. It should be noted that it was Charlie's wife who brought the Balaton cherry to Michigan. 2012 was a bad year for cherry growers in Leelanau Peninsula due to a late freeze. The Balaton crop was sufficient for Cherry Republic's grape wine blends, but to meet its other demands Cherry Republic had to reach beyond Michigan – to Poland.

Cherry Republic was founded in 1989 by Bob Sutherland. He started in summer at the annual Cherry Festival in Traverse City selling T shirts with "Life, Liberty, Beaches and Pie," emblazoned in gold and black below a big red "Cherry Republic." America's motto of Life, Liberty and the Pursuit of Happiness was transformed into Up North Michigan happiness: beaches and pie. The words came before the company.

So Bob graduated to dried cherries in bags – no one had figured how to market the product. Boom Chuggalugga followed, then sodas, jams, jellies and salsas. 99% of their product is sold through their two tasting rooms, which are designed to be friendly to kids as well as adults.

"Life, Liberty, Beaches and Pie." In winemaking, doesn't everything start with the earth and the vine? Not at Cherry Republic, where it starts with the earth and the cherry, Northern Michigan's number one crop. Nowhere are cherries grown better than in northwest Michigan! So that is "life" to Cherry Republic. "Liberty" is the freedom to choose to buy at Cherry Republic or else-where, so they make products that will attract not just adults but kids as well, something not easy for a "straight winery" serving only alcoholic beverages to do. Bob claims to "wear" bare feet to work. That's "beaches." Who wears shoes on a beach? Keep in touch with what is local, and that has to mean beaches, or why else do you come Up North? And "pie." What is more Up North Michigan dessert than cherry pie? Is there any restaurant that doesn't have cherry pie on its dessert menu?

The following is from Cherry Republic's web site, but it bears repeating (with minor adjustment):

A true gift comes with no expectations. One day in spring, two college kids came into Cherry Republic with a loaf of bread. They went over to our sample table and spread both White Chocolate Cherry Peanut Butter and Cherry Almond Butter on the bread and made two sandwiches and left. My staff was irate with the gall of those kids. I shook my head and asked if this had ever happened before. They said no. After talking with them for a while, we all came to the same conclusion. Our generosity doesn't feel right if it has limitations—since we can easily afford it, we can help supply some industrious kids a lunch.

Liberty Sparkling

Cherry White (5% cherry with Pinot Grigio)
Cherry Shook Dessert Wine
Great Hall Riesling (10% cherry)

Cherry Spiced Wine
Cherry Red (20% cherry with Merlot)
Cherry Sangria
Balaton Cherry (100% Balaton cherries)
Abbondanza (45% cherry + Cayuga, Muscat & Viognier)
Conservancy (Montmorency & Balaton cherries.
$1 from every bottle sold goes to
the Leelanau Conservancy)

23. French Valley Vineyards

231-941-7060
Bistro (Tasting Room)
231-271-2675
1338 North Pebble Beach Drive
Suttons Bay, MI 49682
www.vininn.com/frenchvalleyvineyards/index.html

Owner of the French Valley vineyards since 1990 is Stephen Kozelko. Steve tells this author that, at the end of the day, he especially likes to have a bottle of the French Valley Chardonnay just for sipping or paired with fish. The French Valley wines are made at Bel Lago by Dr. Charles Edson.

The Vineyard Inn and adjacent Corky's Bistro feature weddings on the beach and wine tasting in the Bistro. The Vineyard Inn just a few feet away from the 45th parallel on the beach of West Bay is where you will find Corky's Bistro, both owned by Pam Leonard. The French Valley wines are the house wines of Corky's Bistro.

The French Valley vineyard is part of a scenic 75-acre cherry orchard plus vineyard complex. The barn, moved from M72 and rebuilt by Amish craftsmen, can host weddings, corporate events and farm-to-table dinners for up to 400 guests. The winery on the property was built in 2011. Equipment is soon to be installed so that wines will be made on site, creating a true estate winery.

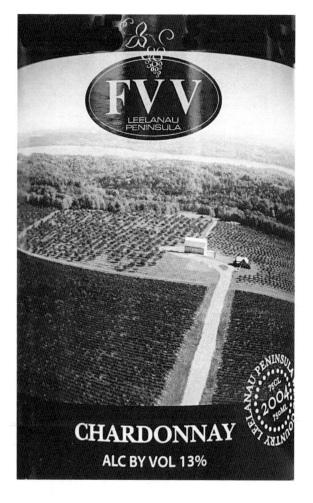

Pinot Grigio   Riesling

Pinot Noir   Cabernet Franc + Merlot

Merlot

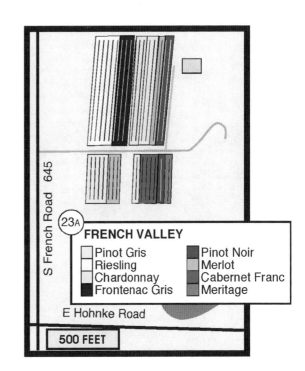

S French Road 645

23A

FRENCH VALLEY

Pinot Gris   Pinot Noir
Riesling   Merlot
Chardonnay   Cabernet Franc
Frontenac Gris   Meritage

E Hohnke Road

500 FEET

61

24. M22

231-334-4425
6298 Western Avenue
Glen Arbor, MI 49636
www.crystalriveroutfitters.com

Proclaiming that "M22 is not just a road, it's a way of life," the M22 winery grows no grapes, but offers exclusive wines for tasting, bottle sales and by the glass. The M22 brand works with Black Star Farms for the wines they offer under a locally iconic moniker, "M22." Look at a map and you will see that M-22 for the most part hugs the Lake Michigan shoreline on the west side of the Leelanau Peninsula and then the shoreline of West (Grand Traverse) Bay.

Please note, also, that Michigan road signs show "M22" but, by law, all Michigan numbered "trunklines" are legally designated "M-n," so M22 is actually M-22. This is a syntax that came into law in 1919, the first year Michigan roadways were signed. Only Kansas of the other forty-nine states follows this syntax.

Brothers Keegan and Matt Myers started the M22 line of clothing after their love of the scenic highway. They licensed the M22 Glen Arbor Store and Tasting Room, that is owned by Matt Wiesen and his wife Katy. This then is operated as Crystal River Outfitters, providing kayaking and biking trips as well as wine. "Since the clothing company is based on the love for and the lifestyle of North-ern Michigan, adding wine to the product line-up was an obvious fit," is how Katy explained the choice to add wine to the M22 product lineup. They first offered M22 wines in 2007 and opened the tasting room in 2010. Now the wine list has grown to nine wines and hard cider.

Bubbly Brut

Pinot Grigio	M22 White *
Chardonnay	Riesling

Rosé

Pinot Noir	M22 Red **
Cherry	Hard Apple Cider

*44% Chardonnay blended with Pinot Gris, Riesling & Pinot Blanc
** Cabernet Franc

25. Tandem Ciders

231-271-0050
2055 Setterbo Road
Suttons Bay, MI 49682
www.tandemciders.com

It was a romantic trip. Nikki Rothwell had earned her Ph.D. so she and Dan Young headed to England to sample beer. Dan Young was partner in a brewery-restaurant, The People's Pint, in Greenfield, Massachusetts, not far from Athol, where he was born. Nikki was an entomologist and who knows how many insects they'd find in England that weren't in central Massachusetts.

Starting in Devon, southwest England, Nikki and Dan tandem-bicycled from town to town. They sampled beer and cider, finding cider more common than beer. Staying in Bed & Breakfasts – which in England are more like a room that becomes available when the owners' child or children have left home than the American B&B - they enjoyed a month on the road and in the pubs.

Back in Massachusetts, Nikki found herself competing with a plethora of other Ph.D's. No job. She complained about this to her mother who lived in northwest Michigan. Two weeks later, her mother phoned: a job was waiting for her at the MSU extension. It had been offered to someone else, but that candidate declined the offer. There weren't many entomologists in NW Michigan, so she was hired. After alternating between central Massachusetts and northwest Michigan for a year, Dan divested himself of his Massachusetts partnership.

Michigan was having a serious surplus of apples and needed a way to use them. In the early part of the millennium the Michigan Hard Cider Initiative (www.Michiganhardcider.org/initiative.htm) was launched, and Dan went downstate to attend. He learned about obtaining a liquor license and the taxation of beverages. A business plan came next. They sold their first cider in 2008.

If a winery produces wine, what does a cidery produce? Cider, of course. No, you may call it that, but it is wine made from apples. Further, the dictionary calls "cidery" a brewery making cider. Cider mill, however, seems to be the proper term.

When Dan applied for membership in the Leelanau Peninsula Vintners Associaton (LPVA) for his cidery, some winemakers objected – what, no grapes? – but under Michigan law, any fruit juice that is fermented to an alcohol content of 7% or higher qualifies as wine. Larry Mawby, who had a background in apples before he planted grapes, supported Dan, and Tandem Ciders became part of the wine tour of Leelanau Peninsula. Mawby also predicted that others would join Dan and then they could break off into their own organization.

In 2013 two more cider mills are predicted for the Leelanau Peninsula!! Huzza Larry.

Dan was quick to note that he had help from Lee Lutes, who first tried to get him to grow grapes. On the cider side, it was Mick Beck at Uncle Johns Cider Mill on US 127 in St. Johns (25 miles north of Lansing) who taught him much.

Apples that are good to eat don't make the best cider. Apples that make good cider are higher in sugar, tannins and acids than table apples, thus bitter. So, on Tandem Ciders' own orchard one will find apples with names such as Ashmead's Kernal, Yarlington Mill, Harrison, Orleans Reinette and Porter's Perfection. As with current production, these apples will soon be custom-crafted in small batches at the Tandem Ciders Cider Mill.

For Toast the Season, Tandem Ciders presented Raclette & Roasted Delicata Squash Crepes with Smackintosh Cider.

For Taste the Passion, Tandem presented Chicken Mole in a Cornmeal Crepe paired with Sweetheart Cider.

The following is a list of (wine) ciders offered by Tandem Ciders. They offer no grape wines.

Scrumpy Little Woody (draft)
Cidre Royal
Early Day   Farmhouse
Ida Gold   Honey Pie
Pretty Penny   Sweetheart
Smackintosh   The Crabster
Pomona

26. Motovino Cellars

231-386-1027
107 W Nagonaba Street
Northport, MI 49670
www.motovinocellars.com

Eric and Deirdre Owen are the owners, with Shawn Walters the winemaker. The Grand Opening was August 11, 2012. Welcome to where the cork meets the road.

So, in 2012 Motovino had their first vintage, from the Norvick Road vineyard. But why the motorcycle on the label, in fact, on all their labels? And why a name like "Cruiser"? If you are asking, you need to talk to a motorcycling riding buddy. Motorcycles and motors are a passion to some, as is wine, and why not?

Says Eric, "at Motovino we love the machines and the wine, so we make wine and invite cyclists to drop by for a glass of Chardonnay, or . . ."

Cruiser (Unoaked Chardonnay)   Thumper (Dry Riesling)
Café (Semi-Dry Riesling)   Dream

F-Head (red)

Scooters Cherry   Scooters Peach

With their first season behind them, Deirdre and Eric are moving the tasting room across the road to a much larger venue. They hope in 2013 to be serving wine by the glass with food.

MOTOVINO

WINETASTING ROOM
SPECIALTY FOODS
MOTORCYCLISTS
WELCOME

S Norvick Road

Richlyn Drive

500 FEET

26A

NORVICK GRAPES

Half rows:
Auxerrois
Muscat Ottonel
Marquette
Gewürztraminer (2 rows)
NY 76 White
Pinot Nolr
Leon Millot
Full rows:
Muscat Ottonel
Pinot Gris (6 rows!)
Short rows:
Pinot Noir
Merlot
Pinot Gris
Cabernet Franc
Muscat Ottonel
and
out front
Riesling
Gewürztraminer
Pinot Gris

27. Laurentide Winery

810-231-1785
56 French Road
Lake Leelanau, MI 49653
www.laurentidewinery.com

Owned by Bill and Susan Braymer. Their winemaker is Shawn Walters.

Just as we were sitting down for breakfast at the 45th Parallel Café in Suttons Bay, Susan Braymer handed Pat and me a sheet of paper. "This is our story. I did this to save time." Two hours later . . .

Bill Braymer is in software at Siemens in Ann Arbor. He and Susan are transitioning into wine making. We were to discuss their operation and Grand Opening on the following Saturday. But first we had to hear how they got here.

It started with Jack Cakebread and a guy named Miljenko "Mike" Grgrich. Yes, the one whose Chardonnay beat the French in 1976. This was when some wine in Sonoma was poured into paper cups for tasting! It was a time when Bill left his wine purchase at the winery and he got a phone call asking if he was the one. Yes. "I'll send it to you," said Jack Cakebread.

Moving from northern California had to be wrenching, but there is a beautiful side. Late in the 1980s Bill and Susan went into a Lake Geneva, Wisconsin wine store and found '85 and '87 Mondavi reds being sold off so the store could bring in "fresh, new wines!" Rather than offer how much they would pay, Bill and Susan asked how much he wanted. $6? "We'll take a case." Then they discovered a '77 Buena Vista wine now known as "The Count," named after the colorful "Count of Buena Vista" who pioneered California's move to production of premium wines. Now Bill and Susan got every wine friend to come and buy the remaining stock.

They got help in choosing their vineyard site from Dan Matthies of Peninsula Properties, Inc. They were shown several sites, but the one off French Road spoke to them. The soil is filled with rocks, shale, limestone and seashells left behind by the Laurentide glacier of 14,000 years ago. They also found a Petosky stone not quite as large as a football. The name of the winery honors both a French great grandfather Charles Laurent and the soil of the glacier. The vineyard is dry farmed (no irrigation). Living in Ann Arbor, they frequent Zingerman's Roadhouse restaurant, where their Pinot Gris is available by the glass. When they brought their second vintage for tasting, Chef Alex took the glass, tossed it down, declared, "It's better," and went back to the kitchen!

The Laurentide vineyards were planted in 2006 and their first full harvest was 2011. One Lawyer To The Stars from Los Angeles, having visited their French Road vineyard, commented: "I've been to a lot of Napa vineyards, but I don't remember their vines being as lush. This is God's country."

And now, I give you what Susan produced from Bill's suggestions:

Our Story

Chapter One of our story started on a glorious spring day at the Arboretum in Ann Arbor, Michigan. Heavily burdened engineering students, a girl from New Jersey and a boy from Kalamazoo met, fell in love, and have been ever since. Our 1st experience with wine was shared on dates where time seemed long and money was short. The fare was simple and the wine as well. Strange shaped bottles from Portugal or blue ones from Germany shared the table with food-the start of our unending fascination of wine/food pairing.

The odyssey that entails our lives continued with the 1st of several moves across the country as our careers commenced. Our 1st life in California was a time of innumerable trips to Napa and Sonoma. We met huge names now, but little-known then. Fantastic wines and flavors fanned the romantic dance between food and wine, becoming our unifying principle. We traveled to France, lingering in Burgundy and loitering in Bordeaux. A deep-seated respect and love grew about the earth, soil, terroir concept and what wine can and should be.

Still, throughout all these years, like homing pigeons, we returned to Michigan to visit family and take a break from hectic lives with side trips to Up North. Bill wanted to show Calla, our daughter, and me the irresistible Great Lake, bay and light that makes Leelanau so special. The seed was planted, so to speak, and the soil was fertile!

Our tastes had already gone through the evolution process that naturally unfolds, from sweet whites to huge "take my body" reds, to sophisticated whites and much dryer wines in general. I had started pursuing a certificate in wine production from U C Davis and completed my work after several years. This complemented my education in Chemical engineering and process control. Meanwhile, Bill worked hard at refining his taste buds (i.e. Bill enjoyed wine). He has tasted and expanded his wine and business knowledge and forged many personal winery relationships. In California, we experimented as garage wine makers with the vines in our backyard. We realized in early 2000 that we wanted to change our hobby to a business and explored California real estate for that potential. Fast forward to one trip Up North when, on one rainy summer day, we decided to go wine tasting in Leelanau. The rest is history . . .

After the epiphany that good wine can be made outside of the northern California zip codes, our minds were buzzing with possibilities. The puzzle was beginning to take shape. Chapter Two commenced on a mountain in northern California on January 1, 2006 when we bought our French Road farm and initi-

ated our final launch sequence back home. This cast the die for our continuing epic venture and Chapter Three, this tasting room and winery.

The unique geography formed by the Laurentide glaciers, along with trellis design, planting density, clonal types, varietal choices, along with the altitude, aspect and microclimate on French Road, constitute a prime location to grow vines. All of these factors allow our grapes to mature into the best expression of Leelanau soil transformed into wine. Wine is history unfolding into your glass and we are happy to be a small part of this grand pageant. Enjoy your time at Laurentide Winery.

Chardonnay (unoaked, French Chablis style)
Pinot Gris
Sauvignon Blanc (no residual sugar)   Riesling
Semi-Sweet Riesling   Emergence White

Pinot Noir

Cherry Wine

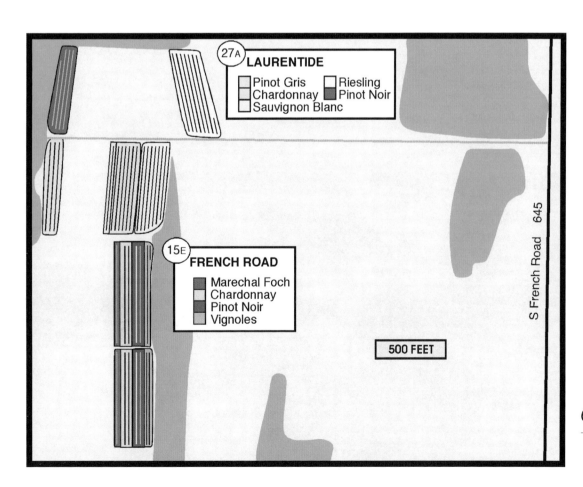

28. Blustone Vineyards

231-256-0146
780 N. Sylt Road
Lake Leelanau, MI 49653
www.blustonevineyards.com

Tom and Joan Knighton are the owners of Blustone Vineyards. Their winemaker is Shawn Walters.

Blustone Vineyards sits on 40 acres in the heart of the Leelanau peninsula. In February of 2010, Tom and Joan Knighton purchased the property that included a 10 acre vineyard that was already five years old. They currently have additional acreage in cover crop with the goal of expanding the vineyard to 15 acres in the coming year. The vines' roots reach deep into granite and limestone giving the soil a unique minerality that is reflected in several of Blustone's wines.

The Knighton's started visiting Leelanau County over 20 years ago. "The simplicity and beauty of this 'tucked away' secret that is Leelanau is something we treasure," says Tom. "We live on the water and have always enjoyed walking the beach in search of Leland Bluestone. It's such a beautiful creation of nature and we're always excited when we find it. Blustone wines are inspired by these unanticipated moments of life."

Having a long time interest in wine and winemaking, the Knighton's watched the wine industry in Leelanau grow and eventually decided to become a part of it. "We received good counsel that was both encouraging and realistic from some of the area's most successful vintners. Dan Matthies and Larry Mawby were especially influential in our decision to move forward and pursue our dreams of opening a winery."

Blustone anticipates producing around 3,000 cases of select wines a year. The winemaking process starts with the core principle: "let the wine express itself". Their focus is on making the highest quality wine possible and creating an experience that exceeds their customers' expectations. At the center of the experience is their new contemporary wood, stone and glass tasting room that has panoramic views of the vineyard and the Leelanau landscape. "We take our wines very seriously," says Tom, "ourselves not so much."

The Blustone tasting room celebrated its grand opening as part of the LPVA Toast of the Season, the first two weekends of November, 2012. For that event, a Caramelized Onion and Apple Tart was served with their 2011 Riesling. Over 1,500 people visited.

For Taste the Passion, in the spirit of the holiday, Blustone served a heart-shaped chocolate-cherry brownie paired with their 2010 Pinot Noir.

Chardonnay	Pinot Grigio	Riesling (dry)
Late Harvest Riesling	Gewürztraminer⁴	Pinot Noir Rosé
Pinot Noir	Winemaker's Red*	Ad Lib**

Opening day at Blustone

Connexion Dessert Wine***
Merlot and Cabernet Franc will eventually join the above offerings.

*** Port-style made from Leelanau cherries.

[4] Half aged in stainless steel, the other in Acacia barrels to enhance the natural spicy character of the grape.

* Cabernet Franc, Merlot, Syrah. ** Pinot noir, Cabernet Franc, Merlot and Regent

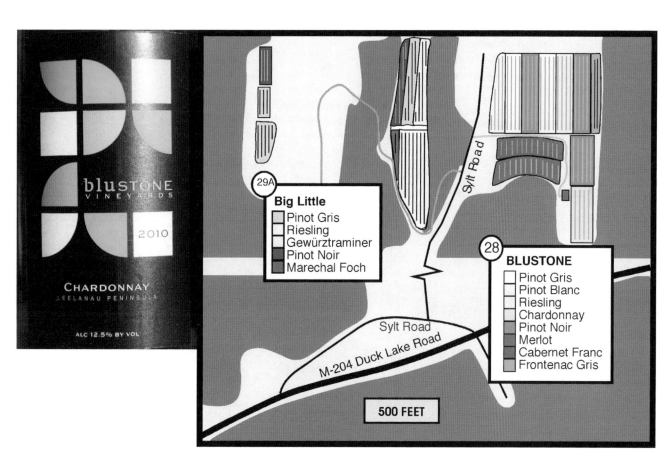

blustone
VINEYARDS

2010

CHARDONNAY
LEELANAU PENINSULA

ALC 12.5% BY VOL

29A
Big Little
- Pinot Gris
- Riesling
- Gewürztraminer
- Pinot Noir
- Marechal Foch

28
BLUSTONE
- Pinot Gris
- Pinot Blanc
- Riesling
- Chardonnay
- Pinot Noir
- Merlot
- Cabernet Franc
- Frontenac Gris

Sylt Road

Sylt Road
M-204 Duck Lake Road

500 FEET

29. Big LITTLE Wines

231-714-4854
4519 South Elm Valley Road
Suttons Bay, MI 49682
www.biglittlewines.com

The brothers Laing, owners; Michael and Peter, the one with the beard. "Big and Little brother, making Big wines from this Little Leelanau Peninsula."

The brothers' story started when, in 2003, their parents planted two acres of Pinot Gris and Pinot Noir. For years, they had been visiting their grandparents in the Leelanau area in all four seasons, seeing the area's beauty year round. By 2010 the brothers were living Up North Michigan and harvesting their grapes. Starting small, a couple of wines only, they are expanding bit by bit. 2013 will see the opening of their tasting room next to that of L. Mawby. Their interest lies in producing unique and bold white table and sparkling wines that reflect their *terroir*.

Tire Swing

Mixtape   Crayfish   Treehouse

The label titles are derived from memories of the two brothers. They remember making mixtapes of tracks carefully organized to convey a specific message to the listener. Mixtape wine was made to capture the idea that the whole is greater than the sum of its parts. Food Pairings: Spicy BBQ, ethnic foods, light appetizers.

Fruit for the other three wines is hand picked and whole cluster pressed.

The brothers remember summer afternoons scouring the creek-bed in search of crayfish hiding under rock and limb. Crayfish wine attempts to re-flect hidden nuances of Pinot Gris. Food Pairings: heavy cheeses, creamy pasta dishes, grilled fish.

The memory that infuses Tire Swing bubbly is of their parents "pushing us on the tire swing in our backyard and the laughter that ensued". Tire Swing is a blend where juice from one year is carried into the next and added to the blend which will, accordingly change every release. The cuve close method is used. Food Pairings: Asian foods, roasted chicken and vegetables.

Treehouse wine is 100% Pinot Noir and its profile derives from the boys climbing the ladder and observing how the view changed on the way up from ground to treehouse. Thus, a different look at the familiar Pinot Noir grape. Several yeast strains were used in producing this wine. Food Pairings: Wood-fired pizzas, Grilled chicken and fish, any dish with bacon in it.

As the vineyards of Big LITTLE are due west of those at Blustone, the vineyard map immediately precedes this listing, namely it is at the end of the Blustone listing.

Peter photographed big brother Michael in the vineyard

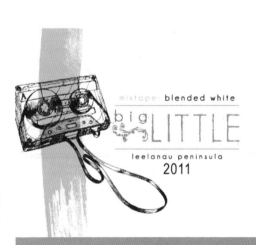

72

30. Bella Fortuna North Restaurant

231-944-2400
104 West Main Street
Lake Leelanau, MI 49653
www.bellafortunanorth.com

Dr Jane Fortune and Dr Robert R Hesse are owners of Bella Fortuna North Restaurant and the Bella Fortuna wine label. Pinot Grigio and Prosecco are planted in their Leland vineyard. They also have a small vineyard outside Florence, Italy, that produces a pure Sangiovese wine. Currently the only wines served are from Italy, but the Pinot Grigio is scheduled for 2013. "Bella Fortuna" translates, more or less, to "beautiful fortune" or "good luck" in Italian (buona fortuna is the more accurate translation) and was chosen by Jane and Bob as a play on Jane's name.

Jane and Bob move between a winter home in Boca Grande, Florida, and homes in Indianapolis, Indiana, Leland, Michigan, and Florence, Italy. In the little town that sits on the river between the two halves of Lake Leelanau and takes its name therefrom, they purchased a building known for its gorgeous mahogany bar that had been shipped to the United States, from Belgium, over 100 years ago. Once called Dan's Powerhouse Tavern, the restaurant was also known as the Key to the County and the LeNaro Pub.

The building has seen extensive remodeling but the original bar remains. A Mugnini wood-fired oven has been installed to keep true to Tuscany roots. Schiacciatas (flatbread pizzas) and many appetizers are made in this oven.

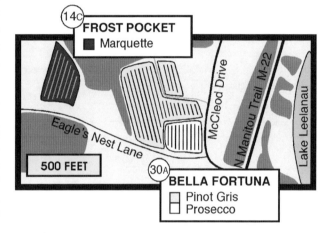

31. Rove Estate Vineyard and Winery

231-421-9171
7237 East Traverse Highway
Traverse City, MI 49684

The Rove Estate tasting room is scheduled to open in 2016 on the vineyard property.

Rove Estate Vineyard and Winery was planted in the spring of 2012 by Ben Braymer of Agrivine. It is the enterprise of Creighton Gallagher. The grapes, when harvested in 2014, will be made into wine by Coenraad Stassen of Brys Estate.

So, the best we can do as of the end of 2012 is to refer the reader to the farm market, which is but a short way from the vineyards. "Gallagher's Farms" is already legendary, and Creighton Gallagher has moved the family into wines at the southern-most border of the Leelanau Peninsula. The site is the highest point on the peninsula at 1,100 feet above sea level, or 520 feet above Lake Michigan. The vineyards are mostly south facing.

In 2013 an additional 5.5 acres will be planted with Gewürztraminer, Pinot Gris, Pinot Blanc and Sauvignon Blanc to bring the total in wine grape vines to about 15 acres.

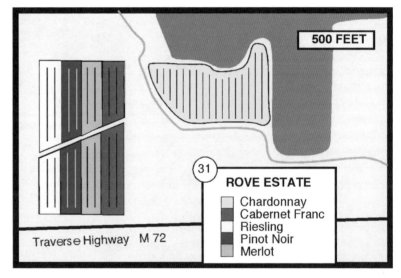

500 FEET

Traverse Highway   M 72

31 ROVE ESTATE
Chardonnay
Cabernet Franc
Riesling
Pinot Noir
Merlot

Driving the end posts for the newly planted grapevines at Rove Estate Vineyard

32. Northwest Michigan Horticultural Research Station

231-946-1510
6686 South Center Highway
Traverse City, MI 49684

The Northwest Michigan Horticultural Research Station is operated by Michigan State University.. No wines are sold. The grapes are processed for Spartan Cellars at Michigan State University.

There are two tests of vines being made. One is a trial of grape varieties to see what will grow in northwest Michigan's climate. The other is a test of spacing of vines and differing methods of trellising the vines for maximum product in terms of quality versus quantity.

The majority of the vines are Riesling, followed by Chardonnay, then Pinot Noir. The following are currently in trial;

Syrah (only a few)
Viognier (only a few)
Ortega

NEWER PLANTINGS OF HYBRIDS;
Vidal
Chambourcin
Noiret
St. Croix
Corot Noir
La Crescent
Brianna
Frontenac
NY 76.0044.24
NY 81.0315.17

OLDER PLANTINGS OF HYBRIDS:
Vignoles
Seyval
Chardonell
Traminette
Valvin Muscat
Regent
Noiret
Phoenix
NY 65

WINES BY THE BAY is a valuable resource for those following the burgeoning growth of the wine industry in northwest lower Michigan. Bill and Pat Storrer have truly undertaken a "labor of love" in their detailed documentation of the wineries and vineyards. The excitement emanating from this emerging wine region is captured in this beautifully presented book.

— Linda Jones, Executive Director, Michigan Grape and Wine Industry Council

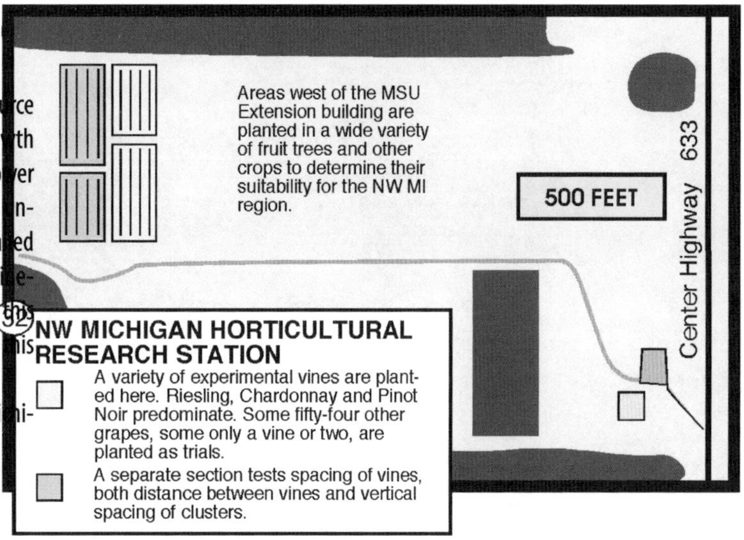

Areas west of the MSU Extension building are planted in a wide variety of fruit trees and other crops to determine their suitability for the NW MI region.

500 FEET

Center Highway 633

NW MICHIGAN HORTICULTURAL RESEARCH STATION

☐ A variety of experimental vines are planted here. Riesling, Chardonnay and Pinot Noir predominate. Some fifty-four other grapes, some only a vine or two, are planted as trials.

☐ A separate section tests spacing of vines, both distance between vines and vertical spacing of clusters.

NEWER PLANTINGS OF VINIFERA;
Dornfelder
Cabernet Franc
Albarino
Cinsault
Zweigelt
Lagrein
Semillon
Teroldego
Rkatsitelli
Tocai Friulano

Gruner Veltliner
Touriga
Fiano
Muscato Giallo
Muscat Ottonel
Orange Muscat
Madeleine Angevine
Muscadella Bordelaise
Moscato Canelli
Siegerrebe
Riesling

The Vineyards of Leelanau Peninsula

The vineyard listings and maps, and to whom the fruit is sold, are based on information provided the author by owners and winemakers following the 2012 harvest. It includes all vineyards known to be in commercial production along with those contracted for such future production.

The listing here and elsewhere in this book identifies each Leelanau Peninsula vineyard with the number/letter combination that is assigned to each providing cross-referencing to its location on the peninsula map with its tasting room. On the individual vineyard maps, the direction of the vine rows is shown. There is no indication of the number of rows. North is always at the top of each map.

1	Brengman Brothers / 15		15A	#2 / 82	
2	Shady Lane / 17		15B	Rick's / 82	
3A	Chateau de Leelanau / 19		15C	#5 / 82	
4	Willow / 21		15D	Crooked Maple Farm / 80	
5	Ciccone / 23		15E	French Road / 69	
6	L Mawby / 25		16A	Boathouse / 45	
6A	Steele's Crossing / 89		17	Circa Estate / 47	
6B	Provemont Hill / 80		17A	Telford Farms / 89	
6C	Yohanda (OMP) / 125		18	Forty-Five North / 49	
7	Black Star Farms / 27		18A	Trillium Hill / 80	
7A	Elm Valley / 81		18B	Schomberg Road / 81	
7B	Isidor's Choice / 81		19	Chateau Fontaine / 51	
7C	Leelanau Summit / 82		19A	Windwhistle Farm / 84	
7D	True North / 83		19B	Wooden Fish / 83	
8	Boskydel / 29		19C	Lakewinds Farm / 80	
8	Raftshol / 31		19D	North Unity / 88	
9	Silver Leaf / 33		19E	Whaleback / 87	
10A	Harvest Moon / 86		19F	Hennessey Harbor / 84	
10	Leelanau Cellars / 35		19G	Twyris / 84	
11A	Pleasant Hill / 81		20	Bel Lago Slope & Overlook / 53	
11B	Route 204 / 83		20A	Farview / 53	
11C	Omena / 35		21	Longview / 55	
11D	Timber Shore / 80		23A	French Valley / 61	
11E	Inman / 82		26A	Norvick / 67	
11F	Bella Vista / 35		27A	Laurentide / 69	
12	Good Neighbor Organic / 37		28	Blustone / 71	
13	Gill's Pier / 39		29A	Big LITTLE / 71	
13A	Edlin Ridge / 81		30A	Bella Fortuna North Restaurant / 73	
13B	Zimmerman / 84		31	Rove Estate / 74	
14A	Matheson / 41		32	NW MI Horticultural Research Sta. / 75	
14B	Swede Road / 83		8m	Old Orchard / 88	
14C	Frost Pocket / 73		E	Drumlin / 87	
15	Good Harbor / 43				

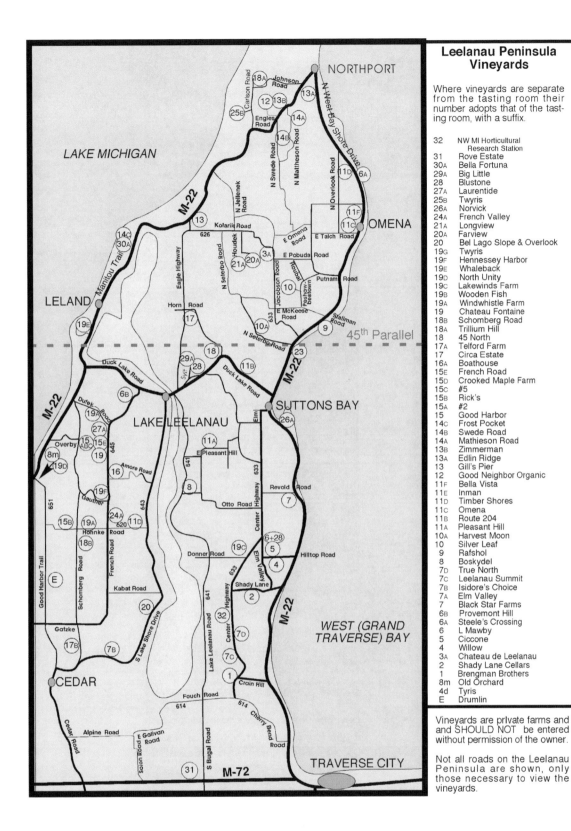

Leelanau Peninsula Vineyards

Where vineyards are separate from the tasting room their number adopts that of the tasting room, with a suffix.

32	NW MI Horticultural Research Station
31	Rove Estate
30A	Bella Fortuna
29A	Big Little
28	Blustone
27A	Laurentide
25B	Twyris
26A	Norvick
24A	French Valley
21A	Longview
20A	Farview
20	Bel Lago Slope & Overlook
19G	Twyris
19F	Hennessey Harbor
19E	Whaleback
19D	North Unity
19C	Lakewinds Farm
19B	Wooden Fish
19A	Windwhistle Farm
19	Chateau Fontaine
18B	Schomberg Road
18A	Trillium Hill
18	45 North
17A	Telford Farm
17	Circa Estate
16A	Boathouse
15E	French Road
15D	Crooked Maple Farm
15C	#5
15B	Rick's
15A	#2
15	Good Harbor
14C	Frost Pocket
14B	Swede Road
14A	Mathieson Road
13B	Zimmerman
13A	Edlin Ridge
13	Gill's Pier
12	Good Neighbor Organic
11F	Bella Vista
11E	Inman
11D	Timber Shores
11C	Omena
11B	Route 204
11A	Pleasant Hill
10A	Harvest Moon
10	Silver Leaf
9	Rafshol
8	Boskydel
7D	True North
7C	Leelanau Summit
7B	Isidore's Choice
7A	Elm Valley
7	Black Star Farms
6B	Provemont Hill
6A	Steele's Crossing
6	L Mawby
5	Ciccone
4	Willow
3A	Chateau de Leelanau
2	Shady Lane Cellars
1	Brengman Brothers
8m	Old Orchard
4d	Tyris
E	Drumlin

Vineyards are private farms and and SHOULD NOT be entered without permission of the owner.

Not all roads on the Leelanau Peninsula are shown, only those necessary to view the vineyards.

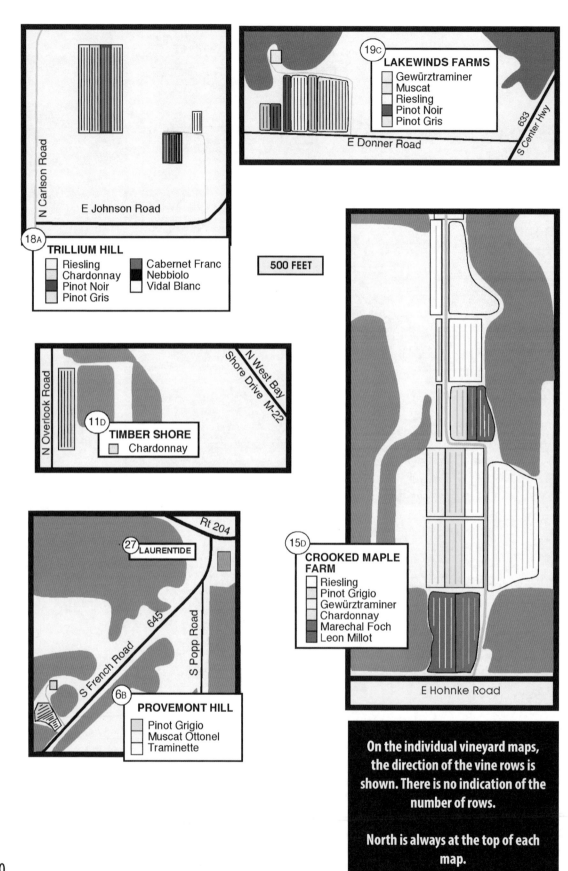

500 FEET

TRILLIUM HILL (18A)
- Riesling
- Chardonnay
- Pinot Noir
- Pinot Gris
- Cabernet Franc
- Nebbiolo
- Vidal Blanc

LAKEWINDS FARMS (19C)
- Gewürztraminer
- Muscat
- Riesling
- Pinot Noir
- Pinot Gris

TIMBER SHORE (11D)
- Chardonnay

LAURENTIDE (27)

PROVEMONT HILL (6B)
- Pinot Grigio
- Muscat Ottonel
- Traminette

CROOKED MAPLE FARM (15D)
- Riesling
- Pinot Grigio
- Gewürztraminer
- Chardonnay
- Marechal Foch
- Leon Millot

On the individual vineyard maps, the direction of the vine rows is shown. There is no indication of the number of rows.

North is always at the top of each map.

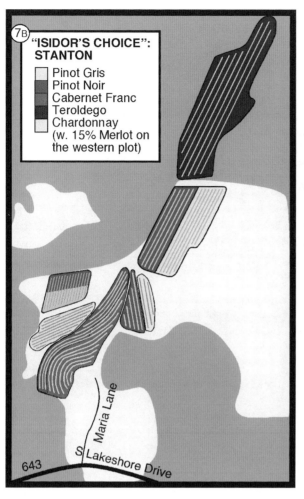

7B "ISIDOR'S CHOICE": STANTON

- Pinot Gris
- Pinot Noir
- Cabernet Franc
- Teroldego
- Chardonnay
  (w. 15% Merlot on
  the western plot)

643
Maria Lane
S Lakeshore Drive

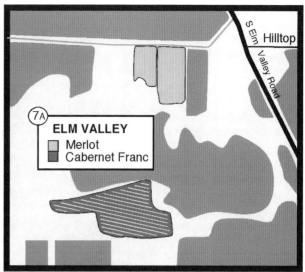

S Elm Valley Road
Hilltop

7A ELM VALLEY

- Merlot
- Cabernet Franc

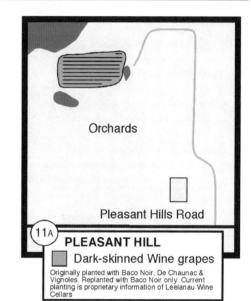

Orchards
Pleasant Hills Road

11A PLEASANT HILL

- Dark-skinned Wine grapes

Originally planted with Baco Noir, De Chaunac &
Vignoles. Replanted with Baco Noir only. Current
planting is proprietary information of Leelanau Wine
Cellars

500 FEET

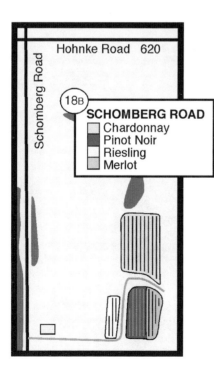

Hohnke Road   620
Schomberg Road

18B SCHOMBERG ROAD

- Chardonnay
- Pinot Noir
- Riesling
- Merlot

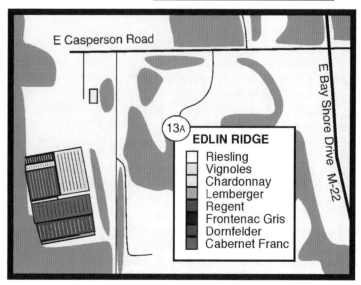

E Casperson Road
E Bay Shore Drive M-22

13A EDLIN RIDGE

- Riesling
- Vignoles
- Chardonnay
- Lemberger
- Regent
- Frontenac Gris
- Dornfelder
- Cabernet Franc

81

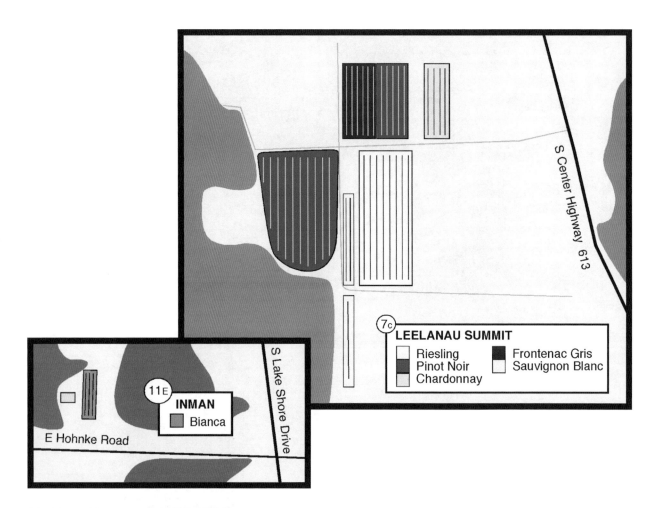

7c LEELANAU SUMMIT

- Riesling
- Pinot Noir
- Chardonnay
- Frontenac Gris
- Sauvignon Blanc

S Center Highway 613

11E INMAN

- Bianca

E Hohnke Road

S Lake Shore Drive

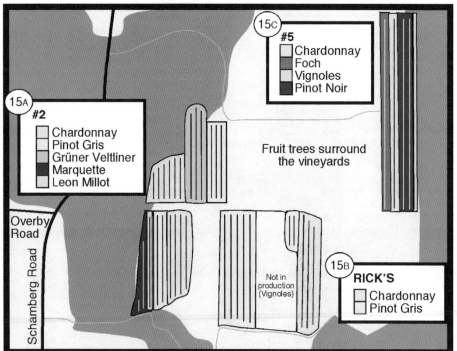

15C #5

- Chardonnay
- Foch
- Vignoles
- Pinot Noir

15A #2

- Chardonnay
- Pinot Gris
- Grüner Veltliner
- Marquette
- Leon Millot

Overby Road

Schamberg Road

Fruit trees surround the vineyards

Not in production (Vignoles)

15B RICK'S

- Chardonnay
- Pinot Gris

500 FEET

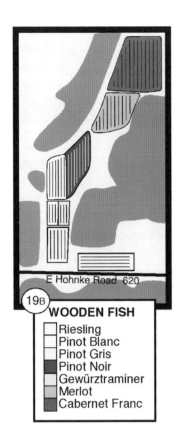

VERTERRA
SWEDE ROAD

14B

- Riesling
- Chardonnay
- Gewürztraminer
- Pinot Blanc
- Vignoles
- Merlot

N Swede Road

633

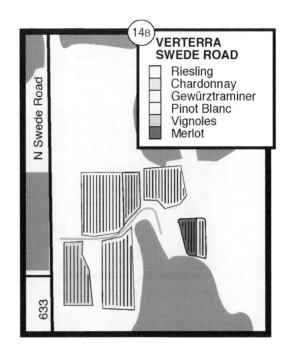

500 FEET

19B

WOODEN FISH

- Riesling
- Pinot Blanc
- Pinot Gris
- Pinot Noir
- Gewürztraminer
- Merlot
- Cabernet Franc

E Hohnke Road 620

S Center Highway

633

E Crimson
Valley Avenue

7D

TRUE NORTH

- Marechal Foch
- Cabernet Sauvignon
- Mixed vines with Merlot

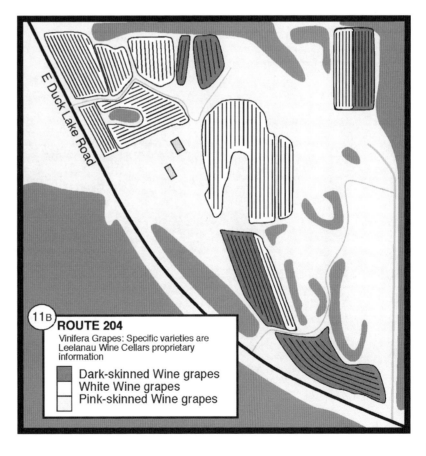

E Duck Lake Road

11B

ROUTE 204

Vinifera Grapes: Specific varieties are
Leelanau Wine Cellars proprietary
information

- Dark-skinned Wine grapes
- White Wine grapes
- Pink-skinned Wine grapes

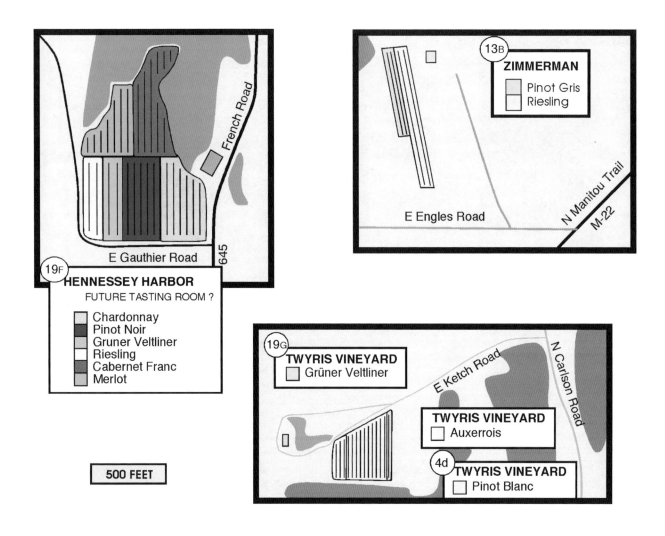

E French Road

E Gauthier Road

645

19F
HENNESSEY HARBOR
FUTURE TASTING ROOM ?

Chardonnay
Pinot Noir
Gruner Veltliner
Riesling
Cabernet Franc
Merlot

13B
ZIMMERMAN
Pinot Gris
Riesling

E Engles Road

N Manitou Trail

M-22

500 FEET

19G
TWYRIS VINEYARD
Grüner Veltliner

E Ketch Road

N Carlson Road

TWYRIS VINEYARD
Auxerrois

4d **TWYRIS VINEYARD**
Pinot Blanc

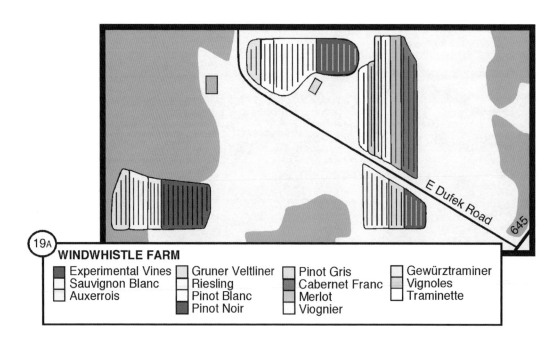

E Dufek Road

645

19A **WINDWHISTLE FARM**

Experimental Vines	Gruner Veltliner	Pinot Gris	Gewürztraminer
Sauvignon Blanc	Riesling	Cabernet Franc	Vignoles
Auxerrois	Pinot Blanc	Merlot	Traminette
	Pinot Noir	Viognier	

84

The Vines: It's Farming

Some Tales, Long, Short, Unvarnished, from Leelanau Peninsula Growers

Ciccone Vineyard and Winery...

... A chair, a chair, my kingdom for a chair.....

When asked, in hopes of hearing from him what his own favorite wine was, "What do you want at the end of the day?" Tony Ciccone came back with, "a chair".

Harvest Moon .....What do you do on your honeymoon?

Montie married Philip Siemer a couple of decades ago. So what to do on their honeymoon? "Plant a vineyard" says Montie. An acre the first year, more thereafter. Pinot Gris, 1,500 plants. Fifty have died off and have been replanted with Bianca, which can handle the chill that did in the Pinot Gris.

This teacher of yoga for a quarter century believes yoga is ageless, so she names her practice, "Ageless Yoga". Montie's oldest student is 84 years old.

The Siemer home looks over their vineyard and a copse of trees off to the left. The turkeys hide there and come out at night. "They are very methodical turkeys," because the grapes between two posts would disappear overnight, then, the next section the following night!

The Siemer's Pinot Gris is from their Harvest Moon vineyard; you'll find it bottled at nearby Silver Leaf Winery.

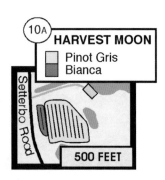

French Valley ..... The necessary dog .....

On arriving at French Valley's vineyards, I was met by the (almost) necessary dog, a border collie who barked vociferously, bared his teeth, but didn't come within six feet of me. Eventually I found Bert Walker, who tends the vineyard for French Valley Winery. Bert is out every day in the vineyards, doing one or another of the many tasks required to manage the vines. He says the acreage is just right for one person to do it all.

Wooden Fish ..... A "wooden fish"?

Randy Woods of Wooden Fish Vineyards gave me the most succinct reason I've ever heard for working his own vineyards, "I like working for me."

Verterra. ....Turkeys tell us when the grapes are ripe.

"They are just the right height to pick the grapes and they know where in the vineyard the ripe ones are!" That's the beginning of Paul Hamelin's vineyard tour for Verterra Winery. (See also Vineyard Tour.)

Whaleback ..... Don't let somebody else run it

Janet Roth is proud of her grapes and the wine made from them by Lee Lutes and Shawn Walters. From a 2007 planting, she now has a second harvest.

Much of what is known as the Whaleback area has been in Janet's family for 80 years, first in cherries, then apples, now vines. She sold off part of the land to the Leelanau Conservancy as the Whaleback Nature Preserve – the Preserve's cliffs and beach are up a trail from the parking lot.

Though Craig Cunningham provides some vineyard management services, Janet insists, "Don't let somebody else run it" but do as much of the work yourself as you can. To Janet, that is the only way to get the quality of grapes that attract purchasers such as Black Star Farms and French Road Cellars.

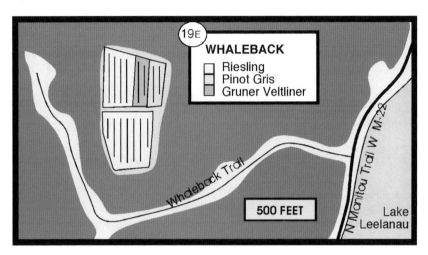

Drumlin ..... What's a drumlin?

Ray and Debbie Kuhn didn't buy a farm with the idea of putting vineyards on the Drumlin (look it up in your Scottish dictionary), it just sort of happened. Point of fact, the east yard off the barn could have offered good seating space for a theatre playing out of the barn. Summer theatre? Or maybe, grapes?

Having spent thirty years traveling around Colorado and its neighbor states for Morton Salt, Ray saw a lot of farming. So, he planted a few rows of grapes, then a few more, and now he has a vineyard, with two Marquette hybrids developed by the University of Minnesota to survive the cold winters. (Ray thinks he was the first to plant the Marquette hybrid). He also has Traminette, a Riesling-like grape that has long thrived in Southwest Michigan.

The Kuhn's do everything they can organically, only varying where extraordinary problems arise, such as a greater than usual insect infestation; then they use whatever will do the job. They have, however, employed a new kind of netting to stop birds and even insects from getting to the clusters. It wraps around the sides of the vines rather than over the top (like traditional bird netting), and can be rolled up from the bottom to reach the clusters at harvest. This is known as permanent netting.

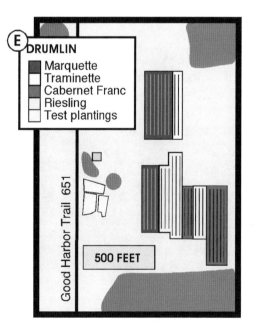

Though they now have four- and three-year vines, and will accordingly harvest enough grapes to make more than their last year's (2011) 30 gallons of wine, they still have no facility to ferment and bottle their juice. There is always something to do, when you do everything by yourself. Someday, there may be a Drumlin wine label. When the 2012 harvest produced a surprisingly large crop, they sold their Marquette grapes to Bel lago — thus joining the commercial wine fraternity.

Old Orchard ..... Making a bargain to get a vineyard .....

The Knight vineyards are the dream of industrialist Charles F. "Chuck" Knight, former Chairman and now Chairman Emeritus of Emerson Electrics. Upon his retirement, Chuck worked with Craig Cunningham to develop a vineyard near Glen Arbor.

Craig wasn't pleased with Chuck's chosen site a short way off Glen Lake, but made a bargain: he would place his little black boxes (that measure daily temperatures) on the site and, after a year, compare them with the results from the best vineyard that he managed. If the result was unsatisfactory, Chuck would have to find someone else to manage his vineyard.

One year later, satisfied, Craig planted the first sections of the vineyard featuring northwest Michigan's only planting of Kerner – Germany's third most planted grape in 1995 and a cross of a red grape, Trollinger, with Riesling.

Knight was a straight-forward businessman, good to work with, says Cunningham. "I'd get a call from his secretary: "Chuck wants to see you at 11:15," and she'd hang up, knowing this meant at Chuck's Up North house.

Via his personal jet, Chuck would fly up from St Louis. "&$%^, Chuck, what do you think this does to my carbon footprint?" was the greeting at the vineyard.

Was it the Kerner, or the quality of the Riesling, that had Bryan Ulbrich interested?

North Unity ..... A Walk to the Manitou Islands .....

Brian Price has eight acres of wine vines, for which he does all the pruning. Back in 1975 he was growing Christmas trees on the property. Before that he was a commercial fisherman, which he didn't give up until 1991. He remembers when Lake Michigan froze over, first in 1977, then in the late 80s, when you could walk to the Manitou islands, or drive a car to them!

The wine grapes are on a former tart cherry site. Brian set out temperature recording devices over two winters before he was satisfied the site was suitable for grapes. Then he planted Chardonnay and Pinot Noir (both Burgundian *vinifera*). The latter is his own favorite drink. He never planted Riesling despite knowing it was the preferred northern white wine grape, because Chardonnay would do fine, and his foremost reason for planting was to enjoy the fruit.

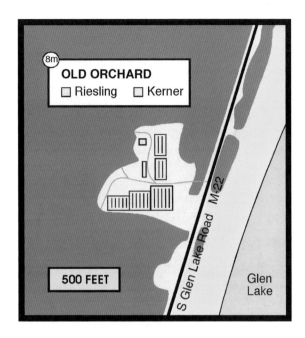

Norvick ..... And then there were more vines .....

Chris Pline was a farmer near Lansing. When he moved north, he still had farming blood, and so begins his tale. Purchasing a few acres on South (why "south," when there is no north?) Norvick Road out on the peninsula that forms the south arm of Suttons Bay, he began planting. A few rows this year, a few more next year. No plan as to doubling one variety; why not instead try something different in the next row?

Meanwhile, Chris and his wife built their home. They went to the local extension service and obtained root stock for their Norvick Road trees that now, after about a decade and a half, have grown to about 20 feet.

And then there were more vines.

Chris is a martial arts instructor and often has only one day off a week. His private vinting has produced an "awesome" Muscat Gewürztraminer blend and a "very smooth" red blend of Merlot and Cabernet Franc. Says his ever-cheerful wife, "These came after Shawn Walters gave Chris some advice and yeast and other chemicals. There are still some bottles in the basement that are close to awful".

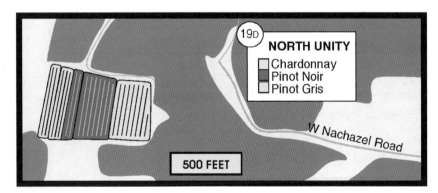

Steele's Crossing ….. The vines pay the taxes …..

The Walkers, Ruth and Scott, come from a long line of farmers. Once their mile-long stretch of West Bay had hogs, cattle and potatoes growing on the poor soil – a soil rich in the calcium left over from an ancient salt water sea on the site. Over time, cherry trees were planted. Eventually, only one year in ten produced a suitable cash crop. Ruth and Scott had been spending weekends Up North, so in 1988 they planted three and a half acres of Chardonnay and one acre of Pinot Noir. In 1991 they sold their crop to Larry Mawby; now, two decades later, they still send their crop to the famous champagne maker. Scott quoted Mawby's oft-quoted or paraphrased line; "Grapes are a weed. Give them water and sun, and they will grow."

Scott has tried several methods of training his vines: first, of course, the traditional "fan" method (great crop, but not sustainable), and finally the "Scott Henry" method, the only Leelanau Peninsula vineyard so trained. Excellent yield, and sustainable.

The vineyard still has remnants of the walnut trees that once ringed the Walker home. Walnuts are "death to vines", so were removed.

In all, Scott says happily, "the vines pay the taxes."

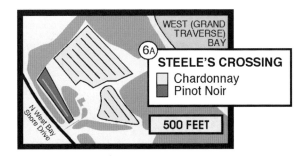

Telford Farms….. Landscaping …..

Telford Farms is owned by a group of nine families who own lots around East Winberie Lane where six of them have homes. Two more families live in Traverse City, and one in Florida.

The original vines were planted by Bruce Simpson of Good Harbor back in the late 80s or early 90s. When the families decided to grow something, Black Star Farms "was the force in suggesting vines as a good choice," according to Jeff Anderson, who lives just beyond the north end of the vineyard and became the vineyard manager. What gave him the needed experience? "Landscaping!" says Jeff.

Black Star Farms' Lee Lutes eventually left the group, and the grapes were then sold to Larry Mawby. The hilly site, which has a hundred foot drop, suffers from frost and the winds are chilly. But Pinot Noir and Vignoles are great champagne grapes, and the bubbly doesn't need high brix, 19 being more than sufficient.

More recently the grapes have gone to Circa Estate, and David Bell oversees vineyard management of what is now an organic vineyard, with local supervision by Jeff Anderson.

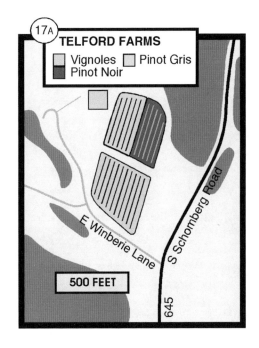

Jeff recalls that, when the sky is gray, it is windy and wet, 30°, then even with coffee and donuts, maybe 40 will show up for the harvest. But get a beautiful blue sky October, 60°, the grape leaves are golden, and the turnout is more like 80!

No, you don't really get into wine grapes for the romance – too much hard work – and you hardly get into it "for the profit," but the harvest dinner brings back some of the romance that got you into it in the first place.

Old Mission Peninsula
and its American Viticultural Area

Vinifera grapes came to Old Mission Peninsula before Leelanau Peninsula. It took only one winery to justify the entire peninsula being named an AVA. So, here is a word about the AVA. An AVA is a unique area in terms of its viticulture. Yes, it was Edward O'Keefe of Chateau Grand Traverse who petitioned AVA status for the Old Mission Peninsula, which was granted June 8, 1987. CGT was the only commercial winery on the peninsula back then.

Vitis Vinifera comes to Up North Michigan

The story of Up North Michigan wine's achieving international recognition starts with Chateau Grand Traverse before its second generation. It is the story of Ed O'Keefe who spent time in Europe. in his youth. Ed was born in Philadelphia at the early edge of the Great Depression. Ed made the first cut for the 1952 Olympics Men's Gymnastic team, having attended Denmark's Ollerup Gymnastics School on a full scholarship, but could not compete; he had suffered a ruptured appendix. Yet, with the team, he was able to tour Europe and come to know its vineyards.

Ed's business acumen was seen in his successfully running nursing homes in the Detroit area, but the call of wine could not be avoided. He moved to Old Mission in 1974. To learn about wine growing, he consulted with the Geisenheim Oenological and Viticultural (Grape Breeding) Institute in Germany on a trip with Dr. Stanley Howell of MSU and Len Olsen of Tabor Hill Winery in Southwest Michigan. The institute's chief viticulturist, Dr. Helmut Becker, came to Michigan and helped O'Keefe contour a 55-acre hill into a southwest slope to take advantage of the afternoon sun and allow cold air to flow out of the vineyard. In 1975 German viticulturist Bernd Philippi came to supervise the first planting of CGT vineyards. Thus, *vitis vinifera* came to Up North Michigan. By 1979 there was a harvest of Riesling – prominent by itself and in various blends with the Chateau Grand Traverse label – Chardonnay and Merlot. Now, with 120 acres in cultivation, he has added Gewürztraminer, Pinot Grigio, Grüner Veltliner, Lemberger, Pinot Meunier and some experimental red wine vines to the mixture. Riesling, however, remains the chief wine, both for Chateau Grand Traverse and the entire two AVA's of the peninsulas.

An unabashed promoter of Michigan wine, Ed can be seen at many wine events, talking up the virtues of wines grown in Up North Michigan.

The Tasting Rooms of Old Mission Peninsula

A Note about tasting room listings and Wine offerings

The headers in the following pages give the name and address, phone number and website information of the named business. Vintages for wines are not provided because often there are two or more vintages of a wine being offered at the same time. Some wines in the listings may be sold out. The listings are designed to show what, in any given year, you might find at each tasting room. The listing of wines offered in each tasting room follows these groupings:

1. Ice wines

2. Sparkling wines

3. White wines, including desert wines

4. Rosé wines

5. Red wines

6. Special blends and unique offerings

7. Fruit wines including cider

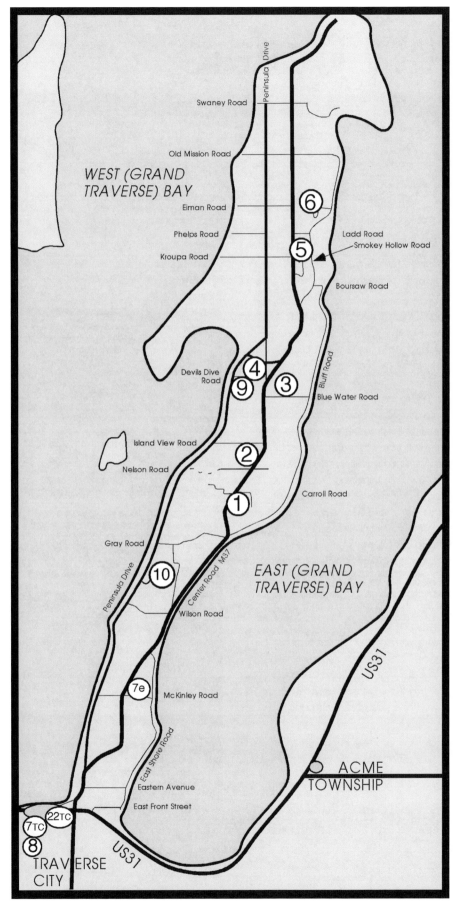

Old Mission Peninsula Tasting Rooms

1 Peninsula Cellars
2 Chateau Grand Traverse
3 Brys Estate
4 Bowers Harbor
5 Chateau Chantal
6 2 Lads
7e TASTES of Black Star
7TC Black Star Farms
   Traverse City
8 Left Foot Charley
9 Mission Table
10 Hawthorne

Vineyards are farms and are private property and should be entered only with permission of the owner.

Not all roads on Old Mission Peninsula are shown. All roads necessary to reach the tasting room are shown.

Tasting rooms in Traverse City are:
7TC TASTES of Black Star Farms
8 Left Foot Charley in The Commons
22TC Cherry Republic on Front Street

A Note about tasting room listings and wine offerings

The list above identifies each Old Mission Peninsula tasting room, with the number that is assigned to each cross-referencing to its location on the peninsula map. Tasting rooms are listed largely in order as one drives up the Old Mission Peninsula from Traverse City, with the following exceptions:

1 Black Star Farms continues numbering from the prime farm on Leelanau Peninsula. 7e is the Black Star Farms Tasting Room on Old Mission Peninsula at the Montana Ruso Vineyards. 7TC is TASTES of Black Star Farms, their Tasting Room in The Village on the Commons in Traverse City's west side.

2 Those tasting rooms and vineyards that have been added to the Old Mission Peninsula following the original members of WOMP grouping follow #8, Left Foot Charley.

1. Peninsula Cellars

Tel. 231-933-9787
11480 Center Road
Traverse City, MI 49686

www.peninsulacellars.com

Dave and Joan Kroupa are the owners. John Kroupa is the general manager and winemaker.

John Kroupa was in the winery office, next the cellar with its steel tanks. Peninsula Cellars "is a winery. We grow the grapes and make the wine" was the way the story of six generations began. Yes, six generations of Kroupas. Kroupa Road! You know you've been around when they name the road after you! With that as a benchmark, John also noted that a good winemaker "should be 6' 2" or taller" as he looked down at my mere 5' 8".

Dave Kroupa, John's father, farms fruit; lots of cherries. Long ago when the family first moved to the north part of Old Mission Peninsula, they had animals and crops. Hay, of course, for the animals, but a range of what could be eaten or sold. Over time, they graduated to stone fruit, peaches, cherries and such and, of course, apples. Again, over time, the apples were phased out and grapes planted. Though much of Peninsula Cellars' wine production comes from grapes grown around Kroupa Road, there is a single vineyard just south of the tasting room, and a few others scattered on the peninsula.

First plantings of vines were in 1991, making Peninsula Cellars one of the oldest wineries on Old Mission Peninsula. By 1994 they had a vintage, and opened a tasting room in the back of Old Mission's General Store. When an old schoolhouse on Carroll Road and Center Highway became available, it was acquired by the Kroupas and converted to a Tasting Room that was opened in 1999.

Peninsula Cellars remains a family run winery not far south of the 45th parallel. The best comparison is with Alsace in France, which also grows Riesling and Gewürztraminer. Peninsula Cellars "Manigold" Gewürztraminer is a name they developed with Rob and Lois Manigold and marketed in 2002. This might be considered their premium wine – still sourced from the Manigolds - rare as it is, because it won accolades unheard-of for a Michigan wine at the time.

John's philosophy toward wine making could be called minimalistic or purist. There is no fussing with secondary or later fermentations; a single, well-chosen yeast starts the fermentation and stays until the right balance of alcohol and sweetness is obtained for their white wines. They use malolactic fermentation for their red wines. Malolactic fermentation, which usually creates a rounder, fuller feel in the mouth, is a process in winemaking where tart-tasting malic acid, naturally present in grape must, is converted to softer-tasting lactic acid.

Peninsula Cellars owns and manages many vineyards other than Maple Grove Vineyard, which is located at their tasting room. See the Old Mission Peninsula Vineyard Maps Section.

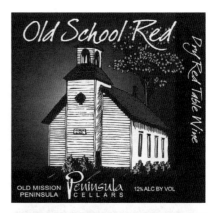

If you think wine-lovers – and especially these winery owners – lack a sense of humor, just look at the labels that they produce that relate to their tasting room, the old school house.

For the Blossom Days event, Peninsula Cellars offered a barrel sample of 2011 Cabernet Franc with some sweets which seemed to be varieties of cheesecake. Their new release was the Pinot Grigio 2011.

Riesling Ice Wine

Reserve Chardonnay
Stainless Steel Chardonnay
Pinot Blanc
Manigold Gewürztraminer
Gewürztraminer
Old School White***
Semi-dry Riesling   Dry Riesling
Select Riesling Homework (rose)

Cabernet Franc/Merlot

Merlot/Cab Franc Reserve
Detention**
Cabernet Franc
Old School Red*

Mélange (Port style)

Kroupa Orchards White Cherry[6]
Apple[4]
Hot Rod Cherry[5]

Dave Kroupa, ever the farmer, mowing the lawn at his Maple Grove vineyard.

* Cab Franc, Merlot Lemberger & Baco Noir   ** Baco Noir, Lemberger & Cab Franc   *** Cayuga, Riesling, Pinot Blanc & Pinot Grigio
[4] Macintosh, Spy, Empire & Greening   [5] Montmorency, Ulster & Balaton   [6] Emperor Francis & Gold

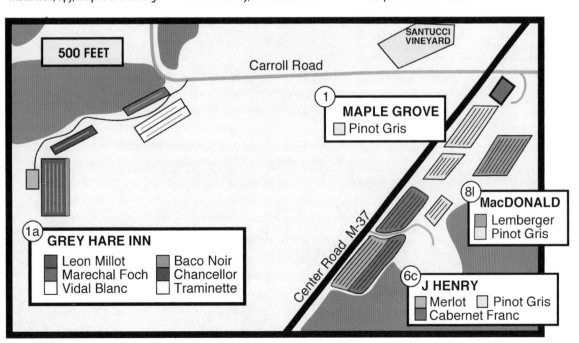

SANTUCCI VINEYARD

500 FEET

Carroll Road

1 MAPLE GROVE
☐ Pinot Gris

Center Road M-37

8l MacDONALD
☐ Lemberger
☐ Pinot Gris

1a GREY HARE INN
■ Leon Millot   ■ Baco Noir
■ Marechal Foch   ■ Chancellor
☐ Vidal Blanc   ☐ Traminette

6c J HENRY
■ Merlot   ☐ Pinot Gris
■ Cabernet Franc

93

2. Chateau Grand Traverse Estate

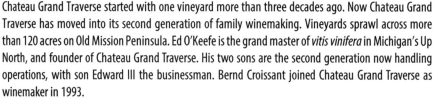

Tel. 231-223-7355
12239 Center Road
Traverse City, MI 49686
www.cgtwines.com

Chateau Grand Traverse started with one vineyard more than three decades ago. Now Chateau Grand Traverse has moved into its second generation of family winemaking. Vineyards sprawl across more than 120 acres on Old Mission Peninsula. Ed O'Keefe is the grand master of *vitis vinifera* in Michigan's Up North, and founder of Chateau Grand Traverse. His two sons are the second generation now handling operations, with son Edward III the businessman. Bernd Croissant joined Chateau Grand Traverse as winemaker in 1993.

Sean O'Keefe is the vineyard supervisor. He had just driven a hamper of grapes to the collection area when this author asked him if 2012 wasn't the greatest year in the history of Up North wine grapes, as many vineyard owners were saying.

"Every year they shout, 'greatest year yet.' Yet this year we had drought conditions." He said that the Pinot Blanc and Gewürztraminer had been harvested and the product was excellent. But others of Chateau Grand Traverse's vineyards would have to be picked bit-by-bit, day-by-day, as the clusters ripened, so uneven would be the ripening during the harvest season.

"Just because the season started a month early, doesn't mean a good harvest," he continued. Cool weather later on, dry spells, all make a difference to the harvest. And the high heat in mid-summer hurt some Riesling vines, which are a cool climate grape.

Chateau Grand Traverse is the oldest and largest commercial winery and vineyard operation in northern Michigan. It never would have happened unless Ed O'Keefe had been in northwest Germany, Mosel Riesling territory.

MSU Extension had decreed that only hybrids would thrive in NW Michigan, but Ed thought the Mosel region's climate was enough similar to Old Mission Peninsula's that he brought back vines. He planted them. They thrived. Everything changed for NW Michigan wines.

Vitis vinifera in NW Michigan became the standard because of Ed O'Keefe's defiance of the experts. Riesling, Chardonnay, Gewürztraminer, the full range of Pinot varieties (Pinot Gris, Pinot Blanc, Pinot Meunier, Pinot Noir), Gamay Noir, Merlot and Cabernet Franc, became the benchmark for the area. Without the waters of East (Grand Traverse) Bay and West (Grand Traverse) Bay moderating the temperature, none of this would have been possible.

Chateau Grand Traverse owns and manages many vineyards other than those located at their estate tasting room. See the Old Mission Peninsula Vineyard Maps Section.

Riesling Ice Wine

Whole Cluster Riesling
Riesling "Lot 49"
Grand Traverse Select NV Sweet
        Harvest Riesling
Semi-dry Riesling
Grand Traverse Select NV
Semidry Riesling
Dry Riesling
Botrytis Riesling
Chardonnay "Barrel Fermented"
Chardonnay "Late Harvest"
Pinot Grigio
Grüner Veltliner
Ship of Fools White Table Wine
Edelzwicher "Noble Blend"***

Pinot Noir Vin Gris

Grand Traverse Select NV Sweet
Traverse Red
Silhouette**
Pinot Noir "Reserve"
Merlot "Reserve"
Gamay Noir
Gamay Noir "Reserve"

Cherry Reserve (Port)

Cherry Wine
National Cherry Festival (Cherry) Wine
Cherry Riesling
Cherry Wine Sangria
Spiced Cherry Wine

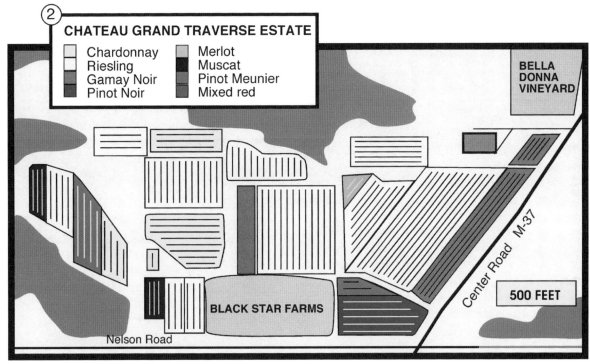

"Real Men wear Pink," shouts to this author by this lively member of the crew in CGT's Old Mission vineyards during the 2012 harvest. Her T-shirt looks for a solution to cancer.

*65% Pinot Blanc, 30% Pinot Gris, 5% Pinot Noir
** Pinot Noir, Gamay Noir, Cabernet Franc, Pinot Meunier, and Merlot

*** Gewürztraminer, Muscat Ottonel, Pinot Gris & Chardonnay.
CGT suggests food pairings for most of its wines.

② CHATEAU GRAND TRAVERSE ESTATE

	Chardonnay		Merlot
	Riesling		Muscat
	Gamay Noir		Pinot Meunier
	Pinot Noir		Mixed red

BELLA DONNA VINEYARD

Center Road M-37

500 FEET

BLACK STAR FARMS

Nelson Road

3. Brys Estate Vineyard and Winery

231-223-9303
3309 Blue Water Road
Traverse City, MI 49686
www.brysestate.com

Walter and Eileen Brys are the owners, Coenraad Stassen the winemaker.

Winemaker Coenraad Stassen had eight years learning wines before he came to America by way of the World Agricultural Exchange. He was "processed" at Ohio State University. He had his choice of working in Virginia, California or Michigan. Silly he, he chose Michigan and arrived in Traverse City on 28 January 2003. The temperature was 7°. Now, that would not have been so bad were it Centigrade, the scale used it seems everywhere but America, but, of course, it was Fahrenheit. The clothes he arrived in were designed for summer. Coenraad Stassen, if you cannot guess it from the name, is a native of South Africa, though he is now fully American. Yet a legend persists that, since the stainless steel tanks for the white wines at Brys Estate Winery are from South Africa, Coenraad Stassen was shipped to Traverse City in one!

After four years at Chateau Chantal, Coenraad was hired by Walter and Eileen Brys. Their desire to follow agricultural practices called "viticulture raisonée" allowed him to follow organic and bio diverse practices that he found suitable to the estate. Also, they grow only *vitis vinifera*, no hybrids. Agrivine does the major agricultural work, such as topping the vines.

But key to the quality of the wines is that at harvest time they pick whole clusters by hand. Machine picking picks all the grape clusters. By hand picking, they can leave clusters damaged by wasps and birds and pick only full healthy clusters.

Brys Estate wines are all but organic. The extreme requirements for agricultural products being certified organic can be prohibitive for reasons often beyond the control of the farmer. It is possible to farm organically yet not gain that title, which has to be proven to the Department of Agriculture. Many farmers simply won't waste the effort, knowing that what they produce satisfies those who desire "organic."

What is "natural" is also contentious. If you are fortunate to take a tour of Brys Estate with Coenraad, you will realize that his standards exceed any requirements the government could put on paper.

It took the Walt and Eileen Brys, from Detroit, then Houston, three decades of dreaming about vineyards and a winery before they realized, retired in Florida, that they wanted to do something wine-related. They traveled the country for two years: California, the Willamette Valley in Oregon, the Finger Lakes region of New York State and the Hill Country of Texas, without much luck. So, after twenty years away from Michigan, they returned. They never left.

What they found on 80 acres was a dilapidated cherry orchard with buildings dating back to the 1890s. Two barns and a pump house survived their renovations, begun in 2000. The farmhouse was rebuilt in 1890s homestead style. One of the barns was turned into a guest cottage. They began planting vines in 2001, 46,500 in all. Three years later, with a first harvest looming, Eileen and Walt began construction of the tasting room, which opened on May 6, 2005.

The staff includes Judy Shaughnessy, Walt's niece, who relocated from Shelby Township, Michigan with her husband and two daughters and Walt's 94-year old mother, to join Brys Estate as the Tasting Room and Wine Club Manager. Son Patrick Brys in the spring of 2010 became the Operations Manager and a new resident on Old Mission Peninsula.

For Blossom Days, Coenraad himself drew a barrel sampling of the 2011 Merlot aging in French Oak, to be released in 2013. This was served with a Bacon Cheese Tart, prepared by Mrs. Brys.

On a July evening in 2012, Coenraad held forth on the farm for a dozen Tasters Guild members. He showed the Chardonnay vines and how they had been topped because they had grown too far above normal height; they were up to several weeks ahead of normal, due to the early hot weeks in spring. From there he explained the process through which the clusters were processed and how at each stage there were waste products that were removed from the juice and composted for later use in the vineyard, thus avoiding chemical fertilizers and pesticides.

Salami, cheese, crackers, tart and sweet cherries, raspberries and chocolate were available during the wine tasting. A 2010 Artisan Chardonnay, then a 2011 Dry Riesling followed a 2011 Pinot Blanc. Two reds were both 2010, Cabernet Franc and Merlot, followed by an inexpensive blend of 2011 Pinot Noir & Riesling. A German style 2011 Gewürztraminer set up the finale, a 2008 "Dry Ice" Riesling Ice Wine with New York style cheesecake.

Coenraad noted that the Pinot Noir/Riesling sold out in six months and 600 cases were made of the Pinot Grigio. He also offered that the Cabernet Franc blend with Merlot was 50:50, and was "wine by the bucket!" The dry Riesling would be "off dry" with 1.2% residual sugar. Bone dry usually suffers from an overbalance of alcohol. 700 cases were made. As to the Gewürztraminer, the French style is dry and "you would have to serve it with dinosaur!" So he does it in a German style that is less oily and reveals less perfume. He also noted that his Gewürztraminer goes with Wasabi!

For more on Brys Estate operations see the section on The Crush, in The Businesses of Wine.

96

Artisan
Brys Estate
VineYard & Winery

Pinot Noir

2 · 0 · 0 · 7

OLD MISSION PENINSULA

ESTATE GROWN

UNFILTERED

ALC. 13.8% BY VOL.

The Chardonnay is a blend of Muscat and Champagne clones, the Gewürztraminer a blend of half the grapes being processed dry and half sweet; an Alsatian style Gewürz, then mixed.

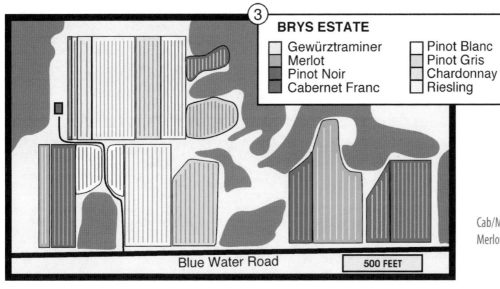

③ **BRYS ESTATE**

Gewürztraminer	Pinot Blanc
Merlot	Pinot Gris
Pinot Noir	Chardonnay
Cabernet Franc	Riesling

Blue Water Road   500 FEET

"Dry Ice" Riesling Ice Wine

Naked Chardonnay
Artisan Chardonnay
DryRiesling
Gewürztraminer
Pinot Blanc
Pinot Grigio
Riesling
Riesling/Gris
Pinot Noir/Riesling (73/27)

Cab/Merlot   Cabernet Franc
Merlot   Pinot Noir

97

4. Bowers Harbor Vineyards and Winery

800-616-7615
2896 Bowers Harbor Road
Traverse City, MI 49686
www.bowersharbor.com

Jack Stegenga was the founder of Bowers Harbor, which is now the farm of Spencer Stegenga and Erica Schoenherr. Bernd Croissant at Chateau Grand Traverse and Bryan Ulbrich at Left Foot Charley serve as winemakers in consultation with Spencer Stegenga.

Spencer is a working farmer, not a businessman owning a farm. He's out in the vineyards, not in the tasting room. That is left to Kristy, Tom and Justin and others as needed. Tom is Tom Petzold, Ten Hands Vineyard, who also directed the Rotary Grand Traverse Region New Release Wine Tasting Event. It can be hoped that it will return.

The history of BHV goes back a long way. Jack Stegenga was told by Ed O'Keefe to buy acreage and plant grapes. Ed saw wine grapes as BHV's future. So the first three "Blocks" (See the map at the end of this article) were established in 1991. When he inherited the operation, Spencer decided that some expansion was needed. "I poured everything I had into the vineyards," says he, "The banks love me." He dedicated the Langley vineyard, first planted in 1998, to his beloved grandfather, Harold Langley. Not long after, he proposed to Erica Schoenherr on a blank canvas of earth. A month after she said "yes," that earth was turned and vines were planted. Spencer dedicated this vineyard to his wife Erica in 2000. The Pinot Grigio from the Erica Vineyard makes up the majority of BHV's flagship wine. Production has reached sixteen thousand cases," he proudly asserts, but he could reach twenty. And he loves working with other winemakers to craft what Bowers Harbor serves.

Sometime in October 2012 Spencer told this author, "Our Cab Franc came in at 24.9 Brix, our Merlot at 23.8." Does this mean a 2012 "2896"? Obviously.

A "Wine in the Vines" dinner shows most everything that Chris Fifarek, one of several vineyard owners who sell his wine grapes to Bowers Harbor Vineyards, can do for the operation. The vegetables are from his garden, the wine from his grapes. That's "local." The idea was synergistic. Chris had left Michigan to see the world, spent many years out west, California, up and down the coast, and Arizona. Eventually the call of Northwest Michigan could not be avoided. Marriage and farmland brought him back to Old Mission Peninsula. Chris has spent much of 2012 in his day job; building Spencer and Erica's home above the Langley vineyards. Living maybe a mile apart, such business relationships turn into personal friendships. Beyond that, every farmer on OMP knows every other farmer, and they help each other as the need arises.

Bowers Harbor offers food-pairing suggestions for each of their wines. Be prepared for them to suggest lobster in the middle of winter. And why not?

For Blossom Days, BHV offered their 2011 Red and Smokey Hollow Riesling, a single vineyard offering. The red was paired with Torta de Carne, a Cuban specialty of ground beef wrapped with yucca root, cabbage and mayo sauce.

For Memorial Day Sunday, BHV produced a pig roasted with their hard cider, plus baked beans and other condiments. Rather than pair it with a specific wine, they let the diner choose a generous glass of any of their wines. Some families bought bottles to share.

The 2896 Langley, Cabernet Franc Erica, Riesling Block II, Riesling Langley, Unwooded Chardonnay and Medium Sweet Riesling are all made at Left Foot Charley. Estate-grown Pinot Gris is used to make Pinot Gris at Chateau Grand Traverse. The estate grown Sparkling, 2896 Brut Rose and Cuvee Evan are made at Left Foot Charley and finished by L. Mawby. The Blanc de Blanc, Brut Chardonnay, Blanc de Noir, Brut Pinot Noir, and Brix Medium Sweet Bubbly are made at L. Mawby. Pinot Gris fruit from vineyards not on the Bowers Harbor estate but elsewhere on Old Mission and on Leelanau peninsulas is used to make Pinot Grigio vinted by Shawn Walters in conjunction with and with advice from Spencer.

Bowers Harbor manages vineyards other than those located at their tasting room. See the Old Mission Peninsula Vineyard Maps Section.

Gewürztraminer Ice Wine[8]

Cuvee Evan Blanc de Noir
Blanc de Blanc, NV Brut Chardonnay
2896, Brut Rosé   Blanc de Noir, Brut
Cuvee Evan Blanc de Blanc   Pinot Noir
Brix Medium Sweet Bubbly[7]

Unwooded Chardonnay
Chardonnay RLS Reserve Wooded
Chardonnay   White Cépages*
Riesling, Block II   Pinot Grigio
Riesling, Medium Sweet   Medium Dry Riesling
Gewürztraminer   Otis**
Riesling, Late Harvest Langley   Cooper[6]

Red Cépages   Bowers Harbor Red***
JT Red[4]   Pinot Noir, Wind Whistle   2896[5] Langley
Pinot Noir, Nicholas   Cabernet Franc, Erica
Claret, Erica & Langley

Spiced Cherry Wine

*Riesling, Pinot Gris, Muscat & 2 other varietals
**Otis was the Official greeter at BHV and first generation BHV vineyard
dog. Otis's wine is a Chardonnay & Riesling blend
***Cabernet Franc & Merlot
[4] 50% Merlot & 50% Cabernet Franc from Wind Whistle and Big Paw
vineyards. = Just That Red
[5] Not available every year: produced only when the grape varietals in the
blend ripen to higher standards
[6] Cooper is the second-genera-
tion BHV vineyard dog, a Bernese
mountain dog
[7] Brix, yet another Bernese
mountain dog, shares his face on
the label
[8] Bowers Harbor Vineyards are
the only producers of Gewürztraminer Ice Wine in the United
States

Bowers Harbor Vineyards

2011
Pinot Grigio
Old Mission Peninsula
Michigan, USA

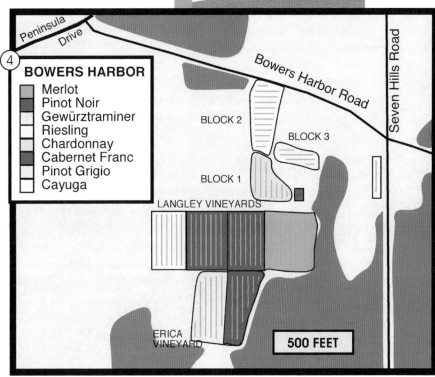

④ BOWERS HARBOR
Merlot
Pinot Noir
Gewürztraminer
Riesling
Chardonnay
Cabernet Franc
Pinot Grigio
Cayuga

Peninsula Drive
Bowers Harbor Road
Seven Hills Road
BLOCK 2
BLOCK 3
BLOCK 1
LANGLEY VINEYARDS
ERICA VINEYARD
500 FEET

5. Chateau Chantal Winery and Inn

231-223-4110
15900 Rue de Vin
Traverse City, MI 49686
www.chateauchantal.com

Travel Center Road up the Old Mission Peninsula and you will pass several tasting rooms on your trek fourteen miles from the center of Traverse City. And you will have no doubt you are there. High on the crest of the backbone of the peninsula is a European style chateau, a winery surrounded by vineyards and a bed and breakfast inn.

It was Mark Johnson, winemaker, who explained the workings of Chateau Chantal after showing me the facilities below the tasting room. Over 115 investors own Chateau Chantal with the majority of shares held by the founding Begin family. Bob and Nadine Begin bought a 60-acre cherry farm in 1983, gradually replaced cherry trees with vines, now covering 35 acres that crowd the site. The winery is named after daughter Marie-Chantal Dalese who is the Director of Marketing. Mark Johnson is the long-time vintner. Brian Hosmer has worked with him in recent years and, late in 2012, became chief vintner for Hawthorne Vineyards that is managed by Chateau Chantal.

Bob Begin had been a priest in Detroit but had been laicized when he phoned his future wife Nadine for their first date. Nadine was a teaching nun. When she and her fellow nuns were told to return to convent life or leave the order, Nadine left. She and Bob were married in 1974 and Marie-Chantal was born in 1978.

As Nadine tells it in her memoir *Feed My Lambs, Feed My Sheep*, Bob left everything to become a farmer; "I see dusty boots, holes in trousers and pockets and a smile from ear to ear!"

Initially four people tested the winery situation but it was Bob Begin and Mark Johnson who stayed with the idea. Mark had studied in Germany, visiting northern Michigan for vacation. His German professors had been to northern Michigan. Mark graduated on a day in June and didn't hesitate to return to the US by July. Opportunities in Germany were only corporate, but he wanted "to grow grapes." So he came to Ed O'Keefe in 1983, worked there 10 years. Bob invested in the vineyards and Mark brought his winemaking knowledge.

Mark instructed this author on the importance of the yeast used to turn sugar into alcohol. There are some 5,000 yeasts for white wine production, and 2,000 types for red. Low-foaming yeast at 10% volume versus one at 15% is a huge savings in gallons of produce. So selecting good yeast is not just about the right yeast to get the flavor profile the winemaker has chosen. Years of experience are all one needs! Yeast is temperature tolerant, but there is a 14% limit of yeast tolerance to alcohol, so any wine above 14% in alcohol has had alcohol added.

Chateau Chantal offers "Northern Hospitality," where wine is something to be enjoyed, not revered.

Chateau Chantal supports the radio program "The New Jazz Archive," hosted by Jeff Haas. Jeff is the son of Karl Haas, widely known for his classical music program, "Adventures in Good Music". It might be said that Jeff is to Jazz what his father was to Classical music. During the summer months, the Jeff Haas Trio performs Jazz at Sunset at Chateau Chantal.

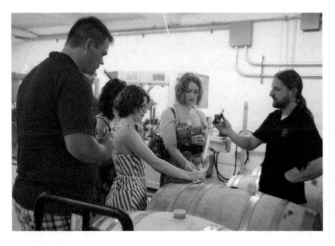

Vineyards surround the Chateau and also at other sites such as M-72 and Blue Water Road, the Lardie brothers vineyards.

For Old Mission Peninsula Blossom Days, Barrel Fermented Chardonnay and Gamay Noir were offered with Boursin cheese tarts.

Chateau Chantal manages many vineyards other than those located at their tasting room. See the Old Mission Peninsula Vineyard Maps Section.

Celebrate   Michigan Sparkling Cherry   Tonight

Pinot Blanc, Hawthorne Vineyard
Proprietor's Reserve Pinot Gris
Unoaked Chardonnay
Proprietor's Reserve Chardonnay
Late Harvest Riesling   Pinot Grigio
Select Harvest Gewurztraminer
Semi-dry Riesling
Naughty White (formerly Virtue)
Nice White (formerly Vice)

Twilight   Malbec Rosé (from Argentina)

Pinot Noir
Proprietor's Reserve Pinot Noir
Naughty Red-Dry
Nice Red-Sweet
Reserve Malbec (from Argentina)

Entice Ice Wine Brandy   Cerise Cherry Port
Cerise Noir Port

Michigan Cherry

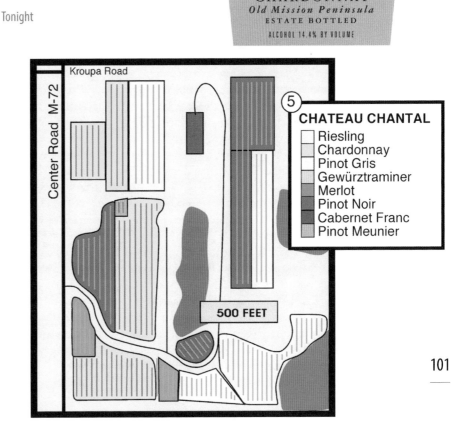

6. Two Lads Winery

231-223-7722
16985 Smokey Hollow Road
Traverse City, MI 49686
www.2Lwinery.com

Cornel Olivier and Chris Baldyga share most all aspects of the winery.

Chris Baldyga was on a roll. The harvest was going well, 70% already picked. Two Lads had just released two Pinot Noirs, one a reserve, their first. He said they would look forward to five Pinot Noir releases each year in the future. Their Pinot Noir Rosé was selling well, and they'd already sold out of two of their white offerings.

Yet was this the best year ever? Depends. They had had to irrigate for some months because of the mid-summer drought, but the Pinot Noir was not affected. Some vineyards on the peninsula were affected, so there may be some impact.

I raised the question of blends, which is the key to great Bordeaux wines. "We blend almost everything. Our Cabernet Franc will have 14% Merlot. Not 15%, because we'd have to call it Cabernet Franc Merlot." When they did label it CFM, their marketing expert said "no," people relate to Cab Franc.

Then we got into the question of *terroir*. Chris doesn't give it much concern. It is the sun, the rain, and the climate that makes the real difference. "We make great Pinot Noir, but it is different from a Burgundy Pinot Noir." It has always been the goal of Two Lads Winery and Vineyards to make great red wines. "Everyone else concentrates on white wines, we concentrate on reds."

Cornel does the vinting, and he doesn't add acid or sugar to adjust pH or sweetness, this being Chris's further explanation of the Two Lads' approach to their wines. "Some wineries make additions to keep the wine the same year after year," but not Two Lads. Each release has its own character.

Two Lads Winery is a 10,500 square foot facility located on 58 acres, 22 of which are established vineyards first planted over a decade ago. Their processing of grapes involves gravity-flow techniques that save energy, reduce noise and preserve aromatics, flavors and colors that can be partially lost when wine is manipulated or handled roughly.

The trellising system used at Two Lads is not the standard for the region. From a single Chardonnay root that is branched into a T, 10 vertical shoots are produced. Each shoot should produce 4 clusters; so one vine yields 40 clusters. Riesling might produce 12 shoots. The branches are held to the horizontal wires with PVC ribbons that stretch as the vine grows. 6.5 tons of fruit can be harvested per acre, which is unusually high.

Born and raised among the beautiful vineyards of Stellenbosch, South Africa, Cornel worked closely with his grandfather on the family farm where "I learned about growing grapes and making wine. After graduating from Elsenburg Agricultural College with a degree in Viticulture and Wine Science, I worked for two wineries in the Stellenbosch area gaining experience in making prestigious wines. In 1999 I moved across the planet to the Old Mission Peninsula and kick-started my career making cool climate wines."

To Cornel, "what I do in the vineyard is more important than what I do after the grapes are crushed".

Chris Baldyga is a local boy, Traverse City. My mother, Terrie, has worked for an Old Mission Peninsula winery since 1985, "so I've been exposed to the vineyard and winery lifestyle since boyhood. I spent time in the summers working in Old Mission Peninsula vineyards when I was too young to work inside a winery and then, when I was old enough, I worked in tasting rooms and as a cellar rat for a few wineries".

Cornel believes in doing as much as he can without outside help. During spring pruning and shaping of the vines he has two regular workers and three seasonal to help.

Chris and Cornel hoe the vineyard but are moving to a mechanical weeder. They have been herbicide-free for three years. Their cover crop has been grass cut tall, but they are moving into alfalfa. They let it grow for two years to ripen the nematodes fully, then plant buckwheat which is a good source of potassium. Nitrogen, phosphorous and potassium are needed. So, they do not fertilize. The one chemical they do use is sulfur (note; all wine contains sulfites) due to the exceedingly high pH of the soil. Their approach attracts ladybugs and other good insects.

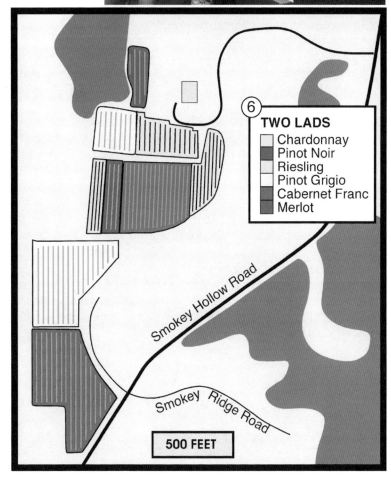

For Blossom Days, Two Lads offered a barrel sampling of 2011 Chardonnay and Pinot Noir with Vichyssoise.

Two Lads works with several other vineyards from which they obtain grapes for inclusion in their offerings. See the Old Mission Peninsula Vineyard Maps Section.

Sparkling Pinot Grigio
Sparkling Reserve*

Chardonnay
Pinot Grigio
Riesling

Rosé (from Cabernet Franc)

Pinot Noir
Reserve Pinot Noir
Merlot
Cabernet Franc

*75% Chardonnay, 25% Pinot Grigio

TWO LADS
Chardonnay
Pinot Noir
Riesling
Pinot Grigio
Cabernet Franc
Merlot

Smokey Hollow Road

Smokey Ridge Road

500 FEET

7TC/7e. Black Star Farms, Old Mission

231-944-1270
Montana Ruso Vineyard
360 McKinley Road
Traverse City, MI 49686
www.blackstarfarms.com

The TASTES of Black Star Farms tasting room is at the Mercato in the Village at Grand Traverse Commons, Traverse City. The numbering of Black Star Farms on Old Mission Peninsula is a continuation of the listing that begins with Black Star Farms on Leelanau Peninsula. There, the suffix is capitalized, here it is lower case.

If you have driven up Center Road as far as Chateau Grand Traverse, you will have seen one of the architectural wonders of the peninsula, the home of Sallie and Kermit Campbell. The slow curve of the copper roof rides high above the house central corridor, with clerestory windows at its long sides providing light to the sculpture gallery. Extensive glazing provides views northwest over the vineyards of Chateau Grand Traverse out to West Grand Traverse Bay.

Mr. Campbell, "Kerm" to his friends, is, with Don Coe, chief co-owner of Black Star Farms, and a producer of grapes. Black Star Farms is operated largely as a cooperative. Profits go to the producers, those who deliver grapes from their vineyards. Only when the grapes have been vinted, bottled and sold, does each producer get his/her share of the profits.

The Chardonnay that grows on the west side of Kerm's house is special. Or you might say, "especially good." Why? He doesn't know, but it produces what seems to him to be a very special wine, so special that in the spring of 2012 cuttings were made and 5,000 new Chardonnay plants were placed in the Leelanau Summit vineyards where there is still much room to expand. The 2012 bottling of Arcturos Chardonnay is a blend of Kerm's grapes with those of Isidor's Choice grapes from the Stanton Vineyards on Leelanau Peninsula.

"Capella" appears on the name of some of Kerm's vineyards. It is a shortening of "a capella," and, yes, Kerm is a singer who once thought of going professional. He is a tenor with high Cs in his range.

Black Star Farms main tasting room is in Suttons Bay (See 7 on Leelanau Peninsula). Black Star Farms also purchases grapes from independent growers.

Some of the vineyards are owned by seriously famous/important people, such as Robert Mampe who builds roller coasters around the world. Roller coasters are so very expensive to build that Mampe is almost alone as a builder. It is Black Star Farms' main vineyards on Old Mission Peninsula, the Montana Ruso Vineyards at the Old Mission Peninsula tasting room that are his.

For Blossom Days, Black Star Farms served BeDazzled Blanc de Blanc. Then their Pinot Noir Rosé with Prosciutto Asparagus Salad Rolls with Fromage Blanc (cow cheese) and Wild Leek Pesto.

The extensive listing of Black Star Farms offerings, which are available at all three tasting rooms, may be found on page 27.

Black Star Farms works with producers whose vineyards are on both peninsulas.

The main farm and tasting room is on Leelanau Peninsula. The Black Star Farms Old Mission tasting room is located at the Montana Ruso Vineyard.

See the Old Mission Peninsula Vineyard Maps Section for additional Black Star Farms Old Mission Peninsula vineyards.

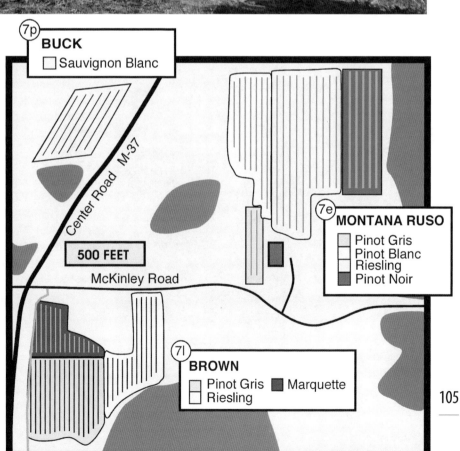

7p BUCK
☐ Sauvignon Blanc

Center Road M-37

500 FEET

McKinley Road

7e MONTANA RUSO
☐ Pinot Gris
☐ Pinot Blanc
☐ Riesling
☐ Pinot Noir

7l BROWN
☐ Pinot Gris   ☐ Marquette
☐ Riesling

8. Left Foot Charley

231-995-0500
806 Red Drive
Traverse City, MI 49684
www.leftfootcharley.com

Bryan Ulbrich and wife Jen own Left Foot Charley. Bryan calls himself the Sherpa, which means he carries the load and points the direction. Drew Perry serves as oenologist.

Bryan claims he was clumsy as a kid. He had an inward pointing left foot that caused him to constantly fall, providing laughs for his mother and uncle, who gave him the moniker of Left Foot Charley.

Bryan produced, in 2002, the first great Gewurztraminer outside of Alsace, while he was winemaker at Peninsula Cellars. This would have been about his third year of winemaking.

Left Foot Charley is unique in owning none of the grapes they make into wine. They rely on independent vineyard owners with whom they work closely, including vineyard management, to achieve quality that is reliable and repeatable. This "system" began in 2004 and is part of Bryan's determination to recognize what he believes is a budding consciousness of "place" in the U.S. wine industry. It also extends to his belief as to how *terroir* affects the tasting experience. "You've got to match the wine with the food it grows next to" is how Bryan stated it to vineyard owner Heather Johnson Reamer of Renegade Vineyard.

A short note from Werner Kuehnis, who provides the Pinot Blanc to Bryan Ulbrich, will illustrate perhaps a humorous note on "place". The Werner Kuehnis Pinot Blanc is planted not north-south but east-west. Why? Because his neighbor likes to look out his window to the East Bay! Bryan, however, also likes it that way. While "Swiss spacing" might be proper for this grape, Werner spaced his vines wide, 9', rather than Swiss style of 4'. The rootstock is planted 5' apart. This gives 20 to 25 shoots per plant, while the Swiss style produces 8-9 shoots. 1,120 shoots per acre, 4,000 bottles of wine. The vines must be watched carefully so as to prune leaves near harvest so the grape clusters on the back (north) side get sun. When a vine dies, Werner takes a shoot and grows a new plant, not one grafted.

106

⅔₀Pinot Blanc

The label identifies the source and the sweetness.
Note residual sugarsof 1% (Dry). 1.3% (Medium-dry) and 2.6%
(which may seem high, but the pH is given to show that it is on
the cusp of medium-dry/medium-sweet.
See "So, How dry is dry" in The Businesses of Wine).
Then note the Pinot Blanc at 0.7%

Vineyard: Island View
Grown in the loam soils of the central hilltops
Grape Grower: Werner Kuehnis

Harvest Date: October 16, 2010
Sugar at Harvest: 24 Brix
Residual Sugar: 0.7%

⅔₀Riesling

Vineyard: Longcore's Yard d'Vine
Grown in very sandy, loam soils facing east
Grape Grower: Jim Longcore

Harvest Date: October 22, 2010
Sugar at Harvest: 23 Brix
Residual Sugar: 1.3%

⅔₀Riesling

Vineyard: Seventh Hill Farm
Grown in loose sand and loam facing south
Grape Growers: Tom Scheuerman

Harvest Date: October 9, 2010
Sugar at Harvest: 22.8 Brix
Residual Sugar: 2.6% ~ TA 9g/L ~ pH 3.03

⅔₀Riesling - Dry

Vineyard: The Terminal Moraine
Grown in hard packed layers of gravel, sand, and clay
Grape Growers: Lisa Reehorst, Cork Eringaard

Harvest Date: October 12, 2010
Sugar at Harvest: 22 Brix
Residual Sugar: 1%

The following list indicates specific sources of vineyard grapes for *vinifera* offerings, each of which is identified on the bottle, followed by blends:

Werner Kuehnis, Island View   Pinot Blanc
Tom Scheuerman, Seventh Hill Farm   Riesling
Lisa Reehorst & Cork Eringaard   Dry Riesling
Jim Longcore   Riesling Yard d'Vine
Robert Manigold   Gewürztraminer, Sauvignon Blanc
Gary & Theresa Wilson, Tale Feathers   Pinot Grigio

Murmur**   Missing Spire Riesling***   Dry Rosé*

*Leon Millot & Pinot Noir from Leelanau & Old Mission vineyards
**Chardonnay, Pinot Gris, Riesling, Gewürztraminer & Traminer
***Vineyards of Chown, Rosi, Eringaard, on Old Mission & Engle Ridge Farms in Williamsburg

Gary and Ann Herzler, Stan Dawson provide Pinot Grigio, Riesling & Cab Franc used in blends

Late in 2012, Pinot Gris and Blaufränkisch from the MacDonald vineyards on Old Mission Peninsula and Sauvignon Blanc from Antrim County appeared on Left Foot Charley shelves.

9. Mission Table;
Bonafide Wines

231-223-4222
13512 Peninsula Drive
Traverse City, MI 49686
www.missiontable.net/mt/bonafide-wine.htm

Have you seen the wine label "Bonafide"? You will find it at Mission Table, the former Bowers Harbor Inn. Since 2006, the inn is owned by Jon Carlson & Greg Lobdell, Old Mission Peninsula natives who invest in restaurants, and managing partner Paul Olson. Olson is also chef at the Mission Table's Jolly Pumpkin restaurant. It is the goal of Jon and Greg to renovate and preserve the Inn as an historic site and award-winning restaurant. Working with the Grand Traverse Regional Land Conservancy and the Michigan Historic Preservation Network, the development rights on the property with a conservation easement now protects historic, scenic and shoreline characteristics of the inn and surrounding property, including the vineyards.

Paul Olson, raised in Bloomfield, Michigan, graduated from Michigan State University and the Culinary Institute of America in Hyde Park, New York, then went on to work at La Cite, La Boheme and Café Luxembourg in Manhattan. Working as executive chef at Luna in Mount Kisco, NY, led to opening five restaurants before his love of Up North Michigan brought him to Mission Table.

Making a standard practice of using everything local as much as possible led to the production of Bonafide wines. Some of the grapes are grown right on the Mission Table property, while the rest are sourced by Peninsula Cellars where

John Kroupa makes the wine. One wine not in the tasting room is the Californian Cabernet Sauvignon that is bottled at Peninsula Cellars, and available only in the Jolly Pumpkin and Mission Table restaurants. It should be noted that the Mission Table website lists twenty-one farms from which they obtain produce other than wine grapes.

The restaurant has a rare liquor license that allows them to sell what they produce, which includes North Peak and Jolly Pumpkin beer and a line of Civilized Spirits from their own Mission Micro Distillery. They also are produced as much as possible from local ingredients. Accordingly, Bonafide wines are served in both the Mission Table restaurant (the restaurant in the former 1880s Bowers Harbor Inn) and in the Jolly Pumpkin restaurant in the slightly younger addition behind Mission Table.

A unique aspect of their tasting room and restaurant wine service is the employment of nitrogen-burst technology. In this, bottles or kegs can be under nitrogen pressure. Nitrogen-burst capability is available to keep wine in opened bottles fresh for days, allowing less-tasted wines to be offered for tasting. The nitrogen is heavier than oxygen, so it settles over the wine, keeping the contents pristine fresh.

The Mission Table restaurant is seasonal, but the tasting room and Jolly Pumpkin operate year-round.

Peninsula White
Chardonnay
Pinot Grigio
Dry Riesling
Late Harvest Riesling
Gewürztraminer

Cabernet Franc Rosé

Peninsula Red
Cabernet Sauvignon•

•Available only in the restaurants

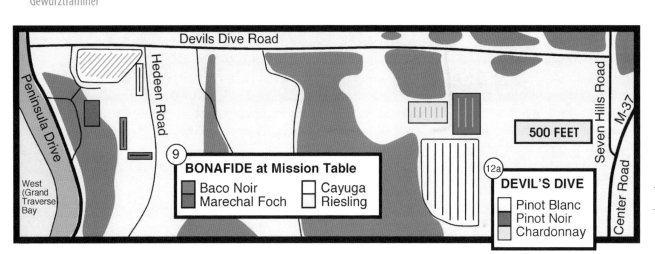

10. Hawthorne Vineyards

231-534-5485
1000 Camino Maria Drive
Traverse City, MI 49686
www.hawthornevineyards.com

Grand opening May 2013. Soft opening 22 September 2012.

Their motto seems to be what John Gay said in 1738; "From wine what sudden friendship springs!"

"My heart is there in northern Michigan," said Cathleen Hawthorne, calling from Florida in early winter. Animated about her experience of serving in the tasting room, she continues, "so different from owning a retail store (as she had), because in a tasting room you make people happy. Tasting wine is a fun thing for them to do!!"

This, from the owners of the new Hawthorne Winery and Vineyards. Buying, from Chateau Chantal, a ready-made vineyard that lacked only a tasting room to be complete, would be daunting to most, but a joy for anyone wishing to return to old haunts!

Then, again, it might be difficult to be more "Michigan" than Bruce, a Dearborn native, and Cathleen Cleary Hawthorne, who met on a blind date. Cathy's great grandmother homesteaded in Benzie County near Platte Lake during Teddy Roosevelt's administration. They owned the Platte Lake Hotel. When it burned down, Cathy's mother, Rosemary Revnell, would see cabins built as the Revnell resort. Revnell Road is still there, south of Platte Lake. Cathy's dad James, a Milford, Michigan, native and Iwo Jima veteran, had a cottage on Crystal Lake near the intersection of Lobb Road and South Shore East. Summers for Cathy meant living next to a Benzie County lake.

Meeting and marrying while still in college, Cathy and Bruce helped each other through their undergraduate years; then Cathy helped Bruce through his graduate years. The couple then lived "in exile" from Michigan, in Atlanta, where Cathy was for 20 years a Master Gardener. Love of gardening is one thing, "gardening" 26 acres of wine grape vines on an 80-acre farm, with plans for 10 more acres of vines, is another; the how-to is yet another step. Cathy spends three hours a day working on her third course in winemaking ("hard work") at California's premier wine institute, the University of California at Davis.

"Hawthorne will not be another Chateau Chantal," explains Marie-Chantal Dalese: Hawthorne wines will come from Hawthorne grapes and be processed at Hawthorne's own facilities by winemaker Brian Hosmer. Lemberger (German for the Austrian Blaufränkisch) varietals are being produced, along with the traditional northern Michigan offerings.

At the Hawthorne tasting room "soft opening," winemaker Brian Hosmer was asked of Hawthorne's first Pinot Noir, "How long will it last?" His reply, "it's in its infancy." "More vines will be planted, with the focus remaining on super-premium, single-varietal wines that reflect the vineyard's specific geographical location on their elevated altitude on the Peninsula," says Hosmer. "It's been an interesting project working with the Hawthorne's," he continues, "they bring a new perspective to the wines being offered from their estate, and it will continue to be an enjoyable challenge to create unique styles of wine for this property."

Cathleen, in return, is enthusiastic in her praise of Hosmer for his choice of yeasts for fermenting the wines and for creating the winery's "unique styles".

"Life is a journey, enjoy it one sip at a time!" is tasting room manager Jan Van Maanen's suggestion.

HAWTHORNE
VINEYARDS

PINOT NOIR
2010 | *Old Mission Peninsula*
ALCOHOL 12.3% BY VOLUME

The temporary tasting room, for the "soft opening" of Hawthorne

Barrel Reserve Chardonnay

Pinot Noir   Lemberger   Merlot/Cabernet Franc

And, in 2013
Gewürztraminer   Pinot Grigio   Unoaked Chardonnay
Pinot Blanc

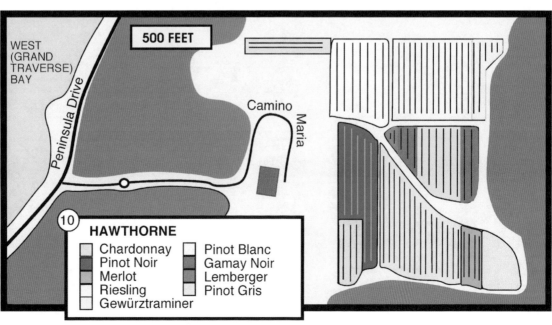

WEST
(GRAND
TRAVERSE)
BAY

Peninsula Drive

500 FEET

Camino Maria

10

HAWTHORNE

☐ Chardonnay	☐ Pinot Blanc
■ Pinot Noir	■ Gamay Noir
■ Merlot	■ Lemberger
☐ Riesling	☐ Pinot Gris
☐ Gewürztraminer	

11. Villa Mari Vineyards

231-633-1277
121 East Front Street, Suite 200
Traverse City, MI 49684
www.villamarivineyards.com

While the Villa Mari vines are but a few miles south of the 45th parallel, the climate of the Old Mission Peninsula is hardly the same as that of Bordeaux, the home of the world's greatest red wines. It comes closer to that of the Italian Piedmont, perhaps the Krasnodar Krai (Russia's Napa Valley) and, who would believe it, to China's Northern Silk Road in the well-known province of Xinjiang. Yet, the desire to create Bordeaux-style wine cannot be suppressed in Up North Michigan.

Under a canopy, also called "hoop house", that raises the temperature as much as 10° Fahrenheit, are planted Bordeaux and north Italian (Piedmont) varieties. The canopy extends the growing season as much as three weeks in the spring and three in the autumn.

The story of "Row 7" and its vineyard is funny — and true. This author has known two versions, but best to stick what is on the bottle, with a bit of additional information from the owner of Mutual Farm Management, Martin Lagina, and the vineyard manager of MFM, Jay Budd.

Martin Lagina was on the hillside across from the Underwood Farms properties. He was planting rootstock. Then came the deluge. Martin quickly contacted every friend who could come and help plant 3,000 vines in the mud.

When the planting seemed to be done, Martin noticed that one box was empty, and he had no idea where the vines had been planted. 'Row 7" came the answer from someone off in the distance. The box had Bordeaux varieties (the other version, perhaps rumor only, said Bordeaux and north Italian reds mixed) and so what was planted was an unknown mix, impossible to replicate. Accordingly, the five barrels of wine from this planting is all that can ever be offered to lovers of this European-style wine. Now, that is what you call a "field blend."

Lagina's business interests include Heritage Sustainable Energy, so Villa Mari "Row 7" is powered by a pair of 7.5 KW windmills." And while his vineyards have been producing wine from Sangiovese, Nebbiolo, Cabernet Sauvignon, Malbec and Syrah grapes, most of his product in 2012 went to Chateau Grand Traverse; only the Row 7 Red Wine was being sold under the Villa Mari label, so named in honor of Martin's maternal grandmother. By the end of 2013 Villa Mari hopes to have a full line of wines.

A tasting room is planned, perhaps for 2014, but the location is not yet determined.

Villa Mari Vineyards owns and manages, through Mutual Farm Management, many vineyards other than those located at their tasting room. See the Old Mission Peninsula Vineyard Maps section.

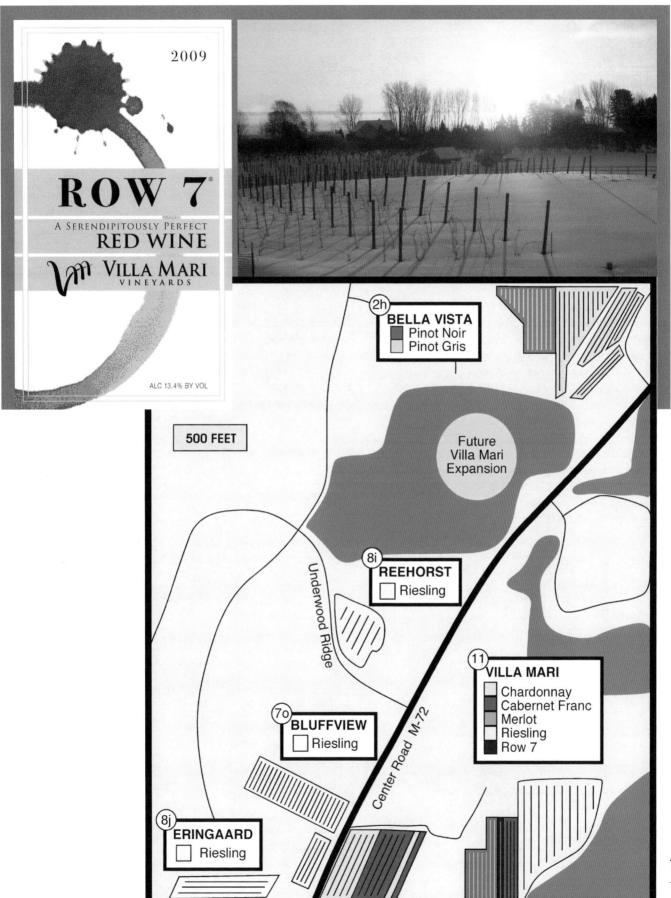

2009

ROW 7 ®

A SERENDIPITOUSLY PERFECT
RED WINE

Vᴍ VILLA MARI
VINEYARDS

ALC 13.4% BY VOL

2h
BELLA VISTA
◼ Pinot Noir
☐ Pinot Gris

500 FEET

Future
Villa Mari
Expansion

8i
REEHORST
☐ Riesling

Underwood Ridge

11
VILLA MARI
☐ Chardonnay
◼ Cabernet Franc
▨ Merlot
☐ Riesling
◼ Row 7

7o
BLUFFVIEW
☐ Riesling

Center Road M-72

8j
ERINGAARD
☐ Riesling

113

12. Oosterhouse Vineyards

Center Highway at Nelson Road
Traverse City, MI 49686.

They have vineyards, but no winery, and no tasting room. But they have wine. They are the Oosterhouse (Oh-stir-house, from Osterhaus) brothers, Todd and Carter

Todd and wife Caroline live on Old Mission Peninsula and tend the vineyards and the business activities, while Carter and wife Amy Smart live in Los Angeles. It is a 50:50 business partnership with the two brothers in daily contact.

Their future plans envision a tasting room next to the vineyards on Nelson Road, done in a style that will be unashamedly Michigan. After all, the brothers were long in the building trades before embarking on wines. Both graduates of Traverse City St. Francis, they have spent most of their lives out of Michigan, with Austin, Texas as a home for Todd and Los Angeles for Carter who is a TV celebrity and producer. Carter's various "fix-it" shows run the gamut from refurbishing bungalows to "Million Dollar Rooms." Carter's wife Amy's parents are locals, living in Omena.

Community service and public projects are a tradition in the Oosterhouse family. For instance, the oldest Santa Claus school in the world is in Midland, and was founded by Caroline's father. Locally, "Carter's Kids" has built children's playgrounds in Greilickville and Frankfort.

Their wine grapes from 40 acres, soon to be 50, are processed by the Two Lads Winery, where they are aging nicely while awaiting the grand opening of the Oosterhouse Tasting Room in 2014. As Todd put it to this author, "we will offer a wine experience like no other. Our wines will knock off some socks."

The Oosterhouse brothers have included the Devil's Dive vineyard in their portfolio.

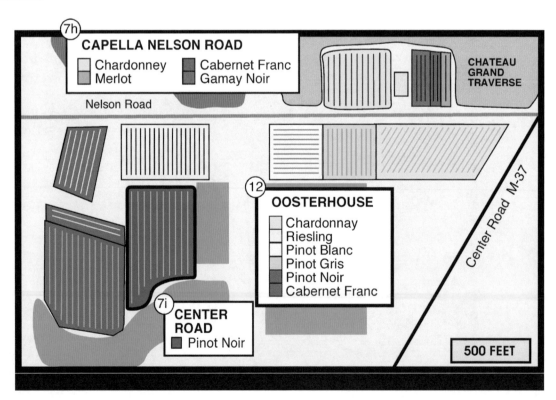

13. O'Brien Vineyards

No tasting room, and a small vineyard. So, arguably, Mr. O'Brien's wine shouldn't even be mentioned here. Except that one of the O'Brien vineyard's grapes has made it to market – O'Mission Riesling, beginning with the 2010 vintage. When Barry O'Brien married Laura Minervini in 1998, he asked her to "find a property with a west-facing slope and a barn". Laura found the property. Barry, then living in New York City, saw only photos, but trusted her. After moving onto the Old Mission property, six years were spent clearing the site and enriching the soil so that the vineyard could be planted. In 2006, they planted "ENTAV-certified" clones on 3309 rootstock. "ENTAV" is an acronym for a French organization (Etablissement National Technique pour l'Amelioration de la Viticulture) that guarantees that clones are virus-free.

Barry O'Brien is a wine importer as well as a wine grower-stylist who was inspired to plant the vineyard by years of work in the wine trade. The wines are marketed under the O'Mission label. He calls his postage stamp sized one-acre vineyard "a proof of concept project". Along with Lee Lutes, winemaker at Black Star Farms, he is an experimenter. Noting that local Riesling can be lean textured, he blends a small amount of Gewurztraminer into his Rieslings to raise the must (freshly pressed grapes, skins, seeds and stems) weight and lower the acidity in order to produce a better balanced white wine. A Riesling at only 19 brix blended with Gewurztraminer at 24 brix works fine.

Yields are strictly limited to produce wines with greater concentration and complexity. Barry has styled his O'Mission Riesling to be off-dry in order to be more appropriate with food. The winemaking team at Black Star Farms, where the O'Mission wines are made, have developed small-scale custom techniques and methods to achieve high levels of quality. O'Brien's self-professed mission has been to make no omissions in pursuit of quality wines. .

There are three wines being produced by O'Brien Vineyards, but only one is currently available at retail, O'Mission Riesling, at Burritts Fresh Market at 509 W. Front Street, Traverse City, Michigan.

O'Brien Vineyard

ALC. 12.3% BY VOLUME

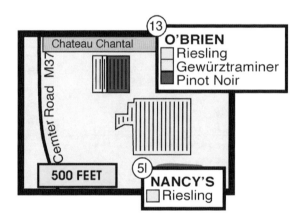

115

The Vineyards of Old Mission Peninsula

The vineyard listings and maps, and to whom the fruit is sold, are based on information provided the author by owners and winemakers following the 2012 harvest. It includes all vineyards known to be in commercial production along with those contracted for such future production.

The listing here and elsewhere in this book identifies each Old Mission Peninsula vineyard with the number/letter combination that is assigned to each providing cross-referencing to its location on the peninsula map with its tasting room.

    Bryan Ulbrich of Left Foot Charley divides the Old Mission Peninsula into three *terroirs*. This narrow peninsula with a central ridge, three miles wide at its widest, has three general microclimates, unlike the wider Leelanau Peninsula whose valleys and hill create multiple microclimates. The number of temperature degree days for growing declines from each *terroir* as one moves north.

1	Maple Grove / 93		5c	Lardie / 132
1a	Grey Hare / 93		5d	Hosmer / 121
1b	Kroupa / 120		5e	Love / 121
1c	Hawkeye / 123		5f	Ochs Orchards / 129
1d	Hogsback / 125		5g	Krupka / 124
1e	Manigold / 121		5h	Three Barns / 134
1f	Ligon / 120		5i	Rigan Estate / 126
2	Chateau Grand Traverse Estate / 95		5j	Urtel / 129
2a	Zafarano / 125		5k	Twin Bay Farms / 125
2b	Bailiwick / 124		5l	Nancy's / 115
2c	Steen / 124		6	2 Lads / 103
2d	Bella Donna / 126		6a	Fouch / 120
2e	Anam Cara Farm / 125		6b	3 Little Bears / 122
2f	Kniss / 124		6c	J Henry / 93
2g	Shangri-La, Too / 126		6d	Twin Bay Farms / 125
2h	Bella Vista / 113		6e	Pratt Farm / 123
2i	Renegade / 134		6f	Ligon / 120
2l	Drop A Wing Farm / 120		7e	Montana Ruso / 105
2m	Porchside / 130		7f	Leorie / 126
2n	Santucci (Carroll Road) / 126		7g	Montague Estate / 105
2o	Roek / 127		7h	Capella Nelson Road / 114
3	Brys Estate / 97		7i	Center Road / 114
4	Bowers Harbor / 99		7j	Capella Old Mission Road / 121
4a	Ten Hands / 122		7k	Haven Hill / 122
4b	Smokey Hollow / 124		7l	Brown / 105
4c	Nicholas / 120		7m	Lone Silo / 127
4d	Twyris (LP) / 84		7n	Twin Bay Farms / 125
5	Chateau Chantal / 101		7p	Buck / 105
5a	Johnson / 122		7q	Peninsula Hills / 134
5b	Pontes / 125		7r	Hagerty / 121
			7s	Pratt Farm / 123

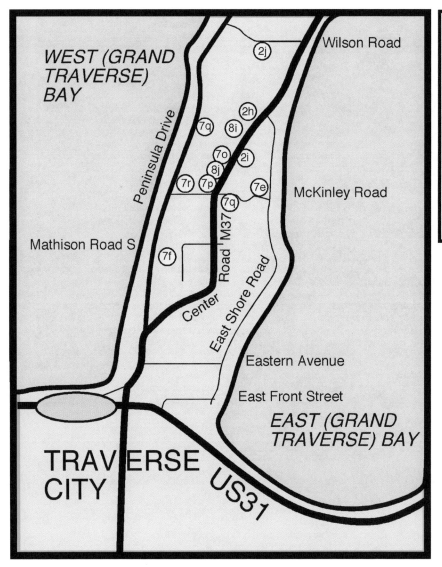

Old Mission Peninsula Southern Terroir Vineyards

2h Bella Vista
2i Villa Mari
2j Alba
7e Montana Ruso
7f Leorie
7l Brown
7o Bluffview
7p Buck
7q Smith
7r Hagerty
8i Reehorst
8j Eringaard

Vineyards are private farms and SHOULD NOT be entered without permission of the owner.

Not all roads on Old Mission Peninsula are shown, only those necessary to view the vineyards.

On the individual vineyard maps, the direction of the vine rows is shown. There is no indication of the number of rows.

North is always at the top of each map.

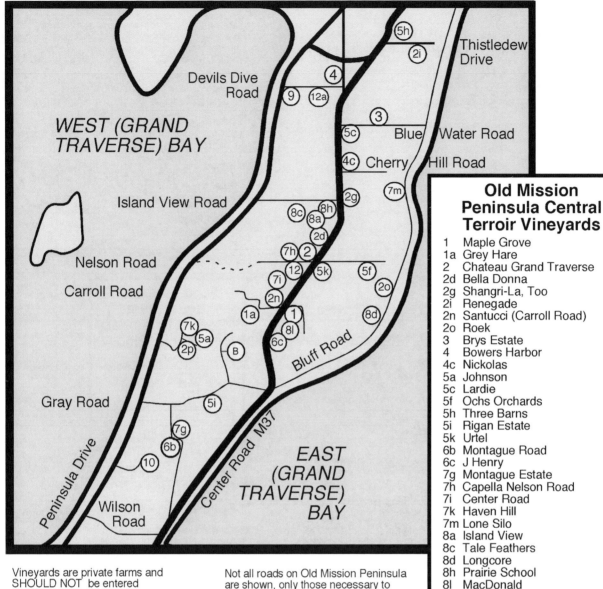

WEST (GRAND TRAVERSE) BAY

Devils Dive Road

Island View Road

Nelson Road

Carroll Road

Gray Road

Peninsula Drive

Wilson Road

Thistledew Drive

Blue Water Road

Cherry Hill Road

Bluff Road

Center Road M37

EAST (GRAND TRAVERSE) BAY

Old Mission Peninsula Central Terroir Vineyards

1	Maple Grove
1a	Grey Hare
2	Chateau Grand Traverse
2d	Bella Donna
2g	Shangri-La, Too
2i	Renegade
2n	Santucci (Carroll Road)
2o	Roek
3	Brys Estate
4	Bowers Harbor
4c	Nickolas
5a	Johnson
5c	Lardie
5f	Ochs Orchards
5h	Three Barns
5i	Rigan Estate
5k	Urtel
6b	Montague Road
6c	J Henry
7g	Montague Estate
7h	Capella Nelson Road
7i	Center Road
7k	Haven Hill
7m	Lone Silo
8a	Island View
8c	Tale Feathers
8d	Longcore
8h	Prairie School
8l	MacDonald
9	Bonafide at Mission Table
10	Hawthorne
12	Oosterhouse
12a	Devil's Drive
B	Crows Crest
D	Harmony Ridge

Vineyards are private farms and SHOULD NOT be entered without permission of the owner.

Not all roads on Old Mission Peninsula are shown, only those necessary to view the vineyards.

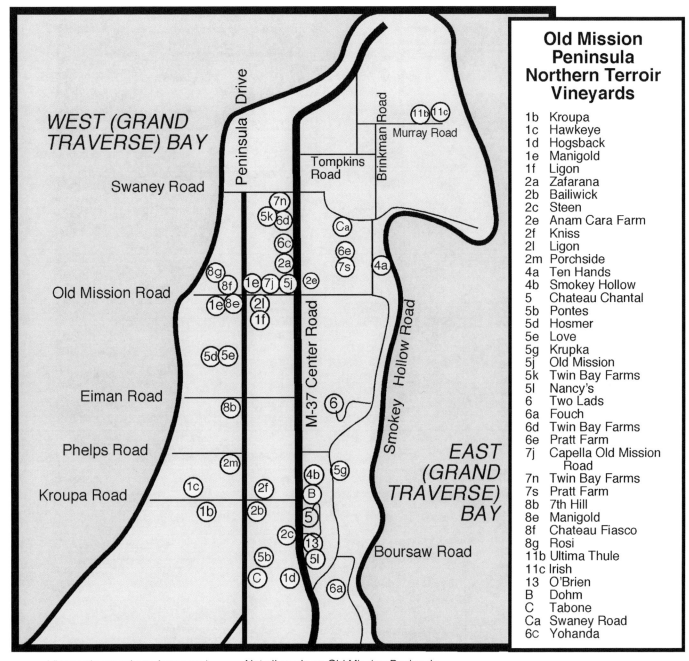

Old Mission Peninsula Northern Terroir Vineyards

WEST (GRAND TRAVERSE) BAY

Peninsula Drive

Swaney Road

Old Mission Road

Eiman Road

Phelps Road

Kroupa Road

M-37 Center Road

Brinkman Road

Murray Road

Tompkins Road

Smokey Hollow Road

Boursaw Road

EAST (GRAND TRAVERSE) BAY

1b	Kroupa
1c	Hawkeye
1d	Hogsback
1e	Manigold
1f	Ligon
2a	Zafarana
2b	Bailiwick
2c	Steen
2e	Anam Cara Farm
2f	Kniss
2l	Ligon
2m	Porchside
4a	Ten Hands
4b	Smokey Hollow
5	Chateau Chantal
5b	Pontes
5d	Hosmer
5e	Love
5g	Krupka
5j	Old Mission
5k	Twin Bay Farms
5l	Nancy's
6	Two Lads
6a	Fouch
6d	Twin Bay Farms
6e	Pratt Farm
7j	Capella Old Mission Road
7n	Twin Bay Farms
7s	Pratt Farm
8b	7th Hill
8e	Manigold
8f	Chateau Fiasco
8g	Rosi
11b	Ultima Thule
11c	Irish
13	O'Brien
B	Dohm
C	Tabone
Ca	Swaney Road
6c	Yohanda

Vineyards are private farms and SHOULD NOT be entered without permission of the owner.

Not all roads on Old Mission Peninsula are shown, only those necessary to view the vineyards.

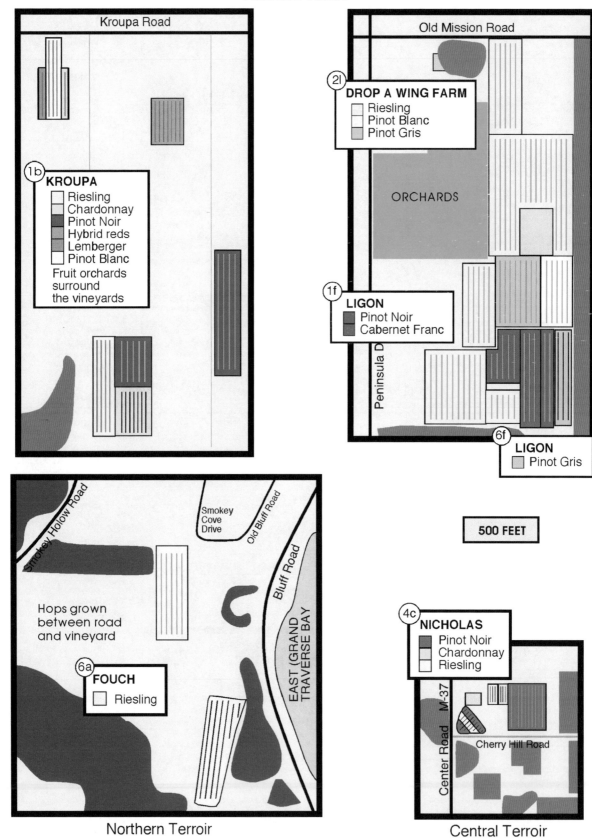

Kroupa Road

1b **KROUPA**
☐ Riesling
☐ Chardonnay
■ Pinot Noir
■ Hybrid reds
■ Lemberger
☐ Pinot Blanc
Fruit orchards
surround
the vineyards

Old Mission Road

2l **DROP A WING FARM**
☐ Riesling
☐ Pinot Blanc
☐ Pinot Gris

ORCHARDS

1f **LIGON**
■ Pinot Noir
■ Cabernet Franc

Peninsula D

6f **LIGON**
☐ Pinot Gris

Smokey Holow Road

Smokey Cove Drive

Old Bluff Road

Bluff Road

EAST (GRAND TRAVERSE BAY)

Hops grown
between road
and vineyard

6a **FOUCH**
☐ Riesling

500 FEET

4c **NICHOLAS**
■ Pinot Noir
☐ Chardonnay
☐ Riesling

Center Road M-37

Cherry Hill Road

Northern Terroir

Central Terroir

Southern Terroir

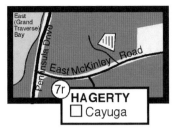

HAGERTY
☐ Cayuga

Central Terroir

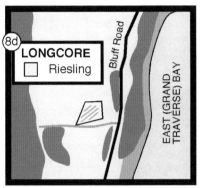

LONGCORE
☐ Riesling

Northern Terroir

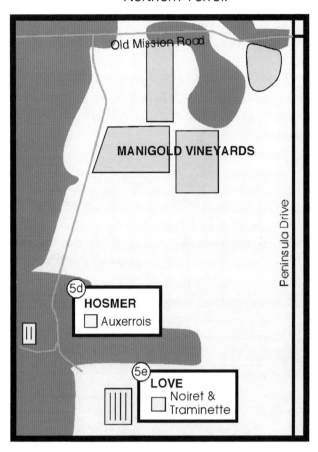

MANIGOLD VINEYARDS

HOSMER
☐ Auxerrois

LOVE
☐ Noiret &
Traminette

Northern
Terroir

500 FEET

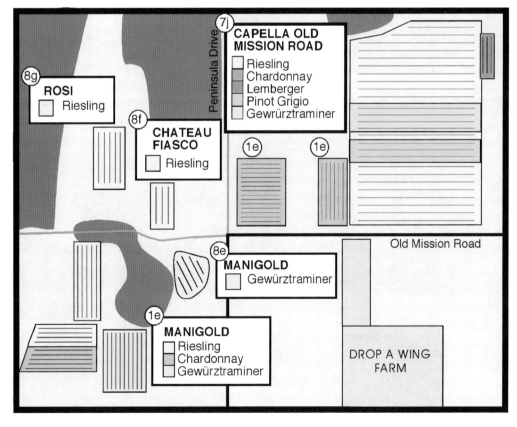

CAPELLA OLD
MISSION ROAD
☐ Riesling
▨ Chardonnay
▨ Lemberger
▨ Pinot Grigio
☐ Gewürztraminer

ROSI
☐ Riesling

CHATEAU
FIASCO
☐ Riesling

MANIGOLD
☐ Gewürztraminer

MANIGOLD
☐ Riesling
▨ Chardonnay
☐ Gewürztraminer

DROP A WING
FARM

Old Mission Road

121

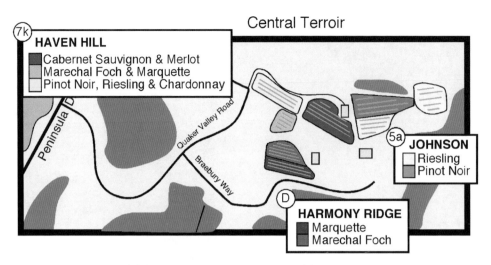

Central Terroir

(7k) **HAVEN HILL**
- Cabernet Sauvignon & Merlot
- Marechal Foch & Marquette
- Pinot Noir, Riesling & Chardonnay

Peninsula D

Quaker Valley Road

Braebury Way

(5a) **JOHNSON**
- Riesling
- Pinot Noir

(D) **HARMONY RIDGE**
- Marquette
- Marechal Foch

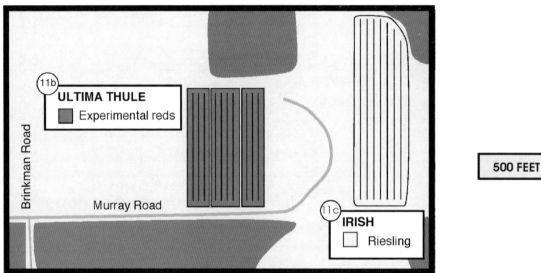

(11b) **ULTIMA THULE**
- Experimental reds

Brinkman Road

Murray Road

(11c) **IRISH**
- Riesling

500 FEET

Northern Terroir

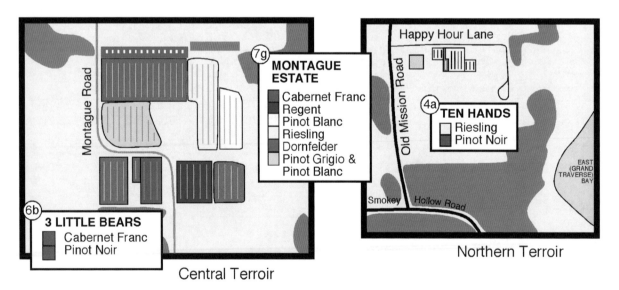

Montague Road

(7g) **MONTAGUE ESTATE**
- Cabernet Franc
- Regent
- Pinot Blanc
- Riesling
- Dornfelder
- Pinot Grigio & Pinot Blanc

(6b) **3 LITTLE BEARS**
- Cabernet Franc
- Pinot Noir

Happy Hour Lane

Old Mission Road

(4a) **TEN HANDS**
- Riesling
- Pinot Noir

EAST (GRAND TRAVERSE) BAY

Smokey Hollow Road

Central Terroir

Northern Terroir

Northern Terroir

Central Terroir

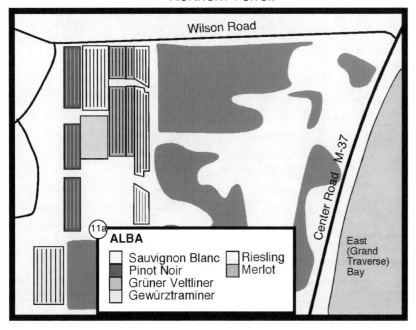

Wilson Road

⑪a ALBA

	Sauvignon Blanc		Riesling
	Pinot Noir		Merlot
	Grüner Veltliner		
	Gewürztraminer		

Center Road M-37

East (Grand Traverse) Bay

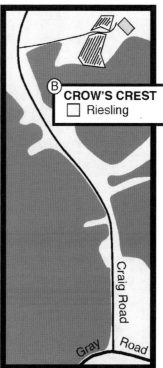

Ⓑ CROW'S CREST
☐ Riesling

Craig Road

Gray Road

500 FEET

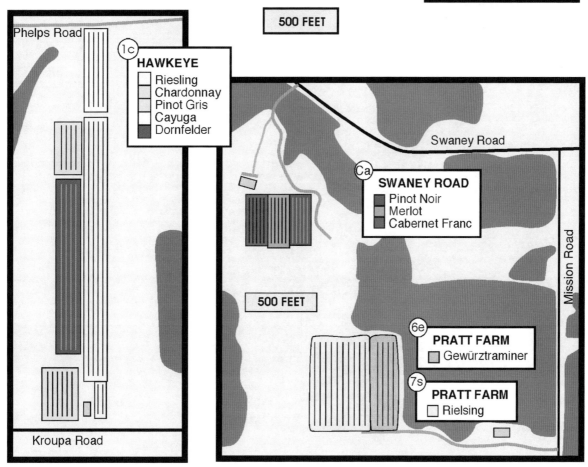

Phelps Road

①c HAWKEYE
☐ Riesling
☐ Chardonnay
☐ Pinot Gris
☐ Cayuga
☐ Dornfelder

Kroupa Road

Swaney Road

Ⓒa SWANEY ROAD
☐ Pinot Noir
☐ Merlot
☐ Cabernet Franc

500 FEET

Mission Road

⑥e PRATT FARM
☐ Gewürztraminer

⑦s PRATT FARM
☐ Rielsing

Northern Terroir

Northern
Terroir

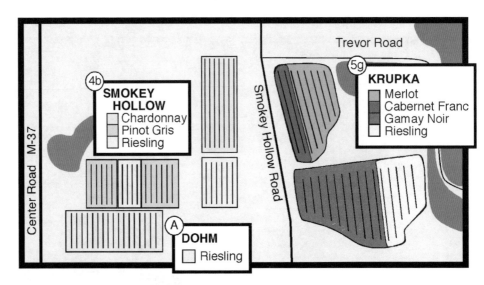

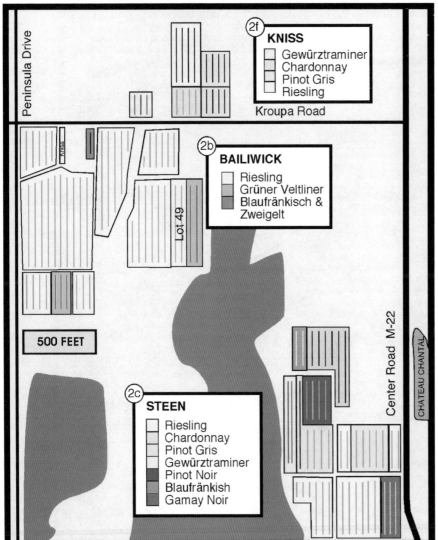

500 FEET

500 FEET

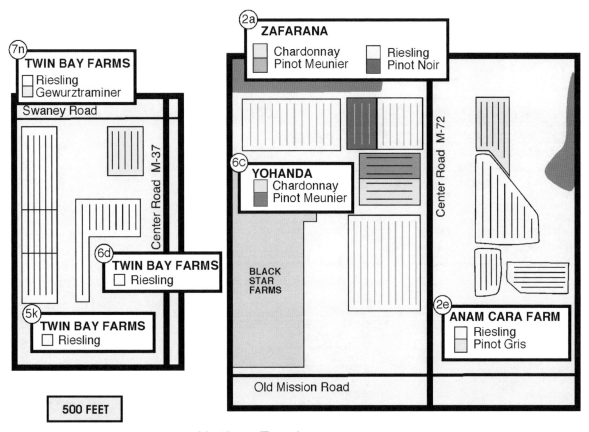

7n TWIN BAY FARMS
- ☐ Riesling
- ☐ Gewürztraminer

Swaney Road

Center Road M-37

2a ZAFARANA
- ☐ Chardonnay
- ☐ Pinot Meunier
- ☐ Riesling
- ■ Pinot Noir

6c YOHANDA
- ☐ Chardonnay
- ■ Pinot Meunier

BLACK STAR FARMS

6d TWIN BAY FARMS
- ☐ Riesling

5k TWIN BAY FARMS
- ☐ Riesling

Center Road M-72

2e ANAM CARA FARM
- ☐ Riesling
- ☐ Pinot Gris

Old Mission Road

500 FEET

Northern Terroir

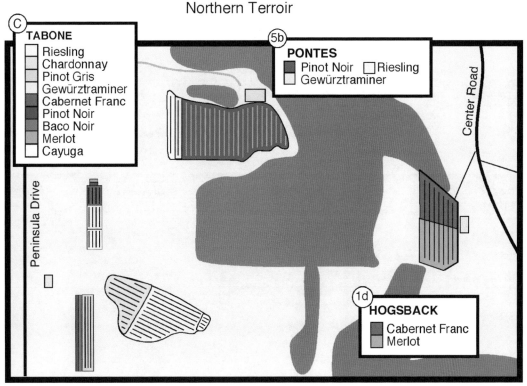

C TABONE
- ☐ Riesling
- ☐ Chardonnay
- ☐ Pinot Gris
- ☐ Gewürztraminer
- ■ Cabernet Franc
- ■ Pinot Noir
- ☐ Baco Noir
- ☐ Merlot
- ☐ Cayuga

5b PONTES
- ■ Pinot Noir
- ☐ Riesling
- ☐ Gewürztraminer

Center Road

Peninsula Drive

1d HOGSBACK
- ■ Cabernet Franc
- ☐ Merlot

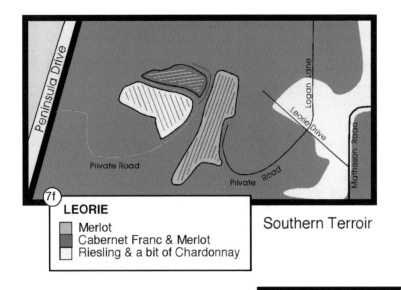

7f LEORIE
- Merlot
- Cabernet Franc & Merlot
- Riesling & a bit of Chardonnay

Peninsula Drive · Logan Lane · Leorie Drive · Matheson Road · Private Road · Private Road

Southern Terroir

500 FEET

2g SHANGRI-LA, TOO
- Pinot Blanc

8c TALE FEATHERS
- Pinot Gris

Island View Road

8h PRAIRIE SCHOOL
- Pinot Blanc

8a ISLAND VIEW
- Pinot Blanc

Experimental vines (personal use):
- Gewürztraminer
- Sauvignon Blanc
- Merlot

M-37 · Center Road

2d BELLA DONNA
- Pinot Gris
- Pinot Blanc

Central Terroir

Gray Road

Montague Road

5i RIGAN ESTATE
- Auxerrois

500 FEET

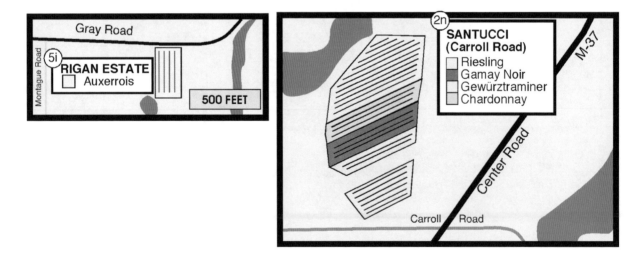

2n SANTUCCI (Carroll Road)
- Riesling
- Gamay Noir
- Gewürztraminer
- Chardonnay

M-37 · Center Road · Carroll Road

126

The Vines: It's Farming

And Now, Some Tales, Long, Short, Unvarnished, from Old Mission Peninsula Growers

Roek ..... Fifty years .....

Jo Roek was the developer of Mission Hills estates. Being Up North for fifty years, she has seen Old Mission Peninsula go from forest and cherry orchards to a land of vineyards and subdivisions. Her own impetus for a vineyard was to improve the value of properties in Mission Hills. She had other possibilities, but eventually settled on vineyards as the best way to raise property values. Her vineyard, which uses irrigation when needed, is 130 feet above West Grand Traverse Bay.

Lone Silo ..... Grüner Veltliner .....

Lawrence Tiefenbach of Lone Silo Vineyard pulled up the cherry orchard on his land some four years ago, then, two years ago, planted Riesling and Gruner Veltliner, the latter because it seemed it could be a valuable addition to the Black Star Farms listings. Ken at Burritts recently asked me if there were any plantings of the Austrian grape, because he thought it would grow well in our climate, and he'd put it on his shelves. Good choice, Lawrence!

Grey Hare ..... Blending, anyone?

The Ruzaks of Grey Hare Vineyard initially planted a few grapes to liven the landscape around their already charming Bed & Breakfast. The views from the two upstairs bedrooms could almost make you think you are in Tuscany – which is why the "hobby" that grew to 2.5 acres is continued. The vines planted are those used mostly for blending: Chancellor (once St Julien Winery's chief red grape), Marechal Foch and Leon Millot (a winter-hardy hybrid from the University of Minnesota Marquette Campus). There is one row of Baco Noir.

Harmony Ridge ..... Honeycrisp grapes .....

Kathryn Bandstra worked in human resources; when she was forced to lay off a large part of the staff, she decided it was time to retire. She and husband Steve lived on sand dunes in western Michigan, then moved north to a larger sand dune, Old Mission Peninsula. But first, they spent time in a Traverse City condo before deciding to build on Old Mission Peninsula. Steve took a long time to research what he might do for a "retirement job." Then, what to do with the front yard down the hill, where they looked over to West Grand Traverse Bay? Well, of course, plant grape vines. But which ones? More time and a decision to grow Marechal Foch next to Marquette, the latter because it could withstand the bitter cold on their cul de sac site. Marquette is to grapes what Honeycrisp is to apples.

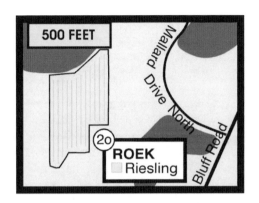

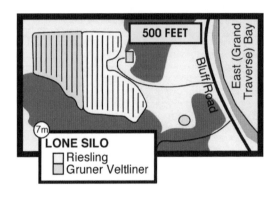

J Henry ..... Winning a dinner .....

Ted Schweitzer, a California native, and Brad Bickle, from Detroit, came to the old Mission Peninsula for a very good reason – it was because of a charity auction. While living in Newport Beach, California, they attended a charity auction at which a seven course dinner, to be prepared and served by acclaimed chef James Boyce of the famous Studio restaurant in the Montage Resort Hotel, was offered. It would be a dinner featuring food and wine pairings. Brad kept putting his paddle up and, eventually, they heard "Sold." They had a year to redeem their dinner and eleven months two weeks later they had not done so. So now they did.

The first course was served, and a sparkling wine accompanied it. The first taste of that wine was like a first kiss! Wonderful! But what was this wine? It was a sparkling wine from L. Mawby, up in northern Michigan.

The Montage has one of the world's great wine cellars, yet here they were serving a Michigan wine because it was as good as any and right for the first course.

So, when Brad, with Ted along, headed to Detroit to see family, they decided to head north and see what L. Mawby was all about.

Of course, those of us who live here, know what that would lead to! The two fell in love with Up North and bought a run-down log house with a Pinot Gris vineyard on the lot. With a local contractor, they brought the house up to their standards, and then planted a second vineyard; Merlot and Cabernet Franc. Now, with some time Up North, and planning to stay year-round, they have planted a third vineyard that is all Cabernet Franc.

Ted, an original owner of Original Windsurfer, is delighted to windsurf on the bays or on Lake Michigan. The wine the two produce (not yet marketed) is from their J Henry Vineyard, so named for Ted's grandfather who had moved from Iowa to Los Angeles.

Nancy's   My wife gets all the credit

Stan Jaroh and his wife Nancy's back yard lawn is a vineyard, looking east to the East Arm, Grand Traverse Bay. They also own orchards, which are cared for by Dean Johnson, a major fruit grower on Old Mission Peninsula. Agrivine helps in the vineyard but the family does everything they can before calling in "the reserves." On their deep slope, they planted three acres of vines, put up the posts, ran the wire six years before the 2012 harvest. Then they waited four years before the first useful harvest. 2011 followed; a great harvest, but the drought of 2012 affected their crop that they called "so-so." Chateau Chantal will blend it, but who gets her name on the label? A Nancy's Vineyard label will grace some bottles for friends.

Chateau Fiasco ..... My wife made me do it .....

Chateau Fiasco is the name of the Chown vineyard! Why did Glen Chown plant a vineyard? "My wife made me do it." Then, "I am good at taking orders".

With statements like that, how seriously can you take the owner of Chateau Fiasco? And he says those things with such a smile.

Glen Chown, executive director of the Grand Traverse Regional Land Conservancy, owns a half acre that produces one and a half tons of Riesling that go to Left Foot Charley as part of their Missing Spire label.

Profits from the sale of the Riesling grapes go into his kids' college fund, so you can expect to see the kids working the vines, mentored by Craig Cunningham. The harvest is a community affair, for with the Chowns, everything is all about family. And when the extended family gathers, there are kids age 8 to 15 in the vineyards! Growing grapes can be fun.

Drop a Wing Farm ..... Who is Scott Henry?

Leonard Ligon and wife Eddie run a large independent fruit farm and vineyards, Drop a Wing Farm. She, a talented artist, has painted the signs and the house and handles the dogs and horses. He handles the fruit.

He uses the Scott Henry spur training system developed in Oregon, while most everyone in the two peninsulas follows the Guyot cane training system. He gets six tons of fruit per acre of fully ripe fruit, while others get the Michigan average of 2.7 tons per acre, more if they go for quantity, less if they work for quality.

Leonard's philosophy stems from his love of growth: "I'm not enamored of standing on concrete and serving visitors at a tasting room," says he. "I like to see the plants grow."

Urtel Orchards ….. Horses produced no income …..

The Urtels came north with horses almost two decades ago. But horses produced no income, so, to get space for vines, they pulled out cherry trees and, then, three years ago, planted their vines. Expecting to wait three years to harvest a first crop, the microclimate/*terroir* proved so perfectly suited to their white wine grapes that they had their first harvest at two years.

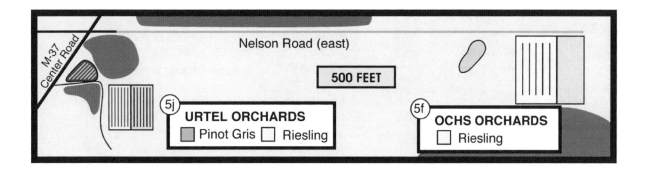

Love ….. Goats …..

Arriving at the Love vineyard way down the Shi-take Trail, you will be met by a Border Collie and goats. All are friendly.

Tale Feathers ….. Feathers …..

"I was the first to sign on with Bryan Ulbrich when he built his Left Foot Charley winery and tasting room in the Traverse City Commons, " said Mr Wilson. "We even named our dog, Charlie" chimed in Mrs. Wilson. Charley for male, Charlie for female.

Ours is a tale. Not Tail feathers, but a Tale, of our being tied-in with Left Foot Charley from the start. "We went to him and asked what he wanted us to grow." Tale Feathers Pinot Gris. Two acres of vines. If you think many of the NW MI wineries are boutique wineries, here is what qualifies as a Boutique Vineyard – like so many others on the Old Mission Peninsula. With this came viticultural practices that met Bryan Ulbrich's standards. Only certain kinds of fertilizer, spread only as needed, nothing overdone. So, too, with everything involving the vineyards. No hired help, just husband and wife in the fields, tending the vines. Pride. Pride in seeing their efforts creating grapes that can bear the family name on the Left Foot Charley label. "Name recognition, that's important," particularly if and when you decide to sell. The prospective buyer sees your property's name on a wine bottle, that helps make the property desirable.

Their Pinot Gris fruit was the first to be processed at Left Foot Charley's new facility. The income paid the taxes, making the Tale Feathers property self-sufficient.

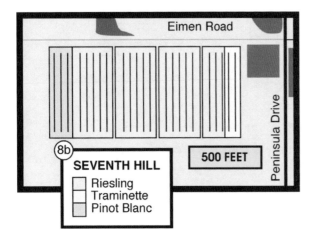

Seventh Hill..... Lucky Seven

So your wife is 7th of fourteen children, and you are 7th of seven. So began Seventh Hill Vineyards' Tom Scheuerman's tale on a cold winter's day. 777 Lucky Seven, it would appear. It all began with his Detroit neighbor's cherry wine; Tom still makes some. He also grows five varieties of garlic so that each ripens at a different time for a year-round supply.

Early a building trades union member, Tom's summer carpentering and brick-laying paid his way through the University of Windsor, Canada. In the summer before his senior year Tom went to his brother's farm in California and there fell in love with farming. In 1994, he and Linda planted a few acres of Riesling and four rows of Traminette on Old Mission Peninsula. Retired after 35 years as a school social worker but still active on social projects, Tom, with Linda, started the Coalition for Civil Rights of Disabled Persons when the State of Michigan was slow to enact the legislation that led to Special Education programs for the disabled. Tom was also a pioneer in founding Parallel 45 Michigan Vines & Wines, a support group for vineyard owners.

When raccoons foraged through the Seventh Hill Vineyards, Tom thought of erecting a "shockers wire" to keep them out. He got no further than the obligatory sign. Drew Perry, Oenologist at Left Foot Charley, on a visit to the vineyards, asked Tom, "what do you expect, the raccoons are going to read that sign and go away?!"

As I was leaving, the ground and drive were covered with snow, so I couldn't see how to get out to Peninsula Drive. Not to worry, was Tom's advice, "I don't grow grass, I grow grapes."

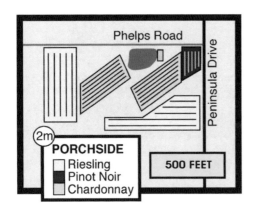

Porchside... Writing the peninsula's standard contract ...

Dave Lenau worked 37 years in the purchasing department at Ford in Dearborn. He and his wife visited Napa often, forming close ties with at least one winery where he thought, "if we were twenty years younger...". Then Up North caught their fancy and on July 11, 2000, they bought their retirement home. Wine grapes followed at the suggestion of Chateau Chantal, though they now sell their grapes to Chateau Grand Traverse. With his business experience, Dave wrote the contract for sale of his grapes and now finds that the contract has found its way around the peninsula to other wineries.

Shangri-La, Too ..... Came the deluge .....

Lou Santucci and Irene Van Harten grow raspberries and other crops besides grapes (which go to Chateau Grand Traverse). They had planted 1,000 Pinot Blanc vines on their west-facing hillside at Shangri-la, Too farm in 2009. It was one incredible day when came the deluge. A massive thunderstorm turned the hillside to mud. It kept raining, and the mud turned to slurry and down the hill came the vines to the flat part of their property. Lou had to dig with his bare hands to find the tiny vines, the root stock of his future vineyard. Gloved hands could not have felt the tiny vines. They lost 200 vines, but replanted the 800 survivors. Those who don't think trial and tribulations pursue even the best of people should take heed - Mother Nature favors no one.

Fouch ..... Hogsback .....

The Fouch family owns a wide swath of land from the hogsback to the East Grand Traverse Bay. The "hogsback" is a stretch of M-37 Center Road starting just north of the Klein's Hogsback Vineyard and runs to south of Chateau Chantal. It once was an up-and-down hilly road, but the dips have been filled in and now form a wall west of the Fouch home across the road from his hops. Dan and Nikki Lynn tend hops, two Riesling vineyards and cherry orchards on this land. The original vineyard was at Dan's parents' cherry orchard. One area was performing poorly, so the trees were torn out and Riesling planted. Along came Cornel (now of 2 Lads but then at Brys Estate); he bought the grapes and put the Fouch name on the label! Dan liked that so, when a second cherry orchard needed replanting, he talked with others. Bryan Ulbrich suggested Muscat, a grape he wanted, but 2 Lads came back with "more Riesling, please." And so it was.

The Fouch's are thinking of other means to diversify (which is why they got into hops) even as 2 Lads ask for more Riesling.

Eringaard ...... Landscaping with vines .....

Cornelius and Sue Eringaard adopted Chinese girl twins 13 years ago. Though their beachfront house near Charleston, SC, was fun for the girls, the family also traveled Up North to Charlevoix. At some point it made more sense to Sue that they live nearer their cottage and they ended up on Old Mission Peninsula. Came time to landscape.

Meanwhile Cornelius, with a Ph.D. in Economics and History, had met James Thomson of Mutual Farm Management, across the road and a winemaker for Black Star Farms. He'd also tasted a marvelous red wine whose grapes were grown under the canopy at MFM. But "Riesling," they said, "it's hardy and wanted by every winery". First, Jim (Thomson) had to remove 2.5 acres of cherry trees before Sue could see the 1.5 acres of vines that "cover the back part of the yard."

The vines grew very well and near the end of the second year there were good-sized clusters of grapes. A harvest in the second year? Then the Mexicans invaded and were picking the clusters and dropping them on the ground! What, removing good grapes? Cornelius learned that this was done to force the roots deeper into the soil and make for a full harvest the next year.

Came the third year. Now a harvest was assured. Then the birds came; flocks of them. They devoured the grapes. After removing the cherry trees, Thomson had done nothing to stop the birds from remaining in the area. The result was only 550 pounds of grapes. Later, Cornelius harvested the remnants and made ice wine! The next year was cold so, again a poor crop, and Sue was ready to plow under the entire vineyard. But one more year, 2011, and 3 tons were harvested, $6,600. They now sell their grapes to Left Foot Charley.

Noting that, to irrigate the vines in the first year, he had to drill a well, and that cost ten thousand dollars, Cornelius comments, "There's no profit, but it is fun." Later, when water and sewer service was extended to the subdivision, he didn't connect to the water. He can water his lawn from his well and not pay Traverse City.

Having their own wine made by Bryan Ulbrich made it all worth the effort.

Dohm ..... Want to buy a vineyard?

With a double gold winning Riesling? Dan and Linda Dohm have just what you want. Dan is about to retire, so the vineyard just north of Chateau Chantal is for sale.

The vineyard was planted by hand over three years in the late nineties. The first year Dan went out and found that they had a very small crop, as would be expected from a first year planting. The next day he came out to pick the grapes, and there were none! The birds had picked the clusters clean!

When they had their first harvest, they turned to local exchange students as well as some Mexicans. They had some 40 pickers who represented nations from Europe, Asia, everywhere else you could think of! Linda made Sloppy Joes for the kids.

Though they were warned they might be picking in wet and cold weather (as low as 30°, one boy turned up in flip flops! As Linda's father-in-law was living in the house on the vineyard property, they had to order a porta-potty to keep the kids from bothering him.

One good note for the perspective buyer; the south-facing vineyard has never had a freeze, even in the year of the great freeze.

Pontes ..... Brazil to Detroit ....

Edson Pontes is a doctor of urology and an investor in Chateau Chantal to which his grapes go at harvest time. At age 20, he left Brazil to study at Wayne State University in Detroit. On getting his degree, he worked in several positions in the northeast before retiring to Up North. It was James Thomson at Chateau Chantal who talked him into planting vines. A few vines at the top of the hill were added to, and added to ......

131

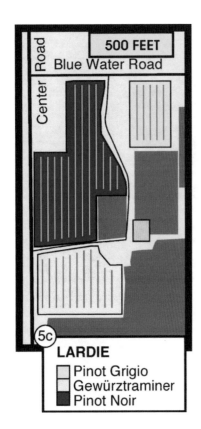

500 FEET
Blue Water Road

Center Road

5c

LARDIE
☐ Pinot Grigio
☐ Gewürztraminer
■ Pinot Noir

Lardie ….. Happy hoe-ers …..

Ken Lardie and his brother Chuck oversee environmentally certified vineyards. I met them over lunch and it wasn't long before they were off to hedge and thin their vineyards on a sunny Saturday in July. While others seemed to think that the 2012 harvest might be the best ever, Ken was not certain it would be as good as 2010.

Ken had wanted a master's degree, but found the only programs in his field were Ph.D.s, at MSU and U of M. The MSU required Greek and Latin, and he dutifully enrolled. Then lack of funding caused the program to be suspended. So he went to U of M, found their Ph.D. program required five languages. So now he is a middle-school teacher in Traverse City, and happy with the choice.

The Lardie brothers date way back on Old Mission. They helped Bob Begin plant Chateau Chantal's first vines. Together they call themselves "two happy hoe-ers." They own 100 acres, 50 of which are in vines.

MacDonald ….. Vines at -15° …..

Bill MacDonald was a real estate appraiser for a bank. Then Bank of America bought the bank and it wasn't many months before Bill was without a job. So, why not try another career?

Back in 1998 or thereabouts, Bill's sister and boyfriend were in Sebastopol, Sonoma County, California. Once a thriving fruit-growing county, its fruit had shifted to grapes, wine grapes, and Bill got roped into crushing grapes at the harvest.

Given that his son was at Northwestern Michigan College in Traverse City, Bill discovered "Up North" and in 2003 bought an existing vineyard. That year the temperature plummeted to -15° and very few vines survived. But the 2004 Pinot Gris won a gold, and the future for his 1,000 plants looked promising. Since then a double gold has been won, and his Lemberger vines thrive.

The next step surprised Bill. Looking for a job, he met Paolo Sabatini, who was looking for someone to make wines from the MSU experimental vineyards. Rather than an interview, Bill was confronted with, "how soon can you start?"

Now, only an infinitesimal number of readers will know of Spartan Cellars. They have no license to sell wines, so what they produce is shared with winemakers at the open house of the Northwest Michigan Horticultural Center of Michigan State University Extension. With MSU professors, too - perhaps one reason to be a professor of MSU rather than U of M!

MacDonald

2008

Lemberger

Estate Grown

Old Mission Peninsula

Tabone ….. Opera …..

Mario Tabone and Tony Ciccone love opera, and in 2011 sponsored an opera festival in Traverse City. The "second annual" will be in 2013, not 2012, as Tabone works to turn his property and a vineyard off Swaney Road just west of Old Mission into major vineyards. Mario bought the vineyard and fruit farm a decade ago. A planned tasting room is still years away: sons Mario A. and Michael will run it. They will do the vinting and the selling. Trevor Gustafson, "little brother" of Joan Ciccone, tends the Tabone vines with farmer Mario.

Mario Tabone, all Italian yet descended from Maltese royalty, so nominally a British subject but wholly American, was a professor of philosophy at the University of Detroit before moving Up North Michigan. His cheerful wife, Mary Ann, a true, light blue-eyed blonde of German extraction broke him free of Dago red and now he drinks Riesling along with his reds. His father gave him his first wine glass when he was four and milk was not allowed in the house thereafter. His mother mixed 7-Up with the wine to make it go further!

Soul Friend ……Anam Cara

Is the name of their vineyards, Gaelic for "soul friend," meaning a place or a person where your soul feels at home? According to John O'Donahue, an accomplished Irish poet, philosopher and Catholic priest, "…You are joined in an ancient and eternal union with humanity that cuts across all barriers of time, convention, philosophy and definition. When you are blessed with an anam cara, the Irish believe, you have arrived at that most sacred place: home."

Shelley Keith, from Iowa, and Tim Quinn, from Southern Michigan, bought a cherry and apple farm in November of 1999 from Dave Murray, who had owned much peninsula land, including what has since become Peninsula Park. Dave had sold the property rights to the Property Development Corporation, which was Peninsula Township's version of a land conservancy. So they could put a house on the property, but not much else. The farm was in disrepair. 3 gallons of cherries and 3 gallons of vodka made a good winter's drink, and was the best way to use cherries. They had already found that they couldn't give their apples away, so they decided to switch to wine grapes. They both worked "more than fulltime," but tried to work the vines. Until they found how much time it took! 3.5 acres of Riesling were planted in 2003, harvested in 2005. They planted Riesling on the advice of Sean O'Keefe, who then bought their grapes. In 2006 they added more Riesling, then Pinot Gris in 2010, again, on Sean's advice. "It pays the taxes."

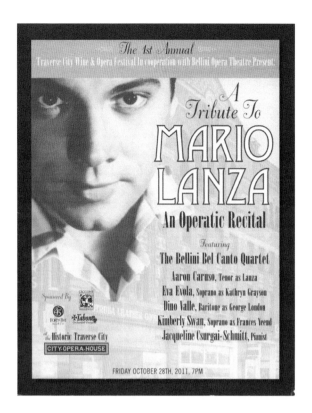

Of course, some of what goes to Chateau Grand Traverse comes back, and Shelley uses her own photographs to make labels. One features Champion, born on the Tuesday after their son competed as member of a MI state champion lacrosse team.

Champion
Anam Cara Farm Riesling 2010

Chill Out

Anam Cara Farm Riesling 2011

133

Lou Smith......My grapes for a castello?

Lou, who grows what is considered a world-class Merlot vineyard, has the "ruins" of a castello on his farm. We would like to call it that, but it is a really a barn. An 18th century barn. A barn that would house equipment needed to service a vineyard. Lou had visited Castello Banfi in Montalcino and met John Mariani, the American owner of this world-famous Tuscan winery. John tasted a bottle of Smith's red and pronounced it "well-balanced ... elegant ... delicious. You've entered world class." Lou came back to the States with a desire to have a place on his west-facing hill reminiscent of his Italian journey, so built the foundations of the barn.

His crop goes to Black Star Farms where it is blended with their offerings and payment to Lou comes back as bottled wine. The label for Lou's 2010 Merlot shows a view from the ruin enclosure down through the vines to West Bay.

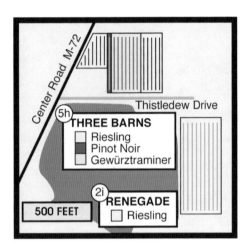

Renegade ..... Have you seen Dad today?

Heather Johnson Reamer remembers the day when her Dad took her to Chateau Grand Traverse and they were escorted into the back rooms. The crush was on and they were given glasses full of 24-hour-old juice. It looked like white mud. "It hit my stomach like a rock," she admitted.

Then, Heather told the story of their Renegade Vineyard: The vines were running down the hillside into the valley! Actually they weren't much as vines yet, having been only recently planted, and there came a downpour. "We were in our mud boots, digging the uprooted vines out of the mud," explained Heather. Grandma chimed in, "Some were under three feet of mud!" So the individual plants were renegades! And so - the name of the vineyard.

Her father, Dean Johnson, had first planted cherry trees. Being cautioned by his father, "Diversification will keep you in business," Dean and his family went on to plant vines. The whole family found that they enjoyed being IN the vines. "It is so calm, so peaceful," continued Heather.

"Have you seen Dad today?" "He's in the vineyard." "Shouldn't we call him up for lunch." "Nope, he just wants to be left alone."

Peace and quiet in the vines. You may not want to believe it, but they talk to you!

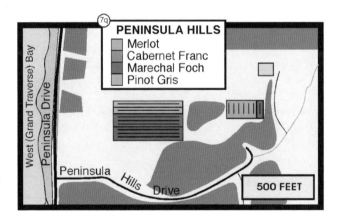

The Businesses of Wine

Wine is a business, the business of selling a product called wine.

Little did I know when I sat down with Don Coe, half-owner and managing partner of Black Star Farms, how much I would learn about the "business" of wine. "One third of wine making is retail," was a starting point. So it begins at the tasting room. It is about "stomachs at the bar."

You build your brand "by generous sampling." Tasting rooms are entertainment venues. You give the visitor an "experience." That, of course, is what "Disney" is all about.

"The world doesn't need another winery." It certainly doesn't need another Michigan winery. There are 7,000 wineries in the United States, only 5,000 fifteen years ago when Don, who has 30 years experience in wine and spirits, "retired" and formed Black Star Farms with Kermit Campbell. Of those 7,000, 10 produce 50% of all the wine and 100 produce 90%. That leaves only 10% of America's wine production to 6,900 wineries.

There are 300,000 wine labels approved by the federal government.

There are three kinds of wineries: Commercial, Aspirational, and Vanity. Don sees these "titles" as self-explanatory.

For commercial wineries, there are basically three business models:

1. "Sell it cheap, stack it high." Namely, produce boodles of wine and fill the grocery stores with it.

2. Quality-price-value. Produce mid-quality wine at a value point. For Black Star Farms, these are wines under $18.

3. World-class. Produce the highest quality wine which, of course, will command a premium price.

Don noted that it is possible to do business at all three levels.

Don also noted that those starting a winery should have long term investment in their program, for they might not turn a profit for eight years, and then have to turn the profit back into the business for the next five. Hopefully, you have children who will inherit what you have created.

The first person you hire should be a top-notch winemaker. Don't just hire him, invest in him (or her, of course). Give him equity in the winery. If you don't, and he becomes known in the business, he will, like star chefs who leave a restaurant to start their own, abandon you and you will have to search for a replacement who is unlikely to be the star you have just lost.

So how do you build consumer loyalty? Charge for the glass with your logo on it! How good is anything that is free? It must be good if you charge for it! Your first taste is free. For $5 you buy a Black Star Farms glass and with it five additional samples. Then you take take the glass with you. Whenever you come back to the winery with your glass (next summer? sooner?), the tastings are free. Guess which winery you will come to first on your return visit. By doing this you create ambassadors for your product. And when your tasting room servers see these ambassadors enter with their glasses, they can call out, "welcome back. Which wine did you like most?" and thus begins a conversation on what they might now like to try.

Now, who do you court in the tasting room? A couple in fancy dress exit a BMW and head to your tasting room. Then a dirt-encrusted pick-up truck arrives with a couple in overalls. You welcome both, of course, but you court the couple in overalls. The BMW couple are probably already sophisticated wine drinkers. Those in overalls may know little, might be coming into a tasting room for the first time and are a bit nervous at what they will find. So you immediately speak to them and engage them in conversation, get them to relax. They are there to learn, and you help them do so.

Don came back to "Why Traverse City." The area has everything needed to attract tourists, so "this was the place to put wineries." When Black Star Farms opened, the average age of a core wine consumer was 57, was college educated and had a $100,000 income. They were only 8 to 10% of the population. They were interested in the three arts - visual, performing, culinary — and the environment. The Traverse City region had all these. Farming began here in the 1860s, and as you drive around the two peninsulas, you will note how many are "Environmentally Certified." All seven wineries of WOMP are environmentally certified.

A great change has taken place since Black Star Farms opened. The average age of the core wine consumer is now in the twenties, for wine has become "hip."

> "If you want to make a small profit in wine, start with a large profit."
> — an ancient wine proverb

The area has a huge tourist industry, much of which is based on "wine and dine." Traverse City is recognized as "a foodie town."

One can cite many local restaurants for their use of local produce and local wines. To name a few of the most prominent: Trattoria Stella, Grand Traverse Pie Company, Amical, The Cooks' House, Boathouse in Bowers Harbor and Mission Table's Jolly Pumpkin Restaurant at the former Bowers Harbor Inn. And, outside of Traverse City, Bluebird in Leland, Blu and Art's Tavern in Glen Arbor, Martha's Leelanau Table in Suttons Bay, Pearl's, and Siren Hall in Elk Rapids.

135

There is an active artistic community with galleries in every Up North Michigan town and the Dennos Museum in Traverse City as an anchor. There is Interlochen with 700 performances every year, with half of these being full public concerts. Local bands play in bars, restaurants and, so it seems, everywhere. There is the Great Lakes Culinary Institute that is developing the next generation of chefs and cooks, many of whom will find a job out of school in the five-county Grand Traverse Region. Now we have "Farm to Table" and "Taste the Local Difference."

My time was up; the parking meter had to be fed. But now I, and perhaps you, the reader, have some idea of what it takes to run a successful (winery) business.

Wine Competitions and Awards

I am looking at an announcement being sent to those in the winemaking business in the mid-west and eastern United States. It is from IEWC, the International Eastern Wine Competition, with a special Riesling championship. No one from the west allowed. It is but one of countless wine competitions, local, regional, national, international (and who knows, planetary . . .)

At every tasting room one visits one sees a string, maybe a whole wall, of awards. This one reason is why they are not listed in this book; there are just too many awards being won by Up North Michigan wine and to list them all, and be fair to the winners, might double the size of this book!!!

Not that it is easy to win an award, but those submitting their wines to competitions or "tasting events" know what they are competing against, and they are not likely to submit a wine they know stands no chance. Why submit a Michigan red wine in a California competition unless you know you had a unique year where your red ripened not just well, but to perfection? Michigan Rieslings and Gewürztraminer compete anywhere, so that is what you submit.

A Vineyard Tour

Paul Hamelin's presentation to visitors on his Verterra vineyard tour covers the length and breadth of the business. So I'll let him do the explaining of the process, starting with a bit of history.

Paul had been thinking about a vineyard for 30 years. In 2005, he and his wife moved to the U.K. to run a pharmaceutical company and while there they hatched a business plan. In May 2007 they planted 27 thousand plants in 10 days on 18 acres. The Matheson vineyards are 3 football fields in length and are now 85% of their production in a former cherry orchard.

In the vineyard, Paul discussed canopy management, which is called pruning/hedging/suckering. A 15-person team does the work in the three Verterra vineyards. His trellising system is called Vertical Shoot Positioning or VSP, which he considers the gold standard, as this has been tested by the best vineyard universities in the world. There are two to three prunings during a typical season.

Mature vine roots go down to 15 feet, and the vines will produce high quality fruit for 50 to 75 years. There is a need to periodically irrigate in Michigan's sandy loamy soils for the first two years when the vines are still quite small and then only in severe drought years.

Pinot, a French word, means "pine cone like," which is the shape of the Pinot Noir, Pinot Gris and Pinot Blanc clusters.

"Veraison" is where the grapes change color from green to their mature colors yellow, bronze, blue, purple . . .

Harvest is usually between September 29 and November 4. Crews work from April 1 through to November 4.

White wine grapevines are planted 4' apart, red 3', both with rows 9 feet apart and, in this vineyard, are oriented North to South allowing for maximum sun exposure through the growing season.

The Matheson vineyard of Verterra

The big three problems are weeds, bugs, and mildew. Paul asserts that it is essentially impossible to grow wine grapes organically in the climates of Northern Michigan due to these three pests/problems.

September and October drought is good for the grapes, as it leads to very small berries, thus, concentrated, aromatic juice.

Just before the grapes ripen or undergo veraison, loud speakers emanating noise are put out to scare birds away as they love to eat grapes. Bluebirds are welcome, as they eat insects, but when the grapes are ripe the birds are preferred to travel in other areas.

Fungicides to reduce the mildew are used right after flowering when grapes set, then when the clusters are ripe and near harvest.

Pinot Noir is grown in windy areas to allow the air to dry the skin surfaces on the grapes helping to reduce mildew. In 2010 Verterrra only produced Pinot Noir but in 2011 they added a Pinot Noir Rosé.

A local, preeminent French restaurant chef and owner had told him they had no American rosé on their wine list: "Nobody makes a decent rosé here in the U.S." After tasting Verterra's initial Rose', the chef/owner said "Finally, a decent rosé" and promptly added it to his two restaurants' wine list.

In a trend that is very common in Napa Valley, several wineries use a common facility to make their wines but generally each winery owns their own tanks and barrels which is what Verterra does to ensure unique wines from their own fruit and wine style.

High acid wines are best for aging (Bryan Ulbrich prefers high acid). "Reserve" usually means "aged in oak."

And so it goes . . .

The Vineyard Season

When a vineyard is planted, that is just the first step before a harvest, at least three years later, is achieved. If it involves removing cherry trees, that means an additional three years, as cherry trees exhaust the earth and the soil has to be prepared and enriched for vines. One way to look at the season is to look at what one independent vineyard servicer does:

Fourth generation farmer Jerry Stanek started with apples and cherries, then vineyards. Then he sold out and moved into servicing the vineyards of others. He soon found himself working on both peninsulas, for Black Star Farms, Forty-Five North, True North and Chateau de Leelanau, a total of 150 acres of vineyards.

Servicing vineyards involves:
Preparing the site
    Planting the vines
       Trellising
          Spraying, often
            Hedging
              Pruning
        Snipping individual leaves
       Culling clusters
     Mowing weeds
   Plowing in the cover crop
And so on and so on . . . . . and on.
Through to the harvest.

Covering multiple vineyards means careful scheduling so you don't fall behind on any one of "your" vineyards.

There are several such service organizations. In addition to Jerry Stanek of J J Farm Services, this author also conferred with Agrivine (Ben and Jen Bramer), Big Paw Vineyard Management (Doug Matthies), Cunningham Viticultural Services (Craig Cunningham), Hamilton Agronomy (Kevin Herman), Wilbur-Ellis Company (Tiffany Steimel) and Mutual Farm Management (Jay Budd).

Several vineyard owners also service vineyards for other owners. Wineries often service the independent vineyards from which they obtain grapes.

The vineyards must be maintained throughout the season. For instance, when the vines grow above their top trellising wire, they must be cut. This is called hedging. To prevent powdery mildew, a major grapevine nemesis (one of several), spraying is needed according to the weather. Leaves must be cut away if they are casting a shadow on the grape clusters.

A young vineyard, perhaps at seven weeks

Those who have visited Black Star Farms' Leelanau tasting room have seen the placards outside the entry. They tell the tale of wine making succinctly, Black Star Farms has graciously provided these for publication here.

MICHIGAN'S CONTINENTAL MARITIME CLIMATE

 Michigan's two peninsulas are surrounded by four of the five Great Lakes, retaining heat under moderating cloud cover to prevent early freezes and extend the growing season.

 Michigan's diverse natural landscape was forged by the Ice Age with alternating glacial ridges (moraines) and till plains providing both ample groundwater and well drained hillsides for fruit production.

 Michigan is in the transition zone between fertile broadleaf deciduous forests of the eastern U.S. and the sandy, clay and loamy needle-leaf evergreen forests of Canada, providing the soil structure necessary for cold climate grape varieties.

Michigan is at the convergence of westerly wind belts from the moist tropical air flows off the Gulf of Mexico, mild dry winds from the western prairies and bitterly cold Arctic currents. This produces both beneficial rain and snowfall.

1

LEELANAU PENINSULA & OLD MISSION PENINSULA VITICULTURAL AREAS

We are located on the 45th Parallel that cuts through some of the greatest wine producing areas of the world such as Bordeaux in France, northern Italy and Oregon.

Our two local peninsulas are both recognized as distinctive American viticultural areas. They are cool climate appellations ideally suited for the growing of classic grape varieties such as Chardonnay, Pinot Gris, Riesling, Pinot Noir and Cabernet Franc.

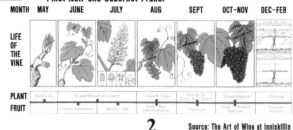

Source: The Art of Wine at Inniskillin

2

VINEYARDS

 Black Star Farms sources 95% of its grapes from its own grower partners on Leelanau and Old Mission Peninsulas. We utilize only Michigan fruit in all of our wines.

Our 5 acres of estate vineyards are planted on the terrace at our entrance. The terrace provides excellent airflow to prevent frozen air pockets and southeasterly and southwesterly slopes to capture maximum sun. Varieties planted include Pinot Noir, Cabernet Franc, Pinot Gris and Pinot Blanc.

3

GRAPE VARIETIES

 CHARDONNAY: (shar-doe-nay) the "king" of Burgundy, producing some of the best-known dry white wines of the world. Widely planted in clay/limestone soil and cool climates. We produce both a "sur lie" style aged entirely in stainless steel, and a barrel-aged style benefiting from 10-14 months in French oak barrels.

RIESLING: (reese-ling) Riesling is to Germany as Chardonnay is to France. Like Chardonnay, one of the "noble" cool climate varieties. By nature high in acid which counters varying amounts of residual sugar and allows the wine to age gracefully. We produce dry and late harvest styles.

 CABERNET FRANC (cab-air-nay fronk) The major constituent of the red wines of the Loire Valley and the great wines of St. Emillion. A late ripening grape that requires a fairly long growing season and clay soils. Our Cabernet Franc ages from 10-16 months in Oak barrels.

PINOT NOIR: (pee-no nwahr) A primary Burgundy and Champagne grape. A very traditional but temperamental grape, producing wines best in well-drained calcareous soils where late season nights are quite cool. Aged from 10-16 months in French Oak barrels.

4

HARVESTING

 A common sight during the harvest is the winemaker and grower checking sugar content with a refractometer. They are checking the degrees Brix to determine disolved solids (sugars) in the juice to define sweetness and potential alcohol production.

MEASUREMENT OF SUGAR CONTENT – GENERAL RULE: DIVIDE BY 2

Brix	20.4	21.5	22.5	40.5
% Potential Alcohol	10.6	11.3	11.9	8.0
		table wines		ice wines

 Picking occurs in each vineyard at the precise time that the grower and winemaker determine will be best for those grapes and the wines to be produced.

A time line is established at time of harvest. This is the point where the clock starts ticking.

 When grapes are harvested and delivered to the winery, they are weighed and inspected again for maturity, sugar content, acid and pH so that the winemaker can determine the first steps in the winemaking process.

The objective is to get fresh grapes delivered within 2 hours. This requires coordination between multiple growers and picking teams.

5

DESTEMMING/CRUSHING

The winemaking process now begins with some sense of urgency. Prolonged contact of the juices with the stems can impart bitterness to the resulting wine. The first step separates the stems from the berries. The stems are collected and added back to the vineyard as organic mulch.

 Grapes are now stacking up near the crush pad as the forklift operator unloads delivery trucks, sorts bins and dumps grapes into the receiving hopper in a choreographed flow.

 For red wine from red grapes or white wine from white grapes, the grapes are gently crushed to insure that seeds containing bitter tannins are not cracked. The resulting "must" is then pumped directly to the press.

If processing white wines from red grapes, the grapes are passed directly to the press without crushing. This is known as "whole cluster" pressing.

6

PRESSING

The "must" flows directly into the press where pure juice is separated from skin, pulp and seeds. We use a Horizontal Pneumatic press; essentially a bladder that rotates and inflates to press the grapes gently against the inside perforated wall of the cage. The pressed, de-juiced "pomace" can be used for distillation of grape brandy or spread back in the vineyards as organic mulch.

It will be a long day, but the pressing crew will stay until the last of the day's harvest is safely pressed and in fermentation tanks.

The freshly pressed white juices are collected as "free run wine" in a receiving bin under the press and pumped to fermenting tanks.
The red wine must from red grapes is pumped to a fermenting tank first for fermentation and color extraction before moving to the press to separate skin, pulp and seeds.

7

FERMENTATION

WHITE WINES

The juice from the press is cooled to 45° – 50° F and settles for 48 hours to allow sediment to drop to the tank floor. The clear juice is then "racked off" the sediment to another tank and is inoculated with a yeast culture for primary wine fermentation. Following inoculation, white juice may ferment in stainless steel tank or in oak barrels depending on the style desired. After primary fermentation, the wine is racked again into a stainless steel tank or oak barrels for further aging.

8

FERMENTATION

RED WINES

The red wine must in the fermentation tank is inoculated with a yeast culture and fermented at 70° – 85° F. Wine color is the result of extraction of color compounds from the skin. Carbon dioxide gas causes the solid portion of the must to rise forming a cap. Color extraction occurs only between the cap and the juice, so the juice is either pumped from under the cap over the top of the cap, or the floating cap is pushed under the juice, "punching," to insure maximum color extraction, tannins and flavor. After primary fermentation, the must is pressed and sent to oak barrels or tanks for malo-lactic fermentation.

9

AGING

Fermented wines may age in stainless steel tanks and in the process will be subjected to "fining" to remove small, suspended particles to clarify the wine. This also stabilizes the wine by removing yeast cells and proteins that can cause cloudiness, spoilage or precipitation later on. The final step is pumping the wine through a filter under pressure to remove any remaining suspended particles. Barrel-aged wines do not necessarily require fining or filtration.

The cost is high at $400-$1000 per 59 gallon barrel, but oak barrels add much of the character and complexity to the finest wines. The changes that occur in barrel aging include extraction of tannins, vanilla, oak lactones and phenolics from the wood. Oxidation also occurs as tannins, acids and other components of the wine react with gradual exposure to oxygen through the grain of the wood.

Our barrel cellar is under ground in a natural hillside that maintains a constant temperature of 50-60°F year around. White wines and red wines are both aged in bottles, and each may be aged in oak barrels for 10-16 months, depending on the vintage and style of wine desired.

10

BOTTLING

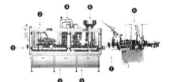

THE FINAL STEP BEFORE THE MARKET

1. Empty Glass: Separate boxed bottles, chosen for the wine to be bottled, arrive to an unloading belt.
2. Bottle Rinser: Bottles are rinsed with filtered water to insure sanitation.
3. Bottle Vacuum: All oxygen is removed and replaced with inert nitrogen before filling to guarantee the wine has no contact with oxygen.
4. Bottle Filler: The fill level is electronically monitored to insure a standard fill.
5. Nitrogen Injector: The head space in each bottle is injected with inert nitrogen to remove any oxygen which might oxidize the wine.
6. Corker: The cork is compressed before entering the bottle and then expands for a tight seal.
7. Capsule Dispenser: Capsules are dropped onto the bottle and shrink sealed.
8. Labeler: The labeler applies front, back and shoulder labels as required.

11

Here is Craig Cunningham with his tractor and two assistants rolling out netting on the side of the vines. This is a fast method that is being adopted widely. It is called side bind netting. The traditional method is throwing the netting over the top of the vines. A third, promising, method is permanent netting, in which the netting is rolled up at the end of the season, and then down at veraison.

Near the end of the growing season, what is called "veraison" happens, namely, the grapes ripen and turn color. This is the time birds, raccoons, deer, turkeys come out to feast. So, what to do? Cover the grapes with netting.

But the goal of all the hard farm labor is the harvest and the crush.

So, when do you know when it is time to harvest? When you have the right

BRIX

Okay, now that you know how to say it, what is it?

Well, at Bowers Harbor, it is Brix, the obligatory dog.

Lots of tasting rooms have dogs, that's true, but unless you are one of the favored dogs, so what?

"Brix" is a measure of sugar in the grape. Take a little more than half the Brix number (55% to be exact) and it equates to the percent of soluble sugar.

But the winemaker measures brix before harvest. It's how the grape tells the winemaker it's time to harvest. Just over 18 brix is all you need for the grape to give you a good bubbly. For still wine, it seems that 21 is good and 24 is winemaker heaven. But brix must be balanced with acid content to produce the flavor profile desired by the winemaker. Such a balancing act is the life of the winemaker. I've been told a pH of 3.6 or less is desired. Ask your family chemist about pH. – or go online.

So, how dry is dry?

How dry I am, how dry I am
It's plain to see just why I am
No alcohol in my highball
And that is why so dry I am
--- Irving Berlin

How dry is dry? And what is "dry"?

Dry is a measure of sweetness. It is the "residual sugar" left after fermentation.

One starts with the grape, which is "sweet," and the sweetness is measured in "brix." (See previous item) Add yeast to grape juice and the sugar is turned into alcohol. If all the sugar is turned into alcohol, you have a wine that is "bone dry." Zero sugar. Lots of alcohol.

Dan Berger writing for the International Riesling Foundation provides guidelines, which are rather technical, for the four standard categories of dryness. The key to "dryness," he notes, is not the actual amount of sugar in the wine, but the balance of sugar to acid. Let us explain this in terms of a Dry Riesling. A wine carrying the designation of "dry" will have a sugar-to-acid ratio not exceeding 1.0. For example, a wine with 6.8 grams of sugar and 7.5 grams of acidity 0.9:1 would be in the same category as a wine with 8.1 grams of sugar and 9.0 grams of acid even though one has 20% more sugar. A wine with 14 grams of sugar and 14 grams of acid would be dry, but has roughly twice the sugar of the other two examples.

Notice also that wines that are totally or "near-totally" dry (such as 4 grams per liter) will have a much lower ratio. For instance, a wine with only 3 grams of sugar and a total acidity of 6 grams per liter will have a ratio of .5, and clearly the wine is dry.)

pH is a measure of acidity, with 7.0 being the dividing line between acid and alkaline. Rieslings come in at a pH between 2.9 and 3.4 with 3.1 the base. 3.1 and 3.2 are dry, but 3.3 makes it medium dry, 3.5 medium sweet.

One must rely on the winemaker to identify his/her wine as dry, semi- or medium-dry, semi- or medium-sweet, or sweet. Learn your own preference by trial. If you can afford it, you might want to try the four styles of Riesling from a single winery.

Adjacent vineyards; before hedging (left, look for the spindly shoots above the "bush"), after hedging (right)

Here is a vineyard as it awaits Spring pruning, nicely hedged from the previous season.

The Rites of Spring

The Rites of Spring are many in the vineyard, but the first thing any vineyard farmer must do is prune last year's vines. Frankly, this is an arduous task, involving one or more (hopefully more) persons who know how to prune, shape the vine to the lateral wires and tie them to the wire. Young vines may need to be treated differently than older vines.

For a winery (and ANY new winery), there is always planning for the future, which includes planting new vines. This involves prepearing the soil, marking the rows, marking the spacing of the vines, plowing the rows, placing the vines along the rows and covering the roots.

Brengman Brothers was doing all this, of course, in Spring. Gerald and family, including Gerald's daughter, were out in the fields. As is written in this books Brengman Brothers listing, "Tengo famiglia."

Pruning the vine

The Brengmans have planted vineyards for many years, extending their plantings year by year. For 2013 they have added a Cedar Lake vineyard which is the focus of The Planting.

Last year's shoot has to be trimmed.

143

Then bent to the wire,
And clipped to the vine.

Here this is done by a "staple gun"
that wraps a wire around the vine
and the supporting lateral wire.

Here is a wire clip (left)

and here a plastic clip (right).

*Many vineyards, without the use of a "gun" to do
the clipping, will use simple wire tie-ons such as
your grocery store uses to close plastic bags!*

Here is an old vine. Pruning is done only to the vertical shoots.

*It is hard to see in this photo, but this cut vine is "bleeding" sap, much
like Michigan's maple trees in Spring.*

The Preparation

Planting a new vineyard can take years. First the soil has to be tested, then proper organic and other materials worked in to make it just right for wine vines. Once the soil is ready, comes the final preparation, then laying out the site, and finally the planting.

Meet the workhorse of the operation. The tractor's multiple discs will till the soil, with the heavy beam dragged behind to level the field. As the work day begins, it has begun to snow! This can happen even in mid-May!

One pass is a start.

A second pass turns more of the cover crop under and further smooths the surface. There is a long day ahead.

Laying out the vineyard

Spacing the rows is done row by row. Spacing can be by the American system that suits "5' tractors," or can be wider or narrower (common in metric Europe) according to owner preference.

Spacing the vines withinin each row achieved, if the land is flat and you are mechanized, by shallow tines marking the necessary width, eight vines at a time. Hilly vineyards may have to be laid out by hand!

Meanwhile, the bundles of plants are waiting in buckets of ice and ice water. This protects them, as the young vines would die if they dried out. These will be selected clones of the variety being planted. Most will have been grafted, namely the varietal clone will be fitted to a different root stock, a necessary precaution against plant diseases.

The Planting

Here is the hero of the day, "The Planter." He holds one vine in his right hand ready to plant, another in his left.

With the plant stock in front of him in bundles, the planter looks down as the tractor pulls the blades that cut a furrow. When the planter sees that he is directly above the cross-cut vine spacings, he pushes the vine into the furrow. That's concentration for you!

The plant is in the ground, but still needs some help.

Another helper follows the planter and tamps down the earth around the new planting.

This completes the Rites of Spring.

147

Here it is, the vineyard planted. That yellow tag on the young vine, lower left, identifies the particular variety and any other pertinent information (such as which clone). Looks rather barren, doesn't it? Rain and sun will have to do their job. It will be three and a half years before this vineyard produces a useful harvest. Next year posts and lateral wires will be put in to hold the year-old plants

So, why are we showing a life-sized honey-bee? To make a point about pollination. Pollination is needed so plants can create fruits and seeds. Fruit trees are pollinated by bees, making bees an essential link in producing our cherries, peaches, apples, pears, and so on. Bees don't fly in rain (they stay home) and they cannot fight the wind. So weather is important. Calm, dry days are perfect for fruit-tree pollination – just like the beautiful Michigan-blue sky pictured. Grape vine flowers, by contrast, are wind-pollinated. So what is needed for grape-vine pollination is enough wind movement to blow the pollen around between the minute grape flowers.

The Harvest

Harvest begins, of course, in the vineyard. Here we have Ben and Jen Bramer's crew harvesting the Black Star Farms Montague Estate Vineyard.

It takes a large crew to snip the clusters in a day that has limited sunshine hours.

Most vineyards use bird netting over the vines, as is seen here where the crew is snipping the clusters.

149

Without these hard-working men and women, there would be no Up North Michigan wine!

Unload the tractor, then load the bin

And drive into the vines to collect the buckets of grapes.

Celebrate the harvest.

The Crush

Harvest time is "vacation time" to Coenraad Stassen. He is wearing a big smile as I arrive at the processing area of Brys Estate where the juice is already flowing. With his guidance and my camera, here is the story of the end part of the harvest, the de-stemming and the "crushing" of the grapes.

This Pinot Gris is straight from the vineyard. Coenraad notes that, even though you order a grape variety from the nursery, out of a thousand plants, there might be one from a different variety, such as the yellow-green clusters in the bin. Pinot Gris clusters are very tight, thus prone to powdery mildew and other problems. Here Coenraad inspects the bin. "This is what you live for."

Weighing the bin needs to be done before and after the produce is emptied into the de-stemmer, to determine the actual weight of the grapes. De-stemming separates the stem and leaves from the grape without breaking the skin of the grape. The intact berries will then be forced through tubing to the crusher. At Brys Estate, this is done not by the oft-seen stomping of the grapes by bare feet, but by a rotating container.

The Crusher

Grapes drop, free of stems, and are carried through a large tube to the "crusher."

Where the clear juice drops into the tray. And is pumped into the stainless steel tank for fermenting into wine!

Of course, the crush is not the end. Next comes the fermenting. In those big steel tanks. That is where the process begins, but for wines that are expected to age, the wine will be removed from the steel and placed in wood barrels.

Fermenting of fruit – grapes, apples, cherries being the Up North Michigan favorites - requires yeast. Of the thousands of yeast varieties, most winemakers stick with no more than a handful. Choice of yeast, or yeasts, can make one vineyard's wines quite different from another's; even the same grape vinted with two different yeasts will produce seriously different taste profiles. This is just one of the choices the winemaker has to make.

When to stop the yeast from turning the grape sugar to alcohol is the winemaker's task. Let the yeast go to completion and die off can get you a wine with no sugar – bone dry.

So the wine has been tasted by the winemaker for the umpteenth time, and is now found to be the desired sweetness you want and balanced with its acidity. Now, it's time for the bottling, labeling and packing into twelve bottle cases for shipping. Yes, shipping, to the tasting room, restaurant, wholesale distributor, or wine club member.

Bon voyage!

Terracing is needed for N-S rows on a steep west-facing hillside

The turnoff on the west side of Center Road just south of Chateau Grand Traverse is there due to GTRLC; it provides a view over protected land.

Conserving the Beauty, Nature and Agriculture of the two AVAs

There are three organizations that preserve land in perpetuity in its existing, natural state, The Grand Traverse Regional Land Conservancy (GTRLC), The Leelanau Conservancy, and the Peninsula Development Authority (Peninsula Township Conservancy).

The GTRLC operations cover five counties, Grand Traverse, Benzie, Antrim, Kalkaska and Manistee, the so-called Fruit Belt. It is the largest and most comprehensive of the three organizations.

The influence of the GTRLC on the wine industry on Old Mission Peninsula is profound. Farmers were facing declining profits just a couple decades ago.

"They were on the edge," says Glen Chown, executive director of GTRLC. The farmers needing capital to convert from mostly cherry farming to grape farming found that capital by selling development rights to the GTRLC. In doing this, their land is protected in perpetuity from being developed for housing and similar uses. Farmland remains farmland.

A marvelous GTRLC postcard, for which third-party usage is unavailable, shows aerial views of old Mission Peninsula and lower Manhattan. "Old Mission Peninsula: 17,856 acres – 5,500 acres protected forever" reads the OMP caption. Then, quoting Michigan's signature motto: "If you seek a pleasant peninsula . . ." The photo of Manhattan, with huge skyscrapers in the foreground is captioned, "Manhattan Island: 14,694 acres – Central Park's kinda nice . . ." I hope you "get the picture."

Three elements came together to diversify the Old Mission Peninsula protections. Two of them were wineries, led by Ed O'Keefe at Chateau Grand Traverse and Bob Begin at Chateau Chantal, along with promotion by the Convention and Visitors Bureau. Chateau Grand Traverse was the first farm protected in Michigan. State funds were employed there. Then they were extended to all the vineyards along Nelson Road including Kermit Campbell's and Todd Oosterhouse's vineyards.

The Old Mission Peninsula Township has its own conservancy program. Initially it followed the usual route of purchasing development rights, but so many farms applied for conservancy protection that money soon ran out. So a different tactic is now employed, where tax abatement is offered to the farms.

The Ticker, an online service info@theticker.tc providing business news daily, published an informative article on the leaders of the two other land conservancies. The full article, used with permission, follows:

Top Land Prize Northern Michigan Bound   By Lynn Geiger
October 1, 2012

Local conservancy leaders Glen Chown (l) and Brian Price.

Last night in Salt Lake City, northern Michigan took center stage.

It was there that Glen Chown and Brian Price, executive directors of the Grand Traverse Regional Land Conservancy (GTRLC) and The Leelanau Conservancy, respectively, accepted the top award from the Land Trust Alliance – the umbrella service organization of more than 1,700 land trusts across the nation.

Why the win? Land preservation successes totaling tens of thousands of acres that have made the two local conservancies leaders in the state, and in the nation, in best practices. Why should northern Michigan care? Two words: The economy.

"Five to ten years ago when we were talking about farmland preservation, it was mainly about being the 'right thing to do,'" says Chown. "It was touchy-feely."

Now, Chown says, it's about the connection to the region's future economic prosperity. "I'm really proud of how our region has led that change and it's one of the reasons we won," he says.

Adds Price, "Michigan has become a real center for excellence in commercial and private land preservation."

Marking the first time the National Land Trust Excellence Award has ever been given to a pair of organizations seems only natural for the two groups – a mere 30 miles apart – that combined have protected more than 40,000 acres of land, both forest and farm, across the six-county region.

"We're innovators in the way we work with land preservation … and both organizations recognize that the economy is tied to the natural assets of the region," Price says.

And ultimately, their collaboration – particularly with farmland – comes down to one simple truth: "If you protect farmland, you continue opportunities to invest in long-term agriculture," says Chown.

He explains it this way: Say you're the owner of a dried cherry plant. Won't you feel a lot better about a $10 million investment that will require 10,000 acres of cherry trees if you know that fruit acreage is protected?

Also, consider this: Across the GTRLC and Leelanau Conservancy's coverage area, agriculture contributes as much as $97.7 million annually to the local economy in the form of agricultural products sold. It employs more than 2,000 farm proprietors with net farm earnings of $6.6 million and more than 3,000 workers with a total payroll of $12.8 million.

The Michigan Agriculture Environmental Assurance Program

MAEAP <www.maeap.org> is an initiative of the Michigan Department of Agriculture and Rural Development and is administered by the Grand Traverse Conservation District.

MAEAP is concerned with the sustainability of agriculture and the natural landscape. Its people go to farms, when asked, and sometimes take the initiative to approach farmers. Each farming operation is examined on several levels for certification of Livestock, Cropping and as Farmstead. Both agricultural and commercial aspects of the business are certified.

When evaluating a winery, MAEAP staff look at the prime vineyard and are concerned with such things as waste water treatment. Looking at the growing operation, they consider runoff of natural and chemical fertilizers.

For Farmstead certification they look at such items as location of fuel tanks. For Cropping they look at the fields and where materials used on the crops are stored. They are proactive in considering the nutrients in the soil and what needs to be added to achieve balance and sustainability.

Verified properties are actively sustaining the landscape including the water we drink, the air we breathe, and the streams and lakes that are part of the recreational activities of the region. The farms so verified produce the highest quality Michigan farm products.

All seven wineries of WOMP are Environmentally Verified, as are many of the individual vineyards. On Leelanau Peninsula, Shady Lane Cellars and Orchards, Black Star Farms, Cherry Bay Orchards (Chateau de Leelanau) and Good Neighbor Farms (Organic Winery) are verified. By the time you read this, there will likely be more!

155

The Leelanau Conservancy maintains a park just north of their offices in Leland in the rectangle bounded by North Main Street and North 1st Street and East William Street and East North Street. In the park is a tree that shades plaques identifying those who have given to the Conservancy to purchase and protect land. Purchases are not just of farmland but of any land that has significant beauty or natural value.

A Few (too often) Untold Stories

In any business there are participants whose stories remain unsung. In "The Vineyard Season" we have already mentioned some. Here are stories that flesh out further aspects of these hidden movers without whom you might not get that nice Up North Michigan wine to your dinner table.

Corks, corks, and more corks . . . plus a bottle or ten

Do you know how many types of closures there are for sealing a wine bottle? Don't be smart and suggest "well, there's new and used." Dan Brick of Brick Packaging, an Up North success story, revealed to Pat and me a whole world of wine bottling that we'd never thought of. But first, a bit of family history.

Dan Brick comes from California, where he got started as a salesman. After creating a successful company involved in corrugated paper boxes in the southwest, Dan came to Traverse City because he didn't want his kids educated in southern California! He had planned a move to Oregon, but came here because there is a Brick family in Up North Michigan. A summer visit to Michigan cousins left his family wanting to come back. The two families, parents and kids, fit together like two hands clasping. There had been tears in all eyes when the California Bricks had to leave the Michigan Bricks.

So the Californians returned to Michigan the next year. Back and forth, two years in Michigan, two back in California, then Dan and family settled here, selling the California business in early 2002 and opening the Michigan business in October of that year.

Dan had wanted to be a manufacturer's rep. He had gone to a huge wine industry trade show. A label company offered him work on a commission basis. "Man alive, I wonder if anyone calls on them [Up North Michigan wineries]."

Soon he discovered just how "closed-shop" was the wine bottle business in the U.S. when Lee Lutes of Black Star Farm told him, "We have a hard time getting bottles." So Dan looked into it and found a glass bottle producer in Mexico that could supply him. He bought from that Mexican producer and he imported special bottles from France, Germany and Italy. He met the needs of our two AVA's wine producers with the support of a wife who wouldn't let him take no for an answer once he decided what he needed to do. She provided accounting and billing services in the early years.

But back to bottle closures. Five is the number, if you only think of corks; Natural, Colmated, Micro-Agglomerated, Technical and Synthetic. And that doesn't include Zorks, which combine a capsule (the seal that covers the cork and top – finish - of the bottle) with a cork. There are some six bottle finishes, or shapes of the bottle top; Cork, Flange, Bar Top, Screw Cap, CT 28-400, and Vino Seal. You get the idea . . .

Decisions, decisions, decisions. Now, with all those possible combinations and permutations, in what bottle shape and color do you put your wine? Brick Packaging shows ten bottle colors besides clear glass. For Bordeaux, they offer eleven styles with bottle weights from 455 g to 970 g. Why such a heavy bottle, you ask? Because a premium wine feels even more premium in a heavy bottle.

Now there are seven Burgundy styles, eight Hocks (Riesling), plus other sizes than the standard 750 ml. So, five corks, six finishes, eleven colors, eleven Bordeaux styles. That is 3,630 choices just to bottle a "Bordeaux blend," such as a Cabernet Franc with Merlot, as offered by several Up North Michigan wineries.

That is what Brick Packaging does not only for the two AVA's around Traverse City but also for wineries across the country though mostly in the Midwest.

So, here is a Michigan success story. Brick Beverages provides not only bottles, corks, capsules, but boxes (the inserts are from recycled newsprint), barrels (he consults on what kind of oak, how much it should be toasted, and so on), almost anything a winery could need to get its precious nectar out to the customer.

Sherlock Holmes, Anyone?

Hamilton Agronomy's Kevin Herman is Paul Drake to Perry Mason, or Spenser (not Spencer of Bowers Harbor) in Robert B. Parker's (no, not "the Nose" Robert M. Parker, Jr.) novels. Is he the sleuth of the vineyards? Kevin's job is to go out in to the vineyards and seek out problems, then recommend cures to the vineyard manager or winery owner. It is a demanding job, and none of it involves tasting wines! Unlucky him!

So, what does a Senior Consultant do for a firm devoted to fostering good agricultural practices? At a simple level, he'd be called a "scout." But that doesn't do justice to the comprehensive services he provides vineyard owners. If this doesn't make sense, think of him as a Sherlock Holmes of the vineyards.

While product information (about fertilizers, pesticides . . .) is provided free, consulting is charged on a per acre basis. This starts at the bud break and ends just before harvest. Kevin, who is degreed in Horticulture and is a Crop Consultant Advisor (a national standard), will not only visually inspect the site but also take soil samples and tissue samples, for example, to identify any disease or insect infestations needing treatment, and then, the fertilizers, fumigations, or other treatments needed to maintain a healthy soil.

Powdery mildew is a fungus, *Erysiphe necator/uncinula necator* that affects grapes and can destroy a crop. It can be treated chemically through foliar spraying. It looks like white or grayish-white dust. It is hard to distinguish, therefore, from calcium with which the vines may have been treated, so it requires a trained eye to judge an infection.

Botrytis, or gray mold (a.k.a. Botrytis bunch rot, *botryotinia cinerea*), is another problem. Noble botrytis in the late stages of ripening can be wonderful, producing an ultra high brix which leads to a sweet desert wine. But botrytis in the early spring is anything but "noble": it is disaster, capable of killing any infected cluster. 60,000 spores can form on plant tissue no larger than a small fingernail, and it propagates and spreads with almost lightning speed in windy or moist conditions. In spring it gets onto the plant bud when the cap pops off leaving raw tissue exposed.

Given that Leelanau and Old Mission peninsulas are N-S oriented with the winds off adjacent water flowing E-W, it would seem natural that vineyards be planted E-W to facilitate wind flow through the vineyard to keep the vines and grape clusters dry. But that denies sunlight to the north-facing grape clusters, while providing south-facing clusters a full day of sun. So, most Leelanau and Old Mission vineyards are planted N-S.

Now we are back to Kevin. He inspects vineyards weekly to determine what is needed to obtain the best possible harvest. Foliar spraying (zinc oxide, boric acid, calcium . . .) may be recommended. If dagger nematodes (*Xiphinema americanum*) are discovered, the soil will not just need fertilizer, but may have to be fumigated – most easily before any vines are planted. This is a serious problem where a cherry orchard has been dug up and grape vines planted. (Did you know that the top foot of average soil on one acre weights two million pounds!) Those new grape growers who buy a cherry orchard, pull out the trees, than dig that two feet and mix the soil do massive damage to their future vineyard, destroying nature's mix. This same damage might even date from when that cherry orchard was first planted.

In sum, Kevin's work is an integral part of the vineyard manager's job, and provides peace of mind to the vineyard owner.

44° 48' 13.79" N, 85° 28' 53,45" W

Isn't GPS wonderful?

Without it, Wilbur-Ellis Company in Williamsburg might be just another family-owned provider of agricultural services. With it, they can - and do - survey vineyards and orchards, acre by acre, with state-of-the-art precision tools.

That number in the header is the GPS coordinates of the center of the Wilbur-Ellis Agribusiness retail building in Williamsburg on US 31 North.

You still don't find many women in the agribusiness, but Tiffany Stiemel, a Suttons Bay farm girl, is Wilbur-Ellis's local TSR (Technical Sales Representative) and jill-of-all-trades. Her company shuts down when the snow arrives and opens as Spring pokes its head through that snow. Then she works 60 hours a week with vineyard managers as well as with other vineyard service providers that need the chemicals and pesticides Wilbur-Ellis can supply.

With MSU interns to assist in her scouting, Tiffany applies technology to sample soil types on one-acre grids. Soil types are recorded by GPS coordinates. Then, when folial sprays or ground fertilizers are applied, the spreader is computer-controlled by the coordinates to modify the amount and type of product dispensed as the soil type changes.

Chemicals. New chemicals every year as the fight against pests and diseases continues. This is a complex problem, especially now that vineyard managers and owners want organic products or newly developed products that are more environment-friendly and, of course, less expensive!

Because the most advanced research in vineyard-related chemistry is in California, Wilbur-Ellis is based in San Francisco. Yet here in Michigan, the far eastern reach of their business, they have a chemical plant in Grant, northeast of Muskegon, and a fertilizer plant in Hart, south of Ludington. Here is where they blend fertilizer, sell chemicals and other agriculture services.

Small particles drift further than large. Wilbur-Ellis uses a process that encapsulates small particles which, when they are sprayed, disperse only upon contact with the plant, thus reducing drift. Not the cheapest process, perhaps, but often the most economical. Just one other benefit of being a part of a company whose base is in the heart of wine country U S A.

As with many Up North Michigan businesses, Wilbur-Ellis knows not just the businesses with which they work, but the families who run them. Orchards as well as vineyards. With almost no fruit crop, 2012 was a difficult year; fruit growers will be hard-pressed in 2013 with little or no income carried over for future expenses. This is the time when developed relationships carry the day - for both sides of our Up North Michigan agricultural scene.

And while we are at it, the business of wine started several millennia ago. We've told the story of Up North Michigan wine, winery by tasting room by vineyard. Here is the rest, the final chapter of how wine got from the old world to the new.

From Water Sanitizer to Elixir of the Gods: A Wine History

For most of its history, from 5,000 B.C.E. (or earlier) to the near present, wine was mostly a very sour liquid that was mixed 3 to 5 parts water to 1 part wine to make the water safe to drink.

Then along came the Cistercian monks and their vineyards at Cîteaux, France, in the Middle Ages. One could argue that they discovered *terroir* (from the Latin *terratorium*). They were zealous at tending their vineyards, as manual labor was central to their order. They marked what vines grew well, and what didn't, and where. They found that their wines had identifiable taste from different plots, and they noted that and developed the best. They grew Pinot Noir in the village of Vougeot in Côte de Nuits of Burgundy. Vougeot wine comes from a vineyard whose surface is taken up by its single Grand Cru, Clos de Vougeot, which at 123 acres is the largest Grand Cru of Côte de Nuits.

Even these wines did not last long. Once a new vintage arrived, any leftover wine from the previous year was quickly discounted. Wine is already a saleable commodity.

The Cistercians moved into Germany and, in 1136, founded a huge monastery, Kloster Erbach, in the Rheingau. Riesling is first mentioned in the 1300s in the Rheingau; with its high alcohol content, it was the first wine that could last beyond a year in casks. These casks could be shipped long distances.

Then in 1660, Arnaud III de Pontac, a French nobleman and first president of his regional parliament, decided that wine from the family estate was not only different, but also distinctive. Instead of selling to the negociants, who would blend it with other reds, he doubled its price, thus guaranteeing that his wine would be drunk straight, not blended. His estate: Haut Brion! His red wine was probably a blend of Cabernet Franc, Carmenère and other grapes, though its now famous label is a much different blend that includes grapes that were not around in his time. Cabernet Sauvignon didn't appear until late in the 18th century, and Merlot even later.

Along the way, however, competition appeared. Coffee, tea and chocolate, plus hopped beer and fortified wines: all with the advantage of not turning sour so quickly. They gained a place at the table. Gin in England, Vodka in Russia and other eastern Europe states, and Rum in the American colonies gained favor.

Between the mid 1700s and the later 1800s, two scientists advanced the quality of wine. Antoine Lavoisier discovered and explained the chemistry of wine: an exchange of oxygen that divides sugar into alcohol and carbon dioxide. Fermentation was now predictable. Louis Pasteur saw, through his microscope, the bacteria in wine which were the cause of wine's souring. Sulfur and sugar (cane sugar from the Americas) proved beneficial additives to wine, helping the liquid to last longer and even improve with age. Modern wine was born.

Another major step forward came with cork stoppers and blown glass bottles. Most wine in the 1700s was sold only in barrels, and the wine started its inexorable road to vinegar as soon as the barrel was tapped. Early glass bottles were globular. To keep them from spilling by falling over, an indentation called a punt was made in the bottom, creating a ring that stabilized the bottle. Such bottles were made in intense heat — coal, not wood, fires — and this turned the glass brown or darker. Gradually the shape changed with the bottle becoming slimmer and taller until the ring was the maximum diameter of the very vertical bottle. The punt was no longer needed, yet remains in many wine bottle styles.

By the mid-1800s, the best wines — from a Bordeaux château, a Burgundy cru, Rhine or Mosel estate, Port lodge or Sherry bodega — were what people wanted and bought as a sign of sophistication. This was the first golden age for wine. Rising prices for the best wines brought forth fraud as bad wine was mixed with good, bottles were mislabeled and so on. Soon powdery mildew at-tacked the vines. This was followed by black rot, and finally phylloxera killed the vines and devastated wine production. Recovery came only slowly when it was discovered that sulfur cured powdery mildew and that America's foxy tasting grapes grew on stock that was immune to the miniscule bugs that sucked the roots dry. Grafting the French grape varieties on to American root stock solved the problem.

With the adulteration of wine and the devastations of disease, wine lost its reputation as the "in" drink. People turned to cocktails – the most famous being, of course, the "dry" martini. Bartenders competed to create new mixes and sophisticates prided themselves on being able to mix the best-known cocktails at home. Between the two world wars, during which many European vineyards were trampled and bombed into oblivion, cocktails ruled even as alcohol was "banned." Prohibition in America came about from well-intentioned people who considered alcohol an evil. The Volstead Act prohibited the manufacture, sale, or transportation of intoxicating beverages. It said nothing about drinking such liquids! Predictably, prohibition didn't work.

Here is a little Michigan story. During Prohibition winters, when the Detroit River froze over, Canadian bootleggers would send three cars carrying liquor and wine across the ice. Three, because the Detroit police had only two cars patrolling the border, so one would always get through while the other two went back across the border to safety, only to try again later.

The Scott-Henry trellising, here in autumn light, spreads the vine in a "V", and produces abundant clusters. The Ligon Drop a Wing Farm uses this trellising almost exclusively.

Meanwhile, Down Under, where high alcohol drinks had long been preferred and European wines were rarely available, technical innovations changed everything. Temperature-controlled stainless steel tanks brought about the ability to produce distinctive wines which, though not as complex as Bordeaux blends or Burgundy varietals, were consistently excellent year after year. First Shiraz, then Chardonnay. Bottled, then in boxes! Price carried the day. Who hasn't heard of Lindemanns or Penfolds?

Early in the post-Prohibition era, University of California professors Alfred Winckler and Maynard Amerine researched the vineyards around their state. In 1935 alone they made over 500 five-gallon batches of wine from state vineyards. From this they identified regions where specific grape varieties would thrive. Few winemakers took notice until after World War II when Beaulieu Vineyards and Inglenook began making wines based on the professors' work. Then came the 1976 Judgment of Paris (celebrated in the movie "Bottle Shock") when Chateau Montelena's Chardonnay from Miljenko "Mike" Grgich and Stag's Leap Wine Cellars Cabernet Sauvignon from Warren Winiarski bested French "equivalents" in a blind tasting by French experts. California wines had arrived on the world scene.

This astonishing success led to other states joining the "wine rush": Washington State with Merlot, New York with Riesling, Oregon with Pinot Noir. Even as this was happening, Bernie Rink was planting vines on Leelanau Peninsula just west of Lake Leelanau.

Classification of wines by source/*terroir* started in France in 1855. The Appellations d'Origine Contrôlée (AOC) system in France was designed to guarantee that a wine came from a specific place and contained a specific varietal or blend. After World II, this system of quality control came of age as it spread across Europe. Wine drinkers, seeking out and buying wines with distinctive and identifiable character, helped fuel the drive for improved quality as winemakers produced wines that spoke of the earth from which the wine grapes came. The European Union has furthered this by setting minimal standards for each member country's wines.

Here in the U.S., our equivalent of AOC is American Viticultural Areas (AVA). Michigan has four AVAs, two in the southwest and the two on our Up North peninsulas. The American standards are less restrictive than the European — this allowing for more experimentation with grape vine breeding and with test plantings of grape varieties in hopes of enriching our local offerings. Lucky us.

So, enjoy our remarkable regional wines!

Wine-related Events

Throughout the year there are wine-related events, from a wide array of sponsors, that are open to the public. While, normally, tasting rooms offer only wine tastings, the special events match food with wine chosen by the wineries. In addition, many wineries offer "wine-dinner" and other special events, sometimes at the tasting room, sometimes at a local restaurant. Ask at the tasting room for dates and locations.

Wine-related Community Events include:
Traverse City Winter Microbrew & Music Festival (February, includes wine and cider)
Leland Wine & Food Festival (June)
Traverse City Wine & Art Festival (June)
National Cherry Festival Global Wine Pavilion (June– July)
Leelanau Wine, Food & Music Festival (Northport, June)
Traverse City Summer Microbrew & Music Festival (August, includes wine and cider from Old Mission Peninsula Wineries)

Leelanau Peninsula Vintners Association (LPVA):
LPVA <lpwines.com>. annually sponsors:
Taste the Passion (February)
Spring Sip & Savor (May: Cinco de Mayo)
Traverse City Wine & Art Festival Winemakers Party (June)
Harvest Stompede (September)
Toast the Season (November)
LPVA Small Plates (TBD)

LPVA is a membership organization. Members join in with wine and food pairings at events normally scheduled over two weekends. Tickets are sold online in advance of the events and are usually limited to 1000 per event. Ticket holders are given a glass with the event printed on it that is used for the entire event. One may visit eight events on Saturday and another eight on Sunday. The events are usually sold out.

LPVA publishes a Leelanau Peninsula map with members' tasting rooms marked.

Wines of Old Mission Peninsula (WOMP):
WOMP www.wineriesofoldmission.com sponsors:
Winter Warm Up (January)
Romancing the Riesling (February)
Cellar Sale (March)
Blossom Day (May)
Divas Uncorked (June)
Great Macaroni & Cheese Bake-Off (November)

The Mad Hatter: Cinco de Mayo 2012

The auction, Tasters Guild table with Culinary Institute "Chefs" along the wall.

Tasters Guild of Northwest Michigan (rhill1129@yahoo.com) or Tasters Guild International at (www.tastersguild.com) offers frequent wine dinners at local restaurants, and the Auction at Northwestern Michigan College/ Great Lakes Culinary Institute (February)

An organization of farmers, Parallel 45 Vines & Wines

p45michigan.com holds educational events for wine grape farmers and anyone else interested in wine and grape farming. Thirsty Third Thursday is an after-work social event held throughout the winter months. Educational events are held during the warmer months. P45 hosts the NW Michigan Orchard & Vineyard Show in January and other events throughout the year.

Aside from all the events, including wine dinners, Traverse City is now a major "foodie town." Two magazines, *Bon Appetit* and *Midwest Living*, have listed TC as a top five food town. Might it be said that internationally recognized Chef Mario Batali has a cottage in Up North Michigan because of the local gastronomy? At least one magazine quotes him as having done such.

Taste the Local Difference: Northwest Michigan, a project of the Michigan Land Use Institute, publishes, each year, information on farms, farmers' markets, wineries, cideries, restaurants and even the dates when produce is being harvested. Fresh is what Up North Michigan is about: the publication indicates the farming practices followed by local farms and the use of local produce by restaurants and/or sale at local markets.

And this certainly is what local restaurants are about, fresh. Fresh everything, and local wines. In a comparative tasting by Burrritt's Fresh Markets in Traverse City early in 2013 for new residents of the area, six Up North Michigan wines won out against six nationally high-rated and price-competitive wines.

Fresh produce and local wines makes the area a destination for diners old and young, rich and not so rich. High-end restaurants are not all that is here, for there are taverns with creative menus and even local resort venues have restaurants catering to all levels of family tastes.

Wine-paired Recipes

from Old Mission and Leelanau Peninsulas

Why add recipes to a vine-and-wine exploration of our two peninsulas? Simple. Many cookbooks do indeed suggest wine pairings — nearly always with the widely distributed wines such as from France, Italy, Spain, California, Oregon, Australia, New Zealand. We wanted to bring the inspiration home to our local foods and wines. Who better to ask for locally inspired "wine-paired" recipes than the wineries of our two peninsulas? Each recipe in this special collection has come from a Leelanau Peninsula or an Old Mission Peninsula winery and is accompanied by a wine pairing suggestion for one of their wines.

In editing and formatting each recipe to a standard format, the editor has sought to retain its writer's "writing style" and sometimes, gently dry, humor.

Thank you to all the winemakers, owners, tasting room staffers, and local chefs, who have contributed recipes. Thank you, too, for your endless patience in answering the editor's questions and for your enthusiastic support.

Appetizers

Bacon Wrapped Dates / 164
Blue Cheese Savory Cookies / 167
Bruschetta / 164
Caramelized Onion and Apple Tart / 165
Charred Shrimp with Mint Sauce / 165
Cherry Smoked Lake Trout Spread / 166
Cherry Wine Jelly Cheese Ball / 164
Creamy Blue Cheese Stuffed Phyllo Shells / 166
Deviled Eggs with Bacon / 166
Grilled Oysters with Spicy Tarragon Butter / 167
Pear, Apple Sausage and Swiss Cheese Bites / 168
Raspberry Goat Cheese Tartlet / 168
Smoked Whitefish Pate / 165
The Goat / 167
Winter Warm-Up Spiced Cherry Meatballs / 168

Soups

Curried Carrot Soup / 169
Gazpacho / 169
Morel Chanterelle Bisque / 170
Red Lentil Soup / 171
Roasted Cauliflower Soup / 170
Salmon Chowder / 169

Salads

Asian Pasta Salad / 172
Sparkling Wine Vinaigrette / 172

Main

Beef Verterra / 182
Cherry Balsamic Short Ribs / 173
Cornel's Rabbit Loins Wrapped in Bacon / 174
Creamy Indian-Spiced Halibut Curry / 175
Green-Chili Enchiladas / 176
Grilled Chicken and Peaches / 175
Grilled Orange-Glazed Pork Tenderloin / 177

Honey Mustard Turkey Burger / 180
Leelanau Cottage Pie / 178
Majaraja Curry (Vegetarian) / 178
Mediterranean Quinoa Salad & Grilled Salmon / 179
Northern Michigan Spring Pizza / 179
Poppy's Chicken Cacciatore (Hunter's Chicken) / 180
Pork Braised in Cider / 181
Pork Chops in Chardonnay / 174
Riesling Chicken / 181
Risotto with Butternut Squash, Pancetta, and Jack Cheese / 176
Roasted Rosemary Pork Tenderloin with Sauvignon Blanc Cream Sauce / 177
Satay Tofu (Vegan) / 173
Winter Warm-Up Spiced Cherry Meatballs / 168

Sides

Asparagus Frittata / 183
Bruschetta / 164
Eggplant Parmigiana / 184
Israeli Couscous with Asparagus, Peas & Feta / 183
Pasta Carbonara / 182
Quiche / 184

Desserts

Nadine's Luscious Apricot Bars / 185
Nutty Cherry Bread Pudding / 186
Omi's Sacher Torte / 187
Ramona's Apple Crisp with Caramel Sauce / 185
Ramona's French Vanilla Pumpkin Squares / 186
Toast the Season Chocolate Truffle Torte / 187

Beverages

Apple Gluhwein (Mulled Wine) / 188

Appetizers

Bacon Wrapped Dates

From bigLITTLE wines, submitted by Michael Laing
Suggested wine pairing: Big Little Crayfish (Pinot Gris)
Makes 24 to 30 pieces

1 package bacon, typically 12 strips (thinner bacon works better)
1 lb dates (about 24 to 30 dates), pits removed
Toothpicks

Soak toothpicks in water.

Preheat oven to 350°F.

Cut bacon strips in half cross-wise. Sauté over medium heat until both sides are beginning to turn brown; but do not cook bacon to the point where it becomes crispy (you will need to wrap it around the dates).

Transfer bacon to paper towel to cool.

After the bacon has cooled, wrap each piece around a date.

Overlap the bacon and secure by poking half of a toothpick through both sides of the date.

Bake in oven until bacon becomes brown and crisp, 15 minutes.

Michael Says: this is a personal favorite, especially for cocktail hour.

Cherry Wine Jelly Cheese Ball

From Cherry Republic, submitted by Jason Homa
Recipe created by Chef Steve Eggleston at Cherry Republic, Glen Arbor
Suggested wine pairing: Cherry Republic Liberty sparkling cherry wine
Makes about 1½ lb

1 lb cream cheese
¼ lb cooked chopped bacon
1 scallion
¼ lb shredded Cheddar Jack cheese
4 oz Cherry Republic Wine Jelly
Chopped roasted pecans, optional

Combine all ingredients I(except optional pecans) in food processor.

Puree until fully incorporated.

Pour the mixture into a bowl or shape it into a ball.

Optionally, cover the mixture, whether in bowl or shaped into a ball, with chopped roasted pecans

Serve with crackers.

Bruschetta

From Ciccone Vineyard and Winery
Suggested wine pairing: Ciccone Pinot Noir
Makes 24 small slices, serving 6 to 10 as an appetizer or 3 to 4 for lunch

6 or 7 ripe plum tomatoes (about 1½ lb)
1 garlic clove, minced
1 Tbs extra virgin olive oil
1 tsp fresh oregano, chopped (dried will work)
Salt and freshly ground black pepper, to taste
1 baguette French bread or similar Italian bread
¼ cup extra virgin olive oil

Prepare tomatoes: Parboil tomatoes for one minute in boiling water that has just been removed from burner. Drain. With small sharp knife, remove peels from tomatoes. Cut peeled tomatoes in halves or quarters; remove seeds and juice; cut out and discard stem area. With thicker skins, fewer seeds and less juice, plum tomatoes are better than regular.

Place oven rack at top position in oven. Preheat oven to 450°F.

While oven is heating, chop tomatoes finely. Put tomatoes, garlic and the 1 Tbs olive oil in a bowl and mix. Add the chopped oregano. Add salt and pepper to taste.

Diagonally slice baguette to make slices about ½-inch thick.

With a pastry brush, coat one side of each slice with olive oil (from the ¼ cup oil). Place each slice on a cooking sheet, olive oil side down. You will want to toast them in the top rack of your oven, so you may need to do them in batches depending on the size of your oven. Once oven has reached 450°F, place a tray of bread slices in oven on top rack. Toast for 5 to 6 minutes, until bread just begins to turn golden brown. Alternatively, you can toast bread without first coating it in olive oil. Toast on a griddle for one minute each side. Take a sharp knife and score each slice three times. Rub some garlic in the slices and drizzle half a teaspoon of olive oil on each slice. This is the traditional method of making bruschetta.

To Serve: Align the bread on serving platter, olive oil side up. Either, place the tomato in a bowl separately with a spoon for people to serve themselves over the bread, or place some topping on each slice of bread and serve. If you do top each slice with the tomatoes, do it right before serving or the bread may get soggy. Delicious with cottage cheese on the side.

Caramelized Onion and Apple Tart

From: Blustone Vineyards, submitted by Joan Knighton.
Suggested wine pairing: Blustone Riesling or Blustone Late Harvest Riesling.
Makes two tarts, each producing about 20 2x2-inch pieces.

2 Tbs olive oil
2 medium sweet onions, slced
2 red apples (Gala are good), not peeled, cut in small pieces
¼ tsp salt
¼ tsp sugar
2 sheets frozen puff pastry, thawed
½ cup sour cream

Heat oven to 400°F.

Heat oil in skillet over medium heat, add onions, stirring till soft and golden, 12 to 15 minutes. Stir in apples, salt and sugar and cook till tender, another 2 minutes.

Place each sheet of pastry on parchment-lined baking sheet and prick with a fork. Spread with sour cream, leaving ½-inch border. Top with onion/apple mixture and bake until crisp, 30 minutes.

To Serve: Cut into pieces and serve as an appetizer.

Joan Says: The tarts can be assembled and frozen up to 1 month in advance. Freeze them unbaked, on parchment-lined baking sheets till firm, then wrap in plastic. To cook, bake from frozen at 400°F for 40 to 50 minutes.

Smoked Whitefish Pate

From Leelanau Cellars, submitted by Carrie Hanson
Suggested wine pairing: Leelanau Cellars Semi-Dry Riesling
Makes about 3 cups

1 lb flaked smoked whitefish (suggest Carlson's Smoked
          Whitefish from Leland, Michigan)
¾ to 1 cup mayonnaise
2 tsp fresh lemon juice
½ cup chopped green onion
2 tsp prepared horseradish
1 tsp minced garlic
1 tsp freshly ground black pepper
2 Tbs chopped fresh curly leaf parsley
2 tsp Cajun Seasoning

Mix all the ingredients together in a bowl.

Cover and refrigerate until chilled.

To Serve: Place in a serving bowl, and serve with grilled Pita bread.

Charred Shrimp with Mint Sauce

From Motovino Cellars, submitted by Deirdre Owen
Suggested wine pairing: Motovino Cellars Thumper dry Riesling
Serves 3 to 4

3 jalapenos, seeded and chopped
Juice of 3 to 4 limes
1 cup packed mint leaves
1 tsp sugar
1½ tsp smoked paprika
12 large shrimp, peeled and deveined
3 Tbs kosher salt
2 to 3 Tbs oil
Cilantro leaves

Place jalapenos, lime juice, mint leaves, sugar and smoked paprika in the bowl of a food processor and mix until smooth. Set aside.

Combine salt and shrimp, let stand ½ to 1 hour.

Heat oil in a wok or large sauté pan over high heat. Place shrimp in wok or pan and toss constantly until cooked (opaque and slightly charred). Do not overcook.

To Serve: Arrange shrimp and sauce garnished with cilantro leaves on a plate.

Deirdre Says: With its spicy smoky flavor, the sauce is not for the faint of heart!

Cherry Smoked Lake Trout Spread

From Cherry Republic, submitted by Jason Homa
Recipe created by Chef Steve Eggleston at Cherry Republic, Glen Arbor
Suggested wine pairing: Cherry Republic Great Hall White Riesling
and Cherry blend
Makes about 1 lb

16 oz smoked lake trout
¼ cup fat free mayonnaise
1 tsp Old Bay Seasoning
¼ Tbs Cherry Republic's KaBOB›s Kick'en Cherry Hot Sauce
    (or substitute, Franks Hot Sauce)
1 Tbs Worcestershire Sauce
½ tsp cracked black pepper
1 Tbs Cherry Concentrate
½ cup dried cherries

Combine all ingredients except dried cherries into food processor. Pulse lightly 3 to 4 times, until mixture is fully incorporated but not totally smooth.

Move to bowl and stir in dried cherries.

Chill.

Serve with crackers.

Deviled Eggs with Bacon

From Chateau Chantal, submitted by Marie-Chantal Dalese
Suggested wine pairing: Chateau Chantal Unoaked Chardonnay
Makes 24 pieces

12 eggs
½ cup mayonnaise
4 slices bacon
2 Tbs finely shredded Cheddar cheese
1 Tbs mustard

Place eggs in a saucepan, and cover with cold water. Bring water to a boil and immediately remove saucepan from heat. Cover, and let eggs stand in hot water for 10 to 12 minutes. Remove from hot water, and cool. To cool more quickly, rinse eggs under cold running water.

Meanwhile, place bacon in a large, deep skillet. Cook over medium-high heat until evenly brown. (Alternatively, wrap bacon in paper towels and cook in the microwave for about 1 minute per slice.) Crumble and set aside.

Peel the hard-cooked eggs, and cut in half lengthwise. Remove yolks to a small bowl. Mash egg yolks with mayonnaise, crumbled bacon and cheese. Stir in mustard.

Fill egg white halves with the yolk mixture and refrigerate until serving.

Creamy Blue Cheese Stuffed Phyllo Shells

From Forty-Five North Vineyard & Winery, submitted by Alanna Grossnickle
Suggested wine pairing: Forty-Five North Cabernet Franc Rosé as appetizer;
Forty-Five North Cherry Dessert Wine as dessert
Makes 24 pieces

Glazed Walnuts:
3 cups walnuts, crushed (pecans work equally well)
Olive oil
¼ cup brown sugar
3 Tbs honey, or 3 Tbs combination of honey and maple syrup,
    according to taste
1 Tbs butter

8 oz cream cheese
3 oz blue cheese crumbles
2 dozen mini filo (phyllo) shells
Dried cherries
Dried cranberries

Prepare Glazed Walnuts:

Preheat oven to 350°F. Place crushed nuts in deep-sided baking pan or foil baking dish, (not a cookie sheet) about 9x13-inch, lightly drizzle olive oil and spread nuts evenly over pan surface. Roast in oven 15 to 18 minutes, stirring once. Leave nuts in pan and keep warm.

Combine brown sugar and butter in a saucepan. Cook, stirring, over low heat until brown sugar melts. Add honey/maple syrup; mix well. Pour mixture, while still warm, over warm roasted nuts in pan and toss gently to coat. Let stand until cool. Break into dime-to-nickel sized pieces before serving.

Mix cream cheese and blue cheese until smooth.

Put cheese mix into a pastry piping bag; pipe cheese into filo shells.

Top cheese-filled shells with Glazed Walnuts, cherries, and cranberries.

Blue Cheese Savory Cookies

From Chateau Chantal, submitted by Marie-Chantal Dalese
Suggested wine pairing: Chateau Chantal Late Harvest Riesling
Makes about 3 dozen cookies

1 cup all-purpose flour
½ cup (1 stick, ¼ lb) butter, at room temperature
4 oz blue cheese, crumbled
Black pepper
Additional 2 oz blue cheese crumbles, for top of cookies

Pre heat oven to 350°F. Line a baking sheet with parchment paper.

Place the flour, butter, 4 oz of blue cheese and a few grinds of black pepper in the bowl of a food processor. Process until the dough just comes together and starts to form a ball.

Dump the dough onto a lightly floured surface and knead a few times to pull the dough together. Roll out to ⅛-inch thick with a floured rolling pin. Cut rounds out of the dough with a floured 1-inch cutter and transfer the rounds to the parchment-lined baking sheet.

Using the back of a round half-teaspoon measure or your knuckle, make an indention in the top of each dough round.

Bake the cookies for 10 to 14 minutes, until the pastry is light golden on the bottom.

After removing the cookies from the oven, sprinkle a few cheese crumbles on top of each cookie.

Cool the cookies, still on the baking sheet, for at least 10 minutes, then remove to a wire rack to cool.

The Goat

From Left Foot Charley, submitted by Meridith Lauzon
Suggested wine pairing: Left Foot Charley Pinot Blanc or Left Foot Charley Pinot Gris
Makes 2 to 3 cups

1 (8-oz) package soft goat cheese
½ (8-oz) package crumbled goat cheese
½ cup sour cream
4 to 8 fresh basil leaves, chopped (remember to wash and dry them!)
1 Tbs dried thyme
1 tsp fresh ground pepper
4 oz dried figs, chopped "chunky"
1 handful of chopped walnuts
A dash of salt

Mix all ingredients together and refrigerate for 20 to 30 minutes.

To Serve: Enjoy spread on rosemary or regular flavored crackers.

Grilled Oysters with Spicy Tarragon Butter

From Bowers Harbor Vineyards, submitted by Justin Leshinsky
Suggested wine pairing: Bowers Harbor Vineyards Cuvee Evan Blanc de Noir (dry Champagne-style sparkling wine)
Makes 6 servings

Tarragon Butter:
½ lb (i.e., 2 sticks) unsalted butter, softened
3 Tbs chopped tarragon
2 Tbs hot sauce
½ tsp kosher salt
¼ tsp freshly ground pepper
3 dozen medium to large oysters, such as Gulf Coast or Bluepoint

Light a grill.

Make Tarragon Butter: In a food processor, pulse the butter, tarragon, hot sauce, salt and pepper until blended.

Transfer the tarragon butter to a sheet of plastic wrap and roll into a 2-inch-thick log. Refrigerate the tarragon butter until slightly firm, about 15 minutes. Slice the butter into 36 pats.

Place oysters on hot grill, flat-side up. Cover the grill and cook until the oysters open, about 5 minutes.

Using tongs, transfer the oysters to a platter, trying to keep the liquor inside. Quickly remove the top shells and loosen the oysters from the bottom shells. (The idea is to loosen the meat but keep it in the bottom shell for serving.)

Top each oyster with a pat of the tarragon butter and return the oysters to the grill.

Cover the grill and cook oysters until the tarragon butter is mostly melted and the oysters are hot, about 1 minute.

Serve immediately.

Pear, Apple Sausage and Swiss Cheese Bites

From Brengman Brothers at Crain Hill Vineyards, submitted by Joni Brengman
Suggested wine pairing: Brengman Brothers Riesling
Makes 40 to 50 pieces

6 Tbs Dijon mustard
2 Tbs honey
12 oz pre-cooked apple sausages, cut into ½-inch pieces
        (you should have 40-50 pieces)
12 oz Swiss cheese, cut into ¾-inch dice (40-50 pieces)
2 firm ripe pears, cored and cut into ¾-inch dice (40-50 pieces)

In a small bowl, whisk together the mustard and honey. Set aside.

Heat a large skillet over medium heat. No oil is needed since the fat from the sausages will suffice. Add the sausages and cook, stirring occasionally, until nicely browned and heated through, 4 to 5 minutes. Transfer the sausages to a plate and set aside to cool slightly.

Meanwhile, drizzle the mustard/honey mixture decoratively on to large platter or, evenly divided, on to individual plates.

When sausage is cool enough to handle, skewer one piece each of cheese, sausage, and pear on to a toothpick. Repeat with remaining cheese, sausage, and pear, arranging the toothpicks on top of the mustard.

Serve warm.

Raspberry Goat Cheese Tartlet

From Chateau Chantal, submitted by Marie-Chantal Dalese
Suggested wine pairing: Chateau Chantal Celebrate! Sparkling Wine
Makes 30 pieces

Raspberry Coulis:
1 (10-oz) package frozen raspberries in syrup, thawed
        (or 2½ cups fresh raspberries)
2 Tbs sugar (or ¼ cup sugar if using fresh raspberries)
1 tsp fresh lemon juice, or to taste
1 (11-oz) package goat cheese
2 packages phyllo shells, each box contains 15 shells

Make the coulis: Purée raspberries with syrup, sugar, and lemon juice in a blender or food processor. Pour mixture through a fine sieve into a bowl, pressing on the solids.

Alternatively, the coulis can be made with fresh raspberries. Use 2½ cups fresh raspberries and ¼ cup sugar.

Mix coulis into cheese and spoon into tart to serve.

Marie-Chantal Says: The coulis will keep for 3 days, covered and chilled.

Winter Warm-Up Spiced Cherry Meatballs

From Chateau Grand Traverse Winery & Vineyards
Recipe created by Tasting Room Manager Hiro Miura and Merchandise Manager Michael Bodus
Featuring: Chateau Grand Traverse Silhouette (dry red wine) and Chateau Grand Traverse Spiced Cherry Wine
Makes 75 meatballs (see Note)

1½ cups CGT Silhouette, or other dry red wine
1½ cups CGT Spiced Cherry Wine
1 (21-oz) bottle Brownwood Farms Cherry BBQ Sauce
¼ cup Brownwood Farms BBQ Mustard
1 cup Brownwood Farms Cherry Salsa
1 bay leaf
75 pre-cooked meatballs (½-oz each)

Mix all ingredients (except meatballs) in large, deep pan or stock pot. Bring to a boil and simmer over medium-low heat for 10 minutes to evaporate alcohol.

Add meatballs and simmer for 30 minutes to heat through. Remove bay leaf.

To Serve: For a buffet occasion, meatballs could be served on toothpicks. Alternatively, they can be served as part of sit-down dinner with vegetable side dish and/or a salad.

Note: This quantity uses one whole bag of pre-cooked meatballs. Serving 6 meatballs per person would make 12+ servings; serving 8 meatballs per person would serve 9+. Or, you could serve 4 people for dinner and freeze the remaining meatballs and sauce for another dinner or a party.

Soups

Salmon Chowder

From Ciccone Vineyard and Winery, submitted by Marcale Sisk
Suggested wine pairing: Ciccone Vineyards Pinot Grigio
Makes 4 to 6 servings

½ cup chopped onions
½ cup chopped celery
½ cup diced red or green sweet pepper
1 garlic clove, chopped
3 Tbs butter
1½ cup diced potatoes
1½ cup diced carrots
3 cups chicken broth
1½ tsp salt
1 tsp dill (fresh or dried)
½ tsp black pepper

1 (15-oz) can salmon, drained
1 (12-oz) can evaporated milk
1 (10-oz) can cream corn

Combine first 11 ingredients in large stock pot. Cover and simmer for 20 minutes.

Add salmon, evaporated milk and cream corn. Mix thoroughly and simmer for 10 minutes.

Enjoy in Good Health!

Gazpacho

From Ciccone Vineyard and Winery, submitted by Joan Ciccone
Suggested wine pairing: Ciccone Vineyard's Pinot Grigio
Makes 6 to 8 cups

4 cups tomato juice
1 green bell pepper, chopped
1 cucumber, chopped
2 lb chopped regular tomatoes, unpeeled
3 Tbs extra virgin olive oil
2 green onions, chopped, with green tops
2 garlic cloves, minced
2 Tbs red wine vinegar
Salt and pepper, to taste

Combine all ingredients in a blender or food processor. Blend until well-combined, but still slightly chunky.

Chill at least 2 hours before serving.

Curried Carrot Soup

From Good Harbor Vineyards, submitted by Taylor Simpson
Recipe created by Patrick Sheerin, Executive Chef, The Signature Room at the 95th, John Hancock Building, Chicago
Suggested wine pairing: Good Harbor Vineyards Late Harvest Riesling
Makes 30 servings

3 yellow onions, peeled and coarsely chopped
5 lb peeled carrots, rough chopped
2" knob of ginger, peeled and thinly sliced
1 cup canola oil
½ cup curry powder
2 Tbs finely minced lemongra
4 kaffir lime leaves
1 Tbs ground coriander
1 tsp ground cumin seeds
1 tsp fenugreek
½ gallon carrot juice
3 (14-oz) cans regular coconut milk
Lime juice, to taste
White soy aka tamari, to taste
Fish sauce, to taste
Brown sugar, to taste

In a very large pot, sweat onions, carrots and ginger in canola oil, until tender-if necessary add water to stop it from burning. Add curry powder, lemongrass, lime leaves, coriander, cumin seeds and fenugreek; toast the spices until fragrant. Add carrot juice and coconut milk, simmer until the vegetables are really soft.

Carefully, puree in the blender adjusting the seasoning with lime juice, fish sauce, tamari and brown sugar (it's all based on taste and the sweetness of the carrots).

Strain through a fine sieve: a chinois will give the smoothest soup.

Chef Patrick Says: This soup freezes successfully.

169

Morel Chanterelle Bisque

From Hawthorne Vineyards, created by Chef Eric Nittolo, Executive Chef, Boat-house Restaurant, Old Mission Peninsula, Traverse City
Suggested wine pairing: Hawthorne Vineyards Pinot Noir
Quantities are "restaurant-sized"; bracketed quantities are "dinner-party" which makes 18-24 servings

5 lb [2½] fresh morel mushrooms (not in pieces) or 1 lb [½ lb] dry morel mushrooms
3 lb [1½ lb] fresh chanterelle mushrooms
3 lb [1½ lb] unsalted butter
1 [½] cup chopped garlic
1 [½] cup chopped shallots
3 [1½] leeks washed, quartered, chopped
1 [½] bottle Chateau d' Origniac (French merlot/pinot dessert wine, Cognac-fortified). B&B is an ok substitute
1 [½] gallon whole milk
3 [1½] gallons heavy cream
Fine ground black pepper, to taste
Kosher salt, to taste
½ lb [¼ lb] unsalted butter, cubed
1 cup [approx ½ cup] all-purpose flour
A lot of patience and love (DON'T HALVE THIS!)

If using dry morels, refresh as follows: place morels and cold water in pot and heat slowly (to not damage the morels) to a temperature that is warm but not boiling. This keeps the flavor in the morels. Drain and save water for other uses.) Dry morels have a more concentrated flavor than the fresh.

In a large heavy bottom pot (minimum 12-quart size for dinner-party quan-tities), slowly melt the butter, being careful not to burn or brown it which changes the flavor. To the melted butter, add garlic, shallots and leeks and allow them to become slightly translucent. Add the mushrooms and sim-mer (i.e., bubbling slightly) for 30 minutes to extract the mushroom flavor. Add the Origniac and simmer for 15 minutes. Stir frequently to prevent burning. Next add milk and cream, and let simmer for 30 minutes.

Once the flavors have melded, season first with pepper and create a subtle peppery bite. Salt is "make or break" of this soup, so "push your limits" - be generous as you add the salt, mixing with a wire whisk to fully dissolve the salt and tasting as you go so you don't over-salt.

To finish: In a small sauce pot bring the ½ lb [¼ lb] butter to a rolling boil and remove from heat, add the flour slowly to dissolve and with a wire whip mix until it forms a paste, it should clump slightly in the whisk. If it all sticks in the whisk add more melted butter and it will be perfect, this is called a blonde roux, and return to the heat on high for about a minute more time to make sure that the roux is incorporated. Add the roux to the soup and simmer soup, stirring occasionally, for 15 minutes. This is your thickener.

Chef Eric Says: (1) Always read through your entire recipe before starting any cooking project. (2) Recipe uses two kinds of mushroom: chanterelles and morels. Portabellas are also good. (3) You could fur-ther decrease the quantities from the smaller [bracketed] quantities, but the result will not be the same. Better to make the restaurant size or the dinner-party size, cooking the recipe right through and freezing what you don't use.

Roasted Cauliflower Soup

From Brys Estate Vineyard & Winery, recipe created by Patrick Brys
Suggested wine pairing: Brys Estate Cabernet Franc/Merlot blend
Serves 6 to 8

2 heads cauliflower, cut into florets
1 large russet potato, cut into 1-inch cubes
1 large yellow onion, cut into 1-inch wedges
Olive oil
8 cups chicken stock
¼ cup heavy cream
Salt, preferably Kosher
Black pepper, freshly ground

Preheat oven to 425°F.

Place the prepared cauliflower, potato and onion on a large sheet pan. Driz-zle with olive oil and sprinkle with salt. Toss. Roast in oven for 30 to 40 min-utes, turning once, until cauliflower is nicely browned.

Transfer roasted vegetables to a large soup pot. Add chicken stock and bring to a boil. Cover and simmer for 20 to 30 minutes, until the vegetables are soft. Puree the soup, using an immersion blender (best and easiest) or a traditional blender or food processor (working in batches).

To the pureed soup, add cream, 1½ to 2 tsp salt (depending on the chicken stock you use) and ¾ tsp pepper and stir to combine.

To Serve: Garnish with fresh-made croutons. To make the croutons, cut up bread of your choice (pumpernickel or multi-grain work well for this soup) into large chunks, toss with a little olive oil, salt and pepper, and then cook in a large skillet over medium heat until browned and crispy on all sides.

Red Lentil Soup

From Storrer Family, submitted by Patricia Storrer
Suggested wine pairing: Cabernet Franc or Cab/Franc blend from Old Mission
Peninsula or Leelanau Peninsula
Makes 6 servings

2 to 3 Tbs extra virgin olive oil
1 large onion, finely chopped
2 to 4 garlic cloves, finely chopped
1 large carrot, finely chopped
1 tsp brown sugar
⅛ tsp chili powder, to start with
⅛ tsp curry powder, to start with
1 (14-oz) can diced tomato, not drained
1 cup red lentils, don't rinse yet or they turn to concrete!
3 pints chicken stock
Salt and freshly ground black pepper, to taste

The Author's Wife, Editor and Co-Author preparing to make her Red Lentil Soup

Heat oil in a heavy pot over medium heat; stir in garlic and onion. When onion begins to change color, stir in carrot, sugar, chili powder and curry powder. Cook for 2 to 3 minutes, and then add the tomato.

Rinse and drain the lentils and immediately pour them into the pot and thoroughly mix with the vegetable/oil mixture. Add stock, stir well, bring to boil, lower heat, partially cover pot, and simmer until lentils have broken up, 45 to 60 minutes.

Adjust the flavoring, if desired, adding up to another ⅛ tsp each of chili powder and curry powder. If needed (this depends on your chicken stock), add salt and pepper. Also, if desired, add a little water to thin your soup. Cook for another 15 minutes to meld the flavors.

To Serve: This soup works well pureed or with its natural slightly chunky vegetable texture. Dress it up, if you like, with a little chopped red onion and/or flat-leaf parsley.

Pat Says: This winter lunch favorite freezes well.

Salads

Asian Pasta Salad

From Leelanau Cellars, submitted by Carrie Hanson
Suggested wine pairing: Leelanau Cellars Dry Riesling
Makes 6 servings

2 cups broccoli florets
1 cup snow peas, fresh (needs blanching) or frozen peas (will thaw when tossed in with salad)
1 (16-oz) package pasta
1 cup Asian-style salad dressing
1 red bell pepper, chopped
1 cup carrot slivers
½ cup diced red onion
1 Tbs minced fresh ginger
1 Tbs minced fresh garlic
Salt and ground black pepper, to taste
1 Tbs sesame oil
½ Tbs sesame seeds, toasted

Blanch broccoli in rapidly boiling water for 3 to 5 minutes. Immediately plunge them in an ice water bath. Remove from the water and drain.

Blanch snow peas (if using) for 1 to 2 minutes. Plunge these in an ice water bath. Promptly remove from water and drain.

Cook the pasta in a large pan of boiling water until al dente. Drain and transfer to a large bowl.

Toss the pasta with the salad dressing. Toss with broccoli, red pepper, carrot, red onion, snow peas, ginger, and garlic. Season with salt and pepper to taste.

Refrigerate for several hours or overnight.

To Serve: Sprinkle with sesame oil and toasted sesame seeds. Enjoy!

Carrie Says: Regarding the choice of pasta - choose between linguini, Asian-style buckwheat soba noodles, or a wide rice noodle. All are recommended. Prepare one of these choices by using the specific package directions. Be aware that rice noodles will cook very differently than egg-based linguini; it is important to follow the directions on the individual noodle package.

Sparkling Wine Vinaigrette

From L.Mawby Vineyards, submitted by Dayna Valpey
Featuring L. Mawby and/or M. Lawrence sparkling wines
Makes 1½ cups

1 tsp Dijon mustard
1 tsp minced fresh garlic
¼ cup of champagne vinegar
½ cup of L. Mawby or M. Lawrence sparkling wine
1 cup extra virgin olive oil
Salt and freshly ground pepper, to taste

Try adding fresh herbs for different flavors.

Whisk together Dijon mustard, garlic, champagne vinegar, sparkling wine. While whisking, slowly add the olive oil until the vinaigrette is emulsified. Season with salt and pepper to taste.

Refrigerate any leftover dressing and use within one week.

Dayna Says: This is a quick and easy way to dress up any of your homemade vinaigrettes. It's also a great way to use up any leftover L. Mawby or M. Lawrence sparkling wines from Brut to Demi Sec.

Main

Satay Tofu

From L.Mawby Vineyards, submitted by Dayna Valpey
Suggested wine pairing: MLawrence Wet Sec Sparkling Wine or LMawby Conservancy Extra Sec Methode Champenoise Sparkling Wine
Makes 4 servings

2 cups jasmine rice

Satay Tofu:
⅓ cup vegetable oil
16 oz firm tofu, coarsely chopped
1 Tbs peanut oil
1 garlic clove, crushed
2 tsp grated fresh ginger
1 medium brown onion, coarsely chopped
¼ cup peanut butter
¼ cup light soy sauce
¼ cup sweet chilli sauce
½ cup hot water
1 (14-oz) can coconut cream
1 Tbs coarsely chopped fresh coriander

Cook rice in large saucepan of boiling water, uncovered, until just tender; drain.

Meanwhile, heat vegetable oil in large frying pan, add tofu; cook, in batches, stirring, until browned all over. Drain on absorbent paper.

Heat peanut oil in large frying pan, add garlic, ginger and onion; cook, stirring until onion softens. Add peanut butter, sauces, water and coconut cream. Bring to boil; reduce heat, simmer, uncovered, about 5 minutes or until sauce thickens. Add tofu and coriander; stir to heat through.

Serve this vegan Satay Tofu dish with the cooked rice.

Cherry Balsamic Short Ribs

From Bowers Harbor Vineyards, submitted by Justin Leshinsky
Suggested wine pairing: Bowers Harbor Vineyards Pinot Noir, Wind Whistle
Makes 6 servings

3 lb beef short ribs, trimmed
Salt and fresh ground black pepper, to taste
4 Tbs olive oil, divided
1 onion, chopped
2 celery stalks, chopped
2 carrots, chopped
1 fennel bulb, sliced
1 cup Burgundy wine (such as a Pinot Noir)
3 sprigs fresh rosemary
8 sprigs fresh thyme
3 bay leaves
2½ Tbs beef demi-glace
4 cups chicken stock
1 cup cherry cola
⅓ cup balsamic vinegar
2 cups frozen pitted tart cherries, thawed
1 Tbs butter

Preheat oven to 350°F.

Sprinkle ribs with salt and pepper.

Heat a heavy cast-iron pot or Dutch oven over medium heat until it just begins to give off wisps of smoke, then drizzle in about 1½ Tbs of the olive oil. Sear 3 ribs in the hot oil until golden brown on all sides. Transfer seared ribs to plate. Heat pot until smoking hot again, drizzle in another 1½ Tbs of the oil, and sear the remaining ribs as before. Transfer remaining ribs to a plate and set aside. Discard used oil.

Place remaining 1 Tbs of the oil in the pot over medium heat, and stir in onion, celery, carrots, and fennel. Sprinkle with a pinch of salt, and cook until the vegetables are soft and the onions are translucent, stirring frequently, about 8 minutes. Pour in Burgundy wine; scrape and dissolve all the browned flavor bits from bottom of pot. Bring mixture to a boil, and cook until liquid is reduced by half, about 10 minutes. Stir in rosemary, thyme, bay leaves, and demi-glace; stir well. Mix in chicken stock, cherry cola, and balsamic vinegar.

Push the short ribs into the vegetable mixture so the ribs are about halfway covered; spread cherries over the ribs. Pour any meat juices over the cherries; bring the entire mixture to a boil over medium heat, and cover.

Place covered pot in preheated oven; cook until meat is tender and falling off the bones, 3½ to 4 hours.

Remove ribs to a serving platter. Skim fat from the cherry sauce, and strain cherries, vegetables, and juices through a fine-mesh sieve into a bowl. Discard the solids, and return liquid to the pot. Bring to a boil, and cook the sauce over medium heat until thickened, about 10 minutes, stirring frequently; whisk in butter.

To Serve: Serve sauce over the short ribs.

Pork Chops in Chardonnay

From Raftshol Vineyards, submitted by Warren Raftshol
Featuring Raftshol Vineyards Chardonnay
Makes 4 servings

¼ tsp salt, or to taste
¼ tsp black pepper, or to taste
½ tsp dry mustard
2 Tbs flour (divided 1 Tbs, 1 Tbs)
4 pork chops (boneless or bone-in)
Butter, about ¼ stick, sufficient to sauté onions in large pan
1 medium onion, diced
1 cup Raftshol Vineyards Chardonnay
1 cup water

Put dry ingredients (salt, pepper, mustard, 1 Tbs flour) in plastic bag and shake to mix; add chops and shake to coat them.

In pan big enough to hold all four chops in single layer, sauté onions in butter over medium heat till onions are translucent.

Increase heat to medium high, add chops and brown on both sides.

Reduce heat to simmer. Pour ½ cup of the wine into pan along with remaining dry ingredients from plastic bag. Cover pan and simmer (but not boil) for about 70 minutes or until meat is tender. Add more wine as needed to keep chops covered.

Remove chops from pan and keep warm.

Make gravy: Thoroughly mix the second 1 Tbs flour with 1 cup water. Add to onions and other ingredients in pan. Raise heat to medium high and cook gravy until brown, stirring frequently until gravy is thick.

To Serve: Serve with frozen green peas (cooked!) and white rice topped with the gravy. And drink the rest of your Chardonnay!

Warren Says: Avoid "oaky" Chardonnays for this recipe because the wine flavors are concentrated by reduction. With their nice acid balance, Michigan Chardonnays work well in this recipe.

Cornel's Rabbit Loins Wrapped in Bacon

From Two Lads Winery, recipe created by Cornel Olivier
Suggested wine pairing: Two Lads Fouch Vineyard Riesling
Makes 2 servings, one loin per person

Marinade Ingredients:
1 garlic clove, chopped
Handful each of fresh flat-leaf parsley and thyme,
      finely chopped
juice of ½ lemon
Salt and freshly ground pepper, to taste
2 rabbit loins, cleaned
1 lb bacon, reserve 2 slices
Dressing: ½ cup strawberries, hulled
1 Tbs Dijon mustard
To Garnish:
½ lemon, sliced
Handful chopped walnuts

Mix marinade ingredients and pour into a plastic bag. Add rabbit loins to the bag; seal, and shake ingredients to coat. Refrigerate for 10-12 hours. (It is sufficient to shake initially and then let it sit.)

Preheat oven to 350°F.

Remove marinated loins from the bag. Without patting them dry, place on large plate and let warm to room temperature.

Wrap the loins in bacon, overlapping the bacon strips by a ½-inch to keep them in place. (You could secure the bacon with toothpicks, but the ends could get in the way; better to overlap the ½-inch and handle carefully with tongs.)

In a large sauté pan (suggest 12-inch minimum) cook the 2 reserved bacon slices until the pan has a good coating of bacon fat, about 5 minutes. Put the cooked bacon aside for another use, retaining its fat in the pan.

Place each bacon-wrapped loin in heated pan, with joint facing down. Sear all sides of each loin by moving it round in the pan and rotating it for 2 to 3 minutes total.

Pour the loins and the bacon fat they were cooked in into an oven-proof glass baking pan. Bake for total 5 to 6 minutes, turning the loans over occasionally. Total cooking time may vary, depending on your oven. The loins are ready when the insides are slightly pink, which is medium rare. Remove bacon-wrapped loins from the oven and let cool for 10 minutes.

Make the dressing. Blend strawberries and Dijon mustard in a food processor until smooth.

To Serve: When the dressing is ready, thinly slice through the loins and their bacon wrapping. Plate on bed of mixed greens and drizzle your dressing over it. Garnish with lemon slices and chopped walnuts. Serve with unpeeled baked fingerling potatoes.

Cornel Says: If you prefer more bacon flavor than you get from the wrapped loins, add some of the bacon fat from the pan to the strawberry dressing. Add this extra bacon fat while blending the ingredients in the food processor.

Creamy Indian-Spiced Halibut Curry

From Bowers Harbor Vineyards, submitted by Kristy McClellan
Suggested wine pairing Bowers Harbor Vineyards Gewürztraminer
Makes 4 (generous) servings

2 Tbs canola
1 onion, minced
2 Tbs finely chopped fresh ginger
4 garlic cloves, minced
1 tsp cayenne pepper
1 tsp turmeric
1 tsp ground coriander
1 cup plain whole-milk yogurt
1 cup heavy cream
1 Tbs Garam Masala
Pinch of saffron threads, crumbled
Kosher salt, to taste
2 lb halibut fillets, skinless, cut into 4-inch pieces
Basmati rice and warm naan, for serving

In large deep skillet, heat oil over moderate heat.

Add onion, ginger and garlic; cook, stirring frequently, till lightly browned, about 6 minutes.

Add cayenne, turmeric and coriander; cook for 1 minute, stirring.

Whisk in yogurt, then add cream, Garam Masala and saffron, and bring to a boil.

Reduce heat and simmer sauce until slightly thickened, about 10 minutes. Season with salt.

Add halibut to sauce; turn to coat. Cook over moderate heat, turning once, till fish is cooked through, about 10 minutes.

To Serve: Serve with basmati rice and warm naan.

Grilled Chicken and Peaches

From Boathouse Vineyards, submitted by Dave Albert
Suggested wine pairing: Boathouse Vineyards "Seas the Day" semi-sweet white wine
Makes 4 servings

Glaze:
1 cup peach spreadable fruit
2 Tbs olive oil
4 tsp soy sauce
1 Tbs ground mustard
1 garlic clove, minced
½ tsp salt
¼ tsp cayenne pepper

4 boneless chicken breasts
8 medium peaches, halved and pitted

In a small bowl, combine the first seven (7) ingredients. Set aside.

Preheat grill to a medium heat. Coat the grill rack with oil.

Grill chicken (covered) over medium heat, 5 to 7 minutes on each side, or until completely cooked. Baste the chicken with the glaze occasionally during grilling – but not before grilling.

Set chicken aside. Keep warm.

Place peaches cut side down on grill. Grill 8 to 10 minutes or until tender. Turn and baste every 2 minutes.

To Serve: Serve with sides of fresh green beans and red skin potatoes, prepared any style that appeals to you.

Dave says: Perfect light fare for summer!

Risotto with Butternut Squash, Pancetta, and Jack Cheese

From Bowers Harbor Vineyards, submitted by Kristy McClellan
Suggested wine pairing: Bowers Harbor Vineyards RLS Chardonnay Reserve
Makes 4 servings

1½ lb butternut squash, peeled, seeded, cut into ½-inch cubes
    (about 3½ cups)
Cooking spray
2 cups fat-free, reduced-sodium chicken broth
1⅓ cups water
1 Tbs minced fresh tarragon
2 Tbs Madeira wine or sweet Marsala
4 oz pancetta, chopped
1 cup finely chopped onion
1 tsp olive oil
2 garlic cloves, minced
¾ cup uncooked Arborio or other short-grain rice
⅔ cup (about 2½ oz) ½-inch-cubed Monterey Jack cheese
½ tsp salt
¼ tsp freshly ground black pepper
2 Tbs pine nuts, toasted
Fresh tarragon sprigs (optional)

Preheat oven to 475°F. Place squash on nonstick jelly-roll pan coated with cooking spray. Bake for 20 minutes or until tender, turning after 10 minutes. Remove from oven and keep warm. Reduce oven heat to 325°F.

Combine broth, water, tarragon and wine in a saucepan; bring to a simmer. Keep warm over low heat.

In large Dutch oven (or other ovenproof pan), cook pancetta, over medium high heat, until crisp. Remove pancetta from pan; drain on paper towel. Discard pan drippings. Add onion and oil to (ovenproof) pan; sauté 10 minutes or until onion is tender. Add garlic; sauté 1 minute. Add rice; sauté 1 minute. Stir in broth mixture; bring to a boil over medium heat.

Reduce heat; simmer, uncovered, for 10 minutes. (Do not stir: rice will have liquid consistency similar to stew.)

Place pan, uncovered, in oven; bake at 325°F for 15 minutes. Remove from oven.

Stir in squash, pancetta, cheese, salt, and pepper. Cover with clean cloth; let stand 10 minutes (rice will continue to cook).

To Serve: Sprinkle with pine nuts. Garnish with tarragon sprigs, if desired.

Green-Chili Enchiladas

From Chateau Fontaine Vineyards & Winery, submitted by Lucie Matthies
Suggested wine pairing: Chateau Fontaine Dry Riesling
Makes 6 servings

1 roasted chicken (such as available at supermarkets), or,
    3 large chicken breasts
2 (10-oz) cans Old El Paso Green Enchilada Sauce (or Meijers
    Green Enchilada Sauce Mild)
1 (4½-oz) can Old El Paso Green Chilies, Chopped
1 cup chicken broth
Garlic powder, salt and pepper to taste
1 cup sour cream
12 to 16 white corn tacos (fresh, locally made, if possible)
2 to 3 (8-oz) bags shredded Mexican blend cheese

Prepare the chicken:

If using "supermarket roasted" chicken (which is already seasoned), shred the flesh and discard the skin. Save legs and wings for another recipe.

Or, if using chicken breasts, season with garlic powder, salt and pepper to taste (so they are not so bland); then, bake or grill them. Shred the meat when cool enough to handle.

Preheat oven to 350°F.

Make the green sauce: In a heavy saucepan, heat the enchilada sauce, chilies, and broth, cooking the mixture down for about 30 minutes. Add garlic powder, salt and pepper to taste, let the sauce cool a bit, then stir in sour cream.

Dip each taco in the green sauce, add some chicken and cheese, roll up and put in casserole dish.

When all tacos are filled, rolled and placed in casserole dish, top with more of the cheese.

Bake for 30 minutes.

To Serve: Serve with extra Green Sauce, sour cream and shredded lettuce on the side.

Lucie Says: This can also be layered lasagna-style if you have trouble rolling the tacos – some mass-produced varieties tend to crack easily. Since this recipe is relatively mild, Hot Green Sauce can be used on top by those who want it "hot".

Grilled Orange-Glazed Pork Tenderloin

From L. Mawby Vineyards, submitted by Michael Laing
Suggested wine pairing: M.Lawrence Green sparkling wine (extra sec, cuve close method)
Makes 4 to 6 servings

Marmalade Glaze:
½ cup orange (preserves-style) marmalade
3 Tbs orange juice concentrate
1 lemon: 2 tsp grated zest plus 2 Tbs juice
2 tsp minced fresh thyme leaves
3 garlic cloves, pressed through garlic press

1 tsp vegetable oil, plus more for grill grate
2 pork tenderloins, 2 lb in total
Salt and pepper, to taste

Mix marmalade glaze: Process marmalade, orange juice concentrate, lemon zest, lemon juice, thyme and garlic in food processor. Or, whisk to combine.

Simmer mixed glaze over medium heat until thick, about 3 minutes.

Transfer ⅓ of the marmalade glaze to 9x13-inch baking dish, for use in the last step.

Heat grill and grate on high for about 15 minutes. Scrape grill and swab vegetable oil onto grate with paper towel held with tongs.

Pat pork dry with paper towels, and then rub with 1 teaspoon of the oil and season with salt and pepper.

Grill pork, covered, for about 8 minutes.

Brush pork all over with the next one third of the marmalade glaze.

Continue grilling, glazing (using the last one third of the glaze) every two minutes until meat reads 140°F internal temperature (another 4 to 8 minutes).

Transfer pork to the baking dish with the marmalade glaze and roll to coat pork with the glaze.

To Serve: Let rest 5 minutes under foil tent. Slice and serve.

Michael Says: Recommended side is red or black beans and rice.

Roasted Rosemary Pork Tenderloin with Sauvignon Blanc Cream Sauce

From Laurentide Winery, Leelanau Peninsula. Submitted by Susan Braymer
Suggested wine pairing: Laurentide Sauvignon Blanc
Makes 4 servings

1 (approx 1 lb) pork tenderloin
2 Tbs dried rosemary
1 tsp dried thyme
Cracked pepper and sea salt, to taste
2 Tbs extra virgin olive oil
1 red onion, sliced
⅔ cup Laurentide Sauvignon Blanc
⅔ cup heavy cream

Season pork with rosemary, thyme, pepper and salt. Let rest on counter until meat is room temperature.

Preheat oven to 425°F.

Heat oil in cast iron skillet large enough to hold the tenderloin.

Sear pork on medium high heat on all sides.

Leaving pork in skillet, add onion and sauté about until softened, about 2 minutes.

Carefully transfer (hot) cast iron pan, with port and onion, to preheated oven.

Roast about 25 minutes or until instant read thermometer reads 150°F.

Remove meat from skillet and cover with foil in warm place as meat continues cooking to 160°F.

On high heat, deglaze pan with the Sauvignon Blanc wine until reduced by about half. Add any captured drippings from the resting meat.

Whisk in cream and simmer (over low heat) until thickened.

To Serve: Slice pork, spoon sauce over and enjoy! Serve with roasted Yukon gold potatoes, fresh green beans.

Susan Says: Simple elegance for fall or spring.

Leelanau Cottage Pie

From Left Foot Charley, submitted by Meridith Lauzon
Suggested wine pairing: Left Foot Charley Dry Riesling
Makes 6 servings

Filling: 2 Tbs olive oil
3 slices thick cut bacon, cubed
12 chicken thighs, not boneless
2 leeks, white part only, thinly sliced
1 shallot, minced
2 carrots, peeled, thinly sliced
 1 cup Left Foot Charley Dry Riesling
2 cups chicken stock
4 cups cremini mushrooms, sliced
3 bay leaves
1 Tbs dried thyme
Salt and pepper, to taste

Topping:
4 lb assorted root vegetables (such as parsnips, squash, rutabaga)
1 Tbs olive oil
1½ tsp salt
¼ tsp freshly cracked pepper
6 Tbs butter
3 large egg yolks

Make Filling: Heat oil in Dutch oven or other heavy bottomed pot (with lid). Add bacon, fry until crispy; remove and set aside. Add chicken thighs and brown on all sides, working in batches if necessary; set aside. Add leeks and shallot, lightly sauté until fragrant, 1 to 2 minutes. Add carrots, sauté for another 1 minute. Deglaze pan with wine and simmer for 1 minute. Return chicken and bacon to the pot. Add stock, mushrooms, bay leaf and thyme. Bring to a simmer, cover and cook 30 to 40 minutes or until sauce achieves gravy-like consistency. (Part way through cooking, check flavor and add salt and pepper to taste.) Remove chicken thighs, pull meat from bone and shred. Return to pot.

Make Topping: Preheat oven to 425°F. Peel root vegetables and chop into uniform pieces. Toss with oil, salt and pepper, place in roasting pan and roast till tender, about 30 minutes. Place roasted vegetable and butter in food processor, puree until smooth. Add yolks and mix till incorporated.

Finish: Reduce oven heat to 350°F. Transfer filling to 9x13-inch baking dish, and then spoon topping evenly over surface. Bake till browned around edges, about 25 minutes.

Majaraja Curry (mah-ha-rasha)

From Gill's Pier Vineyard & Winery, submitted by Laurie Conney
Created by Chef Kristin Karam, Chef de Cuisine/Owner, K2 Events and Edibles.
Traverse City
Suggested wine pairing: Gill's Pier Semi-dry Estate Riesling
Makes 6 to 8 servings

⅓ cup vegetable or canola oil
3 large red onions, peeled, finely minced (or pulsed on its own
        in food processor till fine)
¼ cup fresh ginger, peeled, minced (or, pulse ginger, jalapeño,
        garlic together in food processor)
1 jalapeño pepper, minced fine (see "Chef Kristin Says", below)
1 garlic head, cloves separated, peeled, finely minced

Spices:
3 Tbs Garam Masala
1 Tbs Chat Masala (or substitute 1 pinch each of cumin and turmeric)
1 Tbs ground cinnamon
1 Tbs cayenne (see "Chef Kristin Says", below)

2 cups vegetable stock
2 cups puréed tomatoes: 1 (14-oz) can pureed tomato would do
2 cups cooked chickpeas: 1 (14-oz) can chickpeas, drained, would do
1 cup heavy cream
1 bunch cilantro, coarsely chopped

With burner on medium, heat oil in Dutch oven-style pan or other high-sided, heavy-bottomed 10-inch pan. Add onions to hot oil, and sauté, reducing heat to ensure onions do not burn. With wooden spoon, constantly scrape the fond created at bottom of pan. Continue cooking onion till the oils separate, about 20 minutes.

Add ginger, the four spices, jalapeño and garlic and sweat them into the onion, 2 to 3 minutes. Add spices and toast till they start to separate to the top of the mixture. Add vegetable stock and stir to combine. Add tomatoes and chickpeas, and bring mixture to a simmer. Your curry is now cooked.

Remove from the heat and stir in cream and cilantro to finish your curry.

To Serve: Serve this vegetarian curry over basmati rice; maybe, also, with vegetable kabobs.

Chef Kristin Says: This simple-to-make curry is medium hot. You can reduce the "heat" by (any or all of) reducing the cayenne quantity, by de-seeding the jalapeño, by reducing the jalapeño quantity. The cream and cilantro also help to reduce the heat.

Mediterranean Quinoa Salad and Grilled Salmon

From Leelanau Cellars, submitted by Carrie Hanson
Suggested wine pairing: Leelanau Cellars Baco Noir Rose
Makes 4 to 6 salad servings

Quinoa:
2 cups water
2 cups chicken bouillon
1 garlic clove, chopped
1 cup uncooked quinoa

Salad:
1 large red onion, diced
1 large green bell pepper, diced
1 large red bell pepper, diced
1 cucumber, peeled seeded and diced
1 large carrot, peeled and diced
½ cup chopped Kalamata olives
½ cup crumbled feta cheese
⅓ cup chopped fresh flat-leaf (Italian) parsley
¼ cup chopped fresh chives
Zest of 1 lemon
½ teaspoon salt
⅔ cup fresh lemon juice
1 Tbs balsamic vinegar
¼ cup extra virgin olive oil

Salmon:
1 (6 to 8 oz) fillet of salmon, not skinned, per person
Olive oil
Salt and pepper
Dried Italian Herb Blend (rosemary, thyme, basil)
Lemon slice

Cook Quinoa: Bring water, bouillon, and garlic to a boil in a saucepan. Stir in quinoa. Reduce heat to medium-low, cover, and simmer until quinoa is tender and the water has been absorbed. 15 to 20 minutes. Scrape the quinoa into a large bowl. Let the quinoa cool.

Make Salad: Gently stir the onion, bell peppers, cucumber, carrots, olives, feta cheese, parsley, chives, lemon zest, and salt into the quinoa. Drizzle with the lemon juice, balsamic vinegar, and olive oil. Stir until evenly mixed. Taste. Adjust seasonings if necessary. The salad is best served at room temperature.

Grill Salmon: Preheat grill to a medium high temperature. Brush both sides of each fillet with oil and sprinkle flesh side with salt, pepper, and dried Italian Herb Blend. Put flesh side of each fillet down first and sear on the grill for 3-4 minutes. Turn each fillet over and sear another 3 to 4 minutes until fully cooked (opaque and not translucent in the center).

To Serve: Serve salmon fillets, topped with lemon slices, next to the Mediterranean Quinoa Salad.

Northern Michigan Spring Pizza

From Two Lads Winery, submitted by Caryn Chachulski
Suggested wine pairing: Two Lads Rosé of Cabernet Franc or Two Lads Pinot Noir
Makes one 14-inch pizza

White Sauce:
2 garlic cloves, chopped
2 Tbs butter
1 to 2 Tbs flour
2 cups heavy cream
½ cup Parmesan cheese, grated

Ramp Pesto:
10 to 12 ramps, cleaned and dried, green parts separated
    from white parts
About ½ cup walnuts, toasted, (or, pine nuts or any other
    preferred nuts)
About ½ cup Parmesan cheese, grated
⅓ to ½ cup extra virgin olive oil
Salt and pepper, to taste
1 lb frozen pizza dough, thawed (or your own favorite pizza
    dough recipe)
Large handful fresh morels
½ to 1 Tbs butter
4-6 oz Raclette cheese, shredded

Make White Sauce: Sauté garlic in butter in a pan. Add flour and stir, about 2 minutes. Add heavy cream and continue to stir until sauce comes to a boil. Reduce heat and keep stirring while sauce thickens, another 3 to 4 minutes. Remove from heat and whisk in Parmesan cheese. If sauce seems too thick, thin with a little milk. If it doesn't seem thick enough, stir in a little more cheese. Sauce will thicken as it cools.

Make Ramp Pesto: Chop the white part of the ramps and sauté in a little of the olive oil over medium heat until translucent, 5 to 7 minutes. Toss ramps (green parts and sautéed white parts), nuts, and Parmesan into a food processor. Drizzle oil into the processor as it's running until you get the consistency you want. Season with salt and pepper.

Prepare Morels: Carefully rinse morels, drain, pat dry and then slice, not too thin. Sauté morels in butter over medium heat, 1 to 2 minutes. Drain liquid and butter from morels.

The Pizza: Preheat oven to 450°F. Throw/work dough until it fits on a 14-inch pizza pan (or stone). Partially bake dough until just starting to crisp, 5 to 7 minutes.

Finish Pizza: Remove partially-cooked pizza from oven and top with the white sauce. Scatter the sautéed morels about. Drizzle the ramp pesto around here and there. Top with Raclette cheese and put the finished pizza in the oven until cheese melts and starts to brown (5 to 7 minutes more).

Serve on its own, or with mixed baby greens and (maybe) a poached egg.

Caryn says: (1) The epitome of our Northern Michigan spring, this pizza is a favorite when morels and ramps abound. (2) The Ramp Pesto is also a great base to use tossed with pasta, over salmon, or smeared on a toasted baguette. (3) The same pizza quantities also work on a 12-inch giving a slightly thicker pizza.

Honey Mustard Turkey Burger

From Boathouse Vineyards, submitted by Dave Albert
Suggested wine pairing: Boathouse Vineyards Pinot Grigio or Dry Riesling
Makes 4 servings

Sauce: ¼ cup honey
¼ cup Dijon mustard
Salt and pepper, to taste
1 lb ground turkey
Salt and pepper, to taste
8 bacon strips
4 slices sharp Cheddar cheese
4 buns
1 granny smith apple
Tomato slices
Lettuce leaves

In a small bowl, mix together honey, mustard, salt and pepper. Set aside.

Form ground turkey into 4 even-sized patties. Salt and pepper them to taste.

Cook bacon over medium heat until crisp. Set bacon aside on plate covered with paper towel.

On grill, cook turkey patties on medium high for 4 minutes. Flip and cook for another 2 minutes. Place cheese on patties and cook for the last 2 minutes.

While turkey patties are still on grill, place buns, inside-down, on grill for 30 seconds or until lightly toasted.

Core but do not peel apple. Cut apple in half round its "equator"; then cut two ¼-inch slices from each half. You want the widest part of the apple.

Assemble burgers: On bottom half of each bun, place a turkey patty, then 2 bacon slices, then 1 apple slice, then a tomato slice and finally a lettuce leaf. Spoon sauce over inside of top half of bun and place bun on patty.

Dave Says: This is perfect light fare for summer! Be sure that your turkey patties are cooked to well done.

Poppy's Chicken Cacciatore (Hunter's Chicken)

From Forty-Five North Vineyard & Winery; submitted by Kirstin Policastro
Suggested wine pairing: Forty-Five North Estate Grown Pinot Noir Merlot or Reserve Chardonnay
Makes 4 servings, with plenty left over

2 to 3 Tbs butter, divided
2 to 4 Tbs extra virgin olive oil, divided
6 each bone-in chicken legs and thighs, 12 pieces altogether, fat
        and skin trimmed (skin can be retained for extra flavor)
1 large or 2 medium sweet onions, chopped
1 (12-oz) package fresh mushrooms (button, white, cremini or
        portabella), sliced
½ cup pitted Kalamata Olives
2 Tbs capers, drained
½ cup red table wine, or more depending on pan size and volume
        of ingredients
1 large potato, peeled, chopped (more if needed)
2 (14-oz) cans good quality stewed tomatoes, "rough-chopped"
        and drained. Reserve the drained juice.
Salt and pepper to taste

Note: this recipe is finished in the oven but each of the ingredients is first sautéed or browned on the stove and then combined in a Dutch oven or similar large baking dish (with lid) that can go from oven to table.

Preheat oven to 350°F.

Heat sauté pan over medium heat. Add 2 Tbs of the butter and 2 Tbs of the olive oil. Brown chicken pieces on all sides to seal in juices. Transfer chicken pieces to plate and keep warm.

Drain fat from sauté pan. In the same pan, add as much as you need (maybe none) of the remaining 1 Tbs of the butter and 2 Tbs of the olive oil, then sauté onions and mushrooms, adding the olives and capers at the end of the sauté. Deglaze sauté pan with wine.

In the Dutch oven, assemble all ingredients: chicken, vegetables, wine with deglazed bits from the pan, potato and drained tomatoes. Add enough of the tomato juice so the liquid just covers the other ingredients.

Bake, covered, until chicken falls off the bone, 1 to 1½ hours, depending on your oven. Add more of the drained tomato juice if liquid starts to boil down: you want enough broth to dredge bread at serving time.

Serve with crusty Italian bread.

Kirstin Says: This recipe can easily be increased or decreased as needed.

Pork Braised in Cider

From Tandem Ciders, submitted by Nikki Rothwell
Suggested wine pairing: Tandem Ciders Smackintosh (a sweet cider)
Makes 4 to 6 servings

3 medium carrots, washed, peeled
3 medium garlic cloves
3½ to 4 lb pork center loin or Boston butt
1 Tbs vegetable oil
2 Tbs butter
Flour, spread on a plate
2 Tbs Tandem Ciders Pomona (an apple brandy)
1½ cups, or more, Tandem Ciders Farmhouse Cider (a dry cider)
"Tiny" grating of whole nutmeg (about ⅛ tsp)
2 bay leaves
Several pinches salt
Liberal grindings fresh ground black pepper

Cut carrots lengthwise into sticks ⅜-inch thick or less. Slice the garlic cloves into small stick-like pieces. Take a long, pointed fairly thick tool to pierce the meat at both ends in as many places as you have carrot and garlic sticks (keep the holes about 1 inch apart). Stuff the carrot and garlic sticks into the holes.

Choose a heavy-bottomed or enameled cast iron pot (with lid), just large enough to contain the meat snugly.

Put in oil and butter in pot and turn heat to medium high. When the butter foam begins to subside, turn the meat in the flour, coating it all over, and put into the pot. Brown the meat deeply on all sides. When you have browned the meat, add the Pomona apple brandy. Allow to simmer for a few seconds then pour in the cider until just shy of covering the meat. If the 1½ cups do not suffice, add more, depending on pan size.

Add nutmeg, bay leaves, salt, and pepper. Turn the pork once or twice.

When the cider begins to simmer briskly, adjust heat to a very gentle simmer, and cover the pot tightly. Cook at slow heat for three hours or more, occasionally turning the meat, until it feels tender when prodded with a fork. After 2½ hours, check to see how much liquid remains. If there is a substantial amount, set the lid ajar, and turn up the heat a little.

When done, there should be a small amount of syrupy sauce left in the pot. Transfer the meat to a cutting board, slice it thin and arrange the slices on a warm serving platter. Spoon all the pot juices over the meat and serve at once.

Riesling Chicken

From Shady Lane Cellars, recipe created by Adam Satchwell
Suggested wine pairing: Shady Lane Cellars Dry Riesling or Shady Lane Cellars Semi-Dry Riesling
Makes 4 servings

5 Tbs olive oil, divided
4 oz pancetta, chopped (do not substitute bacon – its smoke curing can overpower the other flavors)
2½ to 3 lb assorted chicken pieces, washed, dried thoroughly (boneless/skinless pieces do not work well)
Salt and pepper, to taste
1 oz brandy
2 cups dry Riesling
2 cups good chicken stock
4 garlic cloves, minced
¼ tsp thyme
1 bay leaf
48 pearl onions (use frozen; the jarred variety get mushy), thawed
½ lb fresh mushrooms, quartered
3 Tbs all-purpose flour
2 Tbs butter, softened
Fresh flat-leaf parsley, chopped

Heat 2 Tbs of the olive oil in large, heavy skillet over medium-high heat, sauté pancetta until lightly browned; set aside.

Season chicken with salt and pepper. Brown on sides, working in several batches to not crowd the chicken.

Return pancetta and chicken to pan, reduce heat to medium-low, cover and cook for 10 minutes, turning chicken once. Remove cover, add brandy, let warm for 10 seconds and then ignite (CAREFULLY!), swirl pan by handle to help the brandy flame completely. Once flames die, add Riesling, chicken stock, garlic, thyme and bay leaf; cover and simmer slowly for 30 minutes or until chicken is done.

While chicken simmers, cook the onions and mushrooms. Unless cooked separately, their liquid will dilute the dish. Lightly brown onions in another 2 Tbs of the olive oil, set aside. Lightly season the mushrooms with salt and pepper. To that same pan, add last 1 Tbs of the olive oil and lightly brown the seasoned mushrooms. Combine with onions. With small amount of liquid from chicken pan, deglaze the onion/mushroom pan, reduce the liquid to almost nothing and combine the resulting onion/mushroom mixture with the chicken simmering in the separate pan.

When chicken is done, remove it and the onions and mushrooms to platter and keep warm. Leave liquid in pan. Increase heat to high and reduce liquid. Combine flour and softened butter thoroughly. When liquid is reduced to 2 cups add flour/butter to liquid and whisk. The resulting sauce should be just thick enough to coat the back of a spoon. If too thin, reduce until desired consistency; if too thick, add a little more chicken stock. Reduce heat under sauce to simmer, add back chicken, onions and mushrooms and warm briefly.

Serve on a platter and garnish with chopped parsley.

Adam Says: This recipe is a variation of the classic Coq au Vin.

Beef Verterra

From Verterra Winery, submitted by Marty Hamelin
Featuring: Verterra Chaos Red Cuvee' table wine
Makes 6 servings

2 lb sirloin steak in ½-inch cubes
1 packet dried onion soup mix
2 tsp garlic powder
2 Tbs butter
3 cups Verterra Chaos Red Cuvee' table wine
2 Tbs parsley flakes
1 bay leaf
½ lb portabella mushrooms
½ lb white mushrooms
1 to 2 cups carrots, thickly sliced, or small whole baby carrots
Pepper, to taste

Shake first 3 ingredients (sirloin, onion soup mix, garlic powder) in a sealed plastic bag for at least 4 hours.

In an electric fry pan at low-medium heat, add butter and sauté the marinated ingredients until browned.

Add the remaining ingredients, except for the carrots

Cook, in the electric fry pan, at 225°F for 1½ to 2 hours, adding carrots for the last 30 minutes of cooking.

Sides

Pasta Carbonara

From Chateau Grand Traverse Winery & Vineyards
Wine pairing suggestion: Chateau Grand Traverse Dry Riesling, or a dry red such as (CGT) Silhouette or (CGT) Gamay Noir
Makes 4 generous servings as main course or 6 as side dish

Pasta:
1 lb spaghetti or rigatoni

Bacon Mixture:
2 Tbs olive oil
1 Tbs butter
4 garlic cloves, crushed
½ lb bacon, chopped in pieces about ¼-inch long
¼ cup Chateau Grand Traverse Dry Riesling wine

Egg/Cheese Mixture:
3 eggs
¼ cup Romano cheese, grated
¼ cup Parmesan cheese, grated
Pepper, to taste
1 Tbs chopped flat leaf (Italian) parsley

Boil water and cook pasta while preparing sauce.

Place oil, butter and crushed garlic into small sauté pan and sauté over low to medium heat until garlic turns deep gold, being careful not to burn it. Remove garlic and discard.

Put the bacon in the pan and sauté until crisp on the edges.

Add the wine and let the mixture boil for 2 minutes, and then turn off the heat.

Into a large bowl, break the eggs, adding the cheeses, pepper and parsley.

When pasta is cooked, drain and pour into bowl with egg/cheese mixture. Add bacon mixture; toss thoroughly and serve.

Asparagus Frittata

From Storrer Family, submitted by Patricia Storrer
Suggested wine pairing: an Up North Michigan Auxerroix or Gruner Veltliner
Makes 2 servings

1 to 2 Tbs butter
⅓ to ½ lb asparagus, washed, trimmed, cut diagonally
      about ⅜-inch thick
3 or 4 eggs
Salt and freshly ground black pepper, to taste
Approx 1 Tbs water
Sprinkle of grated Parmesan cheese

Heat butter in oven-proof 10-inch frying pan, over medium heat, moving melting butter well up the pan sides. Add asparagus, lower heat to low-medium and sauté till bright green and still slightly crisp, 3 to 5 minutes depending on thickness and age of asparagus stalks.

Lightly beat together the eggs, salt, pepper and water.

Turn on your stove's broiler.

Return pan heat to medium and distribute asparagus evenly around pan. Carefully pour in beaten egg, lightly sprinkle grated Parmesan on top of the egg and cook until egg is cooked at edges. (Don't overdo the cheese or it will over-power your asparagus flavor.)

Place pan under hot broiler to finish cooking the frittata until golden brown, 2 to 3 minutes. The pan's handle will become very hot under the broiler — time for an oven mitt.

To Serve: Divide frittata in two halves, slide from the pan and serve immediately.

Israeli Couscous with Asparagus, Peas and Feta

From Brys Estate Vineyard & Winery, recipe created by Patrick Brys
Suggested wine pairing: Brys Estate Naked Chardonnay (an unoaked Chardonnay)
Serves 6 to 8

Dressing:
2 Tbs olive oil
Zest of 1 lemon
Juice of ½ lemon
1 garlic clove, minced
1 tsp salt
½ tsp freshly ground pepper
2 bunches fresh Michigan asparagus, washed and prepared,
      but not diced
Olive oil, salt and pepper

Couscous:
1 Tbs olive oil
1 cup Israeli Couscous
Sprinkle of salt
2 cups chicken broth

Assembly:
1 cup frozen peas, thawed under cold running water
½ cup crumbled Feta cheese
⅓ cup chopped fresh chives
1 tsp dried mint
Lemon wedges, optional, for garnish

Preheat oven to 400°F.

Make dressing: In a small bowl, combine olive oil, lemon juice, zest, garlic, salt and pepper. Set aside.

Prepare asparagus: On a large sheet pan, toss asparagus with olive oil, salt and pepper, and roast in oven until bright green and crisp tender, 6 to 8 minutes. Set aside.

Prepare couscous. In a large pan, heat 1 Tbs olive oil over medium heat. Add couscous and a sprinkle of salt and sauté until golden brown, about 5 minutes, stirring frequently. Add broth and bring to a boil. Cover and reduce heat to low and simmer until the liquid has been absorbed, about 10 minutes. Transfer couscous to a large mixing bowl.

Assemble: Once the asparagus has cooled, chop diagonally into ¾-inch pieces. Add asparagus to the bowl along with the dressing, peas, feta, chives and mint. Toss well and serve.

To Serve: Garnish with lemon wedges. Serve chilled or at room temperature.

Patrick Says: Serve this as a light lunch or as a side dish with shrimp or chicken. Refrigerated, it keeps well for several days.

Quiche

From Chateau Fontaine Vineyards & Winery, submitted by Lucie Matthies
Suggested wine pairing: Chateau Fontaine Chardonnay
Makes one 9-inch diameter quiche, 4 to 6 servings

¼ cup chopped scallions, white part only
1 Tbs butter
1 9-inch deep dish pie shell
1 cup filling, made up of any combination of the following:
      Asparagus: sliced on the diagonal and parboiled 3-5 minutes
      Fresh herbs: 1 Tbs each of chopped tarragon, chives, dill
      Bacon: 3 slices fried and crumbled
      Mushrooms: sliced and sautéed
1 cup grated Raclette cheese, if available (from Leelanau Cheese
      Company); otherwise, Gruyere cheese
3 eggs
1¼ cup half and half
½ tsp salt
¼ tsp pepper

Preheat oven to 375°F.

Sauté scallions in butter until soft.

Pour scallions, with the butter, into the pie shell, add filling of your choice, sprinkle with cheese.

Beat eggs and half and half, add seasonings, pour into pie shell.

Bake in preheated oven 35 to 40 minutes, or firm and slightly golden.

Eggplant Parmigiana

From Ciccone Vineyard and Winery, submitted by Marcale Sisk
Suggested wine pairing: any Ciccone Vineyards dry red wine
Makes 6 to 8 servings

2 (1-lb) eggplants, peeled, trimmed, cut into ¼-inch rounds
½ cup all-purpose flour, for dredging
3 large eggs, lightly beaten
1 cup fine dry breadcrumbs, or more if needed
½ cup olive oil, or more if needed
3 cups tomato basil sauce
8 oz sliced mozzarella cheese
¼ cup grated Parmesan cheese

Preheat oven to 375°F.

Dredge eggplant slices in flour, then dip in beaten egg and then in breadcrumbs. Sauté eggplant slices, both sides, in olive oil over medium heat until golden brown. Drain eggplant slices on paper towels.

Season eggplant slices with salt and pepper.

Arrange half the eggplant slices in greased casserole dish, 9x13-inch. Cover this layer with half the tomato basil sauce, half the mozzarella and half the Parmesan cheese.

Arrange the remaining ingredients in a second layer, repeating the procedure above.

Bake, uncovered, for 20 to 30 minutes.

Desserts

Ramona's Apple Crisp with Caramel Sauce

From Willow Vineyard & Winery, submitted by Jo Crampton
Suggested wine pairing: Willow Vineyard Semi-Dry Pinot Gris
Makes 8 servings

4 to 5 apples, peeled, cored, sliced (suggest granny smith,
     or other tart variety)
"Crisp":
1 cup flour
1 cup oatmeal
½ cup sugar
½ cup brown sugar
¼ lb (1 stick) butter, melted

Caramel Sauce:
2 cups sugar
½ cup corn syrup
¼ cup water
1½ cups heavy cream
¼ lb (1 stick) unsalted butter
2 tsp vanilla extract

Apple Crisp: Preheat oven to 350°F. Place apples in 9x13-inch cake pan and sprinkle the "crisp" over the apples. Bake for approximately 30 minutes or until apples are tender and the "crisp" is brown.

Caramel Sauce: In saucepan, combine sugar, corn syrup and water. Cook over low heat, stirring occasionally, until sugar dissolves, about 10 minutes. Increase heat and stir until liquid begins to turn golden brown, about another 30 minutes, totaling about 40 minutes from when you start. Remove from heat, stir in cream and then the butter until butter is melted. Return to heat (on simmer) and stir in vanilla. Let cool for about 30 minutes.

To Serve: spoon warm Caramel Sauce over the Apple Crisp.

Jo Says: This recipe is named for Jo's mother, Ramona, whose recipe it was.

Variation: To make a Strawberry Crisp, follow the Apple Crisp recipe, substituting 1¼ lb frozen strawberries, thawed and drained, for the apples and, optionally, adding 1 tsp cinnamon to the "crisp". Cook 30 to 35 minutes. Serve with whipped cream, or chocolate sauce, or ice cream. Pair with Willow Vineyard Pretty 'N Pink Rosé.

Nadine's Luscious Apricot Bars

From Chateau Chantal, submitted by Marie-Chantal Dalese
Suggested wine pairing: Chateau Chantal Late Harvest Riesling
Makes 12 pieces

½ cup Gewurztraminer wine
1 cup dried apricots
¼ lb (1 stick) unsalted butter, softened
¼ cup granulated sugar
1⅓ cups all-purpose flour, divided
1 cup packed light brown sugar
2 large eggs
1 cup chopped walnuts
½ tsp baking powder
½ tsp vanilla
¼ tsp salt
Confectioners' sugar for dusting

Preheat oven to 350°F.

Simmer apricots in Gewurztraminer wine (enough to cover the apricots) in a small saucepan, covered, for 15 minutes. Drain, then cool to room temperature and chop finely.

Beat together butter, granulated sugar, and 1 cup of the flour with an electric mixer on medium speed until mixture resembles coarse crumbs. Press evenly over bottom of a greased 8-inch square metal baking pan (nonstick) and bake in middle of oven until golden, about 25 minutes.

Beat together, in same bowl, chopped apricots, brown sugar, eggs, walnuts, baking powder, vanilla, salt, and remaining flour on medium speed until combined well. Pour topping over crust and bake in middle of oven until topping sets and becomes golden for about 25 to 30 minutes more. Cool in pan on a rack and cut into 12 bars. Dust with confectioners' sugar.

Marie-Chantal Says: This recipe comes from *Feed My Lambs, Feed My Sheep* by Nadine Begin. (Traverse City, MI: Prism Publishers, 2009.) Quoted with permission.

Ramona's French Vanilla Pumpkin Squares

From Willow Vineyard & Winery, submitted by Jo Crampton
Suggested wine pairing: Willow Vineyard Pinot Gris
Makes one 9x13-inch cake, giving about 20 pieces

Bottom layer:
1 package French Vanilla Cake Mix (save 1 cup for topping)
1 egg
½ cup butter
Batter: 1 large can Libby Pumpkin Pie Mix
2 eggs
⅔ cup milk

Topping:
1 cup of remaining Cake Mix
1 tsp cinnamon
¼ cup sugar
½ cup firm butter

Preheat oven to 350°F.

Mix bottom layer ingredients and press into 9x13-inch pan at least 2 inches deep.

Mix batter ingredients and add to pan.

Mix topping ingredients until crumbly and add to pan, being careful not to mix into the batter.

Bake 45 to 55 minutes.

When cold, cut into approx 2x2-inch (or smaller) pieces.

To Serve: The Caramel Sauce, described in Ramona's Apple Crisp recipe, served warm, goes well with the Pumpkin Squares.

Jo Says: This recipe is named for Jo's mother, Ramona, whose recipe it was.

Nutty Cherry Bread Pudding

From Chateau Grand Traverse Winery & Vineyards
Featuring Chateau Grand Traverse Spiced Cherry Wine
Makes 6 servings

½ cup dried cherries
2 Tbs Chateau Grand Traverse Spiced Cherry Wine
¾ cup evaporated milk
¼ cup water
1 cup 2% milk
¼ cup (4 Tbs, or ¼ lb) butter
3 cups white bread cubes
¼ cup sugar
½ cup chopped pecans
½ tsp cinnamon
⅛ tsp salt
2 eggs, beaten
Cherry syrup, to drizzle

Preheat oven to 350°F.

Heat cherries in wine until medium warm and let soak for 20 minutes.

In a saucepan, heat evaporated milk, water, 2% milk and butter till butter is melted.

In a large bowl, combine the next six ingredients (bread cubes, sugar, pecans, cinnamon, salt, eggs) with the undrained cherries. Add milk mixture and stir gently.

Spoon mixture into greased baking dish, 1½ to 2-quart in size. Place dish in pan of hot water.

Bake for 45 to 55 minutes or until knife inserted one inch from edge comes out clean.

To Serve: Serve warm with cherry syrup drizzled on each serving. If desired, top with whipped cream and a sprinkle of almonds or toasted pecans.

Toast the Season Chocolate Truffle Torte

From the Winery at Black Star Farms, submitted by Coryn Briggs
Created by Chef Stephanie Wiitala, the Inn at Black Star Farms
Suggested wine pairing: Black Star Farms Sirius Raspberry Dessert Wine
Makes one 9x13-inch pan, number of pieces depends on piece size

1¾ cups whipping cream, chilled
1 lb quality semi-sweet chocolate chips
3 oz strong coffee, cooled
1 Tbs BSF Sirius Raspberry Dessert Wine, or other dessert wine
4 Tbs unsalted butter
1 cup heavy whipping cream - not whipped
1 tsp flavorless granulated gelatin

In a mixing bowl, beat the 1¾ cups chilled whipping cream to medium peaks. Put back in refrigerator until needed.

Using a bowl in the top of a double boiler, or microwave safe bowl, combine chocolate chips, coffee, dessert wine and butter and melt together until smooth.

Pour the 1 cup of whipping cream that was not whipped into a metal bowl and sprinkle in the gelatin. Allow the gelatin to "bloom" for 10 minutes. Then carefully heat by swirling the bowl over a low gas flame. Do not let the gelatin boil. Stir mixture into the cooled chocolate and set aside to finish cooling.

Separate the whipped chilled heavy cream in half and add to the chocolate mixture in two batches; place mixture in 9x13-inch pan or dish and freeze until solid.

To Serve: Cut the torte into any form you like or use cookie cutters to make shapes. Finish with chocolate ganache or any sauce you like. Fruit sauces work well, too.

Chef Stephanie Says: For the coffee in the recipe, use leftover coffee from your morning brew!

Omi's Sacher Torte

From Motovino Cellars, submitted by Deirdre Owen
Suggested wine pairing: Motovino Cellars Scooters Cherry wine
Makes one 9-inch diameter cake

Cake:
2½ oz unsalted butter
6 eggs, separated
6 Tbs sugar
5 oz Bakers Sweet German Chocolate

Filling:
3½- 4 oz Bakers Sweet German Chocolate
2 heaping serving spoons confectioners' sugar (about ⅔ cup)
3 egg yolks
1 cup whipping cream
Extra chocolate, grated, to decorate sides of cake

Preheat oven to 350°F.

Butter bottom and sides of three round 9-inch cake pans. Dust with flour or cocoa powder; or line pan bottoms with parchment and butter the parchment. (Parchment is best because the cake is delicate and will break if it sticks to the pan.)

Make the cake: Whip up butter until light and fluffy. Mix egg yolks with sugar and beat until light, whitish in color. Melt chocolate and let cool down. Add to butter and mix well. Add butter/chocolate mixture to egg/sugar mixture and mix well. In a separate bowl, beat egg whites until stiff. Gently fold egg whites into the chocolate mixture until well combined. Spoon or pour batter into the cake pans. Place in oven and bake until sides pull away from pan, about 20 minutes. Carefully lift the cakes out of their pans (this is where the parchment helps you) and cool on racks. The cakes need to be completely cool before they are filled and frosted.

Make filling: Melt chocolate and let cool. In the top of a double boiler over barely simmering water, beat 3 egg yolks and the confectioners' sugar until light and thick. Add the melted chocolate, take from heat and beat constantly until mixture ic completely cool. Whip up the whipping cream until stiff. Fold a bit of the cream into the chocolate mixture to loosen up the chocolate (it can be quite stiff!) then fold the rest in and blend well. Chill until firm enough to spread evenly on cake.

Fill and decorate the cake: Fill between layers and frost sides and top. Sprinkle sides with grated chocolate if desired.

To serve: Refrigerate the cake before serving.

Deirdre Says: Because of its whipped cream filling, this cake must be refrigerated. This recipe is Erik's Austro-Hungarian grandmother's version of the classic Sacher Torte, creamier and richer than the original. During cooking, the cakes will puff up very prettily then sink in on themselves. Don't panic! That's just what they do!

Beverages

Apple Gluhwein (Mulled Wine)

From Peninsula Cellars, submitted by Tom Owens
Featuring Peninsula Cellars Apple Wine
Makes 3¼ to 3½ cups

1 bottle Peninsula Cellars Apple Wine
2 cinnamon sticks
Peel of ½ orange
1 apple, quartered, cored, unpeeled
¼ cup sugar
¼ tsp vanilla extract

Heat all ingredients in slow cooker to 135°F.

Hold at that temperature for at 1½ to 2 hours; it tastes better with the longer cooking time. Maintaining the 135°F retains the alcoholic content.

Serve: in warmed mugs or glasses. Perfect after shoveling snow!

Tom Says: A slow cooker is the easiest way to make this recipe: it brings the mulled wine to temperature and maintains it without overheating. The recipe can be made in a regular pot, keeping the liquid below simmer point: the alcoholic content will be lost, but its character will still flavor the mulled wine. The mulled wine keeps in the refrigerator up to one week and reheats successfully.

A Very Selective Bibliography

Only items that have shaped the authors' knowledge of wines, grape farming and, ultimately, the business of wine, are included.

Baldy, Marian W., Ph.D. *The University Wine Course.* (San Francisco, CA: The Wine Appreciation Guild, 1995 2nd ed.).

Beeler, Jaye. *Tasting and Touring Michigan's Homegrown Food: a culinary roadtrip.* (Traverse City, MI: Arbutus Press, 2012).

Benson, Janice, Jane Kowieski and Becky Hill. *Taste The Local Difference, Northwest Michigan: Discover Local Food and Farms.* (Traverse City, MI: Michigan Land Use Institute, 2012).

Borrello, Joe. (Lapeer, MI; Spradlin & Associates, 2002).

— *Recipes from Gold Medal Wineries.* (Lapeer, MI; Spradlin & Associates, 2005).

Clarke, Oz. *'Let me tell you about wine.'* (New York: Sterling Publishing, 2009).

— *New Encyclopedia of Wine.* (New York: Harcourt, Brace &Company, 1999).

Culinary Institute of America, The; Stephen Kolpan, Brian H. Smith, and Michael Weiss. *Exploring Wine; The Culinary Institute of America's Complete Guide to Wines of the World.* ((New York: John Wiley & Sons, 2nd Edition. 2002)

Goldstein, Sid. *The Wine Lover Cooks with Wine: Great Recipes for the Essential Ingrediant.* (San Francisco: Chronicle Books, 2004).

Hathaway, Lorri, and Sharon Kegerreis. *The History of Michigan Wines: 150 Years of Winemaking Along the Great Lakes.* (Charleston, SC: The History Press, 2010).

— *From the Vine: Exploring Michigan Wineries.* (Ann Arbor, MI: Ann Arbor Media Group LLC, 2007).

Johnson, Hugh, and Jancis Robinson. *The Concise World Atlas of Wine.* (New York: Octapus Books, 2009).

Lukacs, Paul. *Inventing Wine* (New York, W. W. Norton & Company, 2012).

MacNeil, Karen. *The Wine Bible.* (New York, Workman Publishing, 2001).

Parker, Robert M., Jr. and Pierre-Antoine Rovani: *Parker's Wine Buyer's Guide.* (New York; Fireside, 2002).

Robinson, Jancis. *The Oxford Companion to Wine.* (New York: The Oxford University Press, 1994).

— Julia Harding and José Vouillamoz *Wine Grapes, A Complete Guide to 1,335 Vine Varieties, Including Their Origins and Flavours.* (New York: Harper Collins Publisher, 2012)

Stevenson, Tom. *The Sotheby's Wine Encyclopedia.* (London, Dorling Kindersley: 4th Edition, 2005).

Walton, Stuart. *Understanding, Choosing and Enjoying Wine.* (London: Hermes House, 2007).

Werlin, Laura. *The All American Cheese and Wine Book: Pairings, Profiles & Recipes.* (New York: Stewart, Tabori & Chang, 2003).

Zraly, Kevin, ed. *The Ultimate Wine Companion.* (New York: Sterling Publishing, 2010).

DVD
Simonetti-Bryan, Jennifer. *The Everyday Guide to Wine.* (Chantillyl, VA, The Teaching Company, 2010).

Movies
"Bottle Shock." Randall Miller, Jody Savin, Ross Schwartz. Directed by Randall Miller. 20th Century Fox Entertainment, 2008.

"Sideways." Alexander Payne, Jim Taylor (based on *Sideways* by Rex Pickett). Directed by Alexander Payne. Fox Searchlight, 2004.

Magazines, Newsletters, Pamphlets
American Wine Society Wine Journal www.americanwinesociety.org
Bon Appetit www.bonappetit.com
Food & Wine www.foodandwine.com
Grape and Wine Newsletter grapes.msu.edu
QRW (Quarterly Review of Wines) www.qrw.com
Riesling Rules www.RieslingRules.com
Traverse City Business News www.tcbusinessnews.com
Vineyard & Winery Management tcaputo@vwmmedia.com
Wine Advocate www.erobertparker.com/entrance.aspx
Wine Spectator www.winespectator.com
Wines & Vines www.winesandvines.com

Internet
www.winepros.com (Professional Friends of Wine)
www.erobertparker.com/entrance.aspx (*Wine Advocate* magazine)
www.michiganwines.com (Michigan Grape and Wine Industry Council)
www.theticker.tc (*Traverse City Business News* online)
www.ttb.gov (U.S. Department of the Treasury's Alcohol and Tobacco Tax and Trade Bureau)
www.winerambler.net (a Mosel Riesling wine lover's ramblings)

And the websites associated with the commercial wine producers of Leelanau and Old Mission Peninsulas as well as interviews and Conversations with Winemakers, Winery Owners, Vineyard Managers are much too numerous to list individually. They will be listed as seems fit with their Winery/Vineyard listing. One must, however, admit that it all started at a Tasters Guild tasting at Left Foot Charley with Bryan Ulbrich.

Photo Credit: Kevin Blais

William Allin Storrer A.B. Harvard '58, M.F.A. Boston University '62, Ph.D. Ohio University '68, a native of Dearborn, Michigan, lives in Frankfort, Michigan. He holds the position of Adjunct Professor of Architecture at the University of Texas at Austin. A world expert on the architecture of Frank Lloyd Wright, his two books, *The Architecture of Frank Lloyd Wright*, a complete catalog and *The Frank Lloyd Wright Companion*, have sold a hundred thousand copies and the latter work has been translated into Italian, Japanese, Mandarin Chinese and Simplified Chinese. Storrer has directed over 40 theatrical works in college and community theatres. For 40 years he was a critic for the British magazine *Opera*, and authored over 400 articles on theatre, music and related arts in magazines and newspapers. Exhibiting his nature and architectural photography in America and Great Britain, he is also a voracious reader (science fiction and mysteries), an itinerant birdwatcher, an energetic world traveler (70 countries in two 'round-the-world journeys and various other sojourns) and a gregarious film buff. He serves as webmaster of both his Dearborn (Mich.) high school and Harvard College classes and has maintained the only web site that allows a comparison of the Perry Mason TV series with the books upon which many of the TV episodes were based.

His latest endeavour, like his earlier ones, is comprehensive. It is the first presentation of a wine region with maps of every vineyard, stories of the winemakers and winery owners, recipes from the tasting room and winery staff and detailed statistics of what is grown on Michigan's American Viticultural Area parallel peninsulas. An all-in-one handbook compendium of the wines of the area, this book explains how to tour the tasting rooms, how to taste and store your wines, as well as presenting some special recipes with which to drink your wines.

Bill and Pat met in Norway. Once they started talking, they never stopped. Their courtship occurred over the Pacific Ocean between South Carolina and New Zealand, until it was decided they both should live in America.

While Bill was out on the two peninsulas, Pat was researching grape varieties and proof reading the book texts.

Patricia is from New Zealand, with a family background of dairy farming and then commercial beekeeping. She describes herself as a life-long professional computer geek who enjoys music, choir singing (soprano), gardening, cooking and history. And, oh yes, she enjoys writing and editing.

Pat says working with Bill on this book has been a pleasure and a privilege: so many new and wonderful friends!

Made in the USA
Charleston, SC
26 October 2013